Dancing on the Color Line

Dancing on the Color Line

African American Tricksters in Nineteenth-Century American Literature

Gretchen Martin

UNIVERSITY PRESS OF MISSISSIPPI / JACKSON

www.upress.state.ms.us

The University Press of Mississippi is a member of the Association of American University Presses.

Manufactured in the United States of America

First printing 2015
∞
Library of Congress Cataloging-in-Publication Data

Martin, Gretchen, 1966–
Dancing on the color line : African American tricksters in nineteenth-century American literature / Gretchen Martin.
pages cm
Includes bibliographical references and index.
ISBN 978-1-4968-0415-0 (hardback) — ISBN 978-1-4968-0416-7 (ebook)
1. American literature—19th century—History and criticism. 2. African Americans in literature. 3. African American arts—Influence. 4. Tricksters in literature. 5. African Americans—Folklore—History. I. Title.
PS217.B55M37 2015
810.9'352996073—dc23

2015019118

British Library Cataloging-in-Publication Data available

For the tellers

Contents

Acknowledgments

I owe an enormous debt of gratitude to my colleagues Marla Weitzman, Kaye Weitzman, Sara Vanover, Sara Davis, Brian McKnight, and John Mark Adrian at the University of Virginia's College at Wise for reading all or part of this manuscript at various stages as well as offering advice, insight, and guidance through this process. This project would not have been possible without their endless support. Thanks also to the anonymous reviewers for their careful attention and insightful suggestions. I am also deeply grateful to John Mark Adrian in his role as department chair for arranging a research sabbatical for me during the spring 2013 semester. I am also tremendously indebted to Professor Edward Piacentino for inviting me to serve as a guest editor for a special issue in the journal *Studies in American Humor* in 2009, which led to further investigation and thinking regarding the role of black tricksters in American literature. Professors Edward Piacentino, M. Thomas Inge, Scott Romine, and Karen Weyer have also been incredible sources of information and support over the years as I worked through the various stages of this project, and I am truly grateful for their expertise and assistance. I am also grateful to my students, current and former, for their support and interest in this project. Thank you Matthew Donlevy, Emahunn Campbell, Autumn Lauzon, Danielle Roberts, Connie Little, John Dotson, Terri Konstantinou, Jacki Maloyed, Heather Pearson, Kylene Rinkewich, Katie Beth Brooks, and Makayla Gamble. Thanks also to my family, Amanda Martin, the Woods family, Holly, John, Kaitlyn, Madelyn, and Luke, and to Gail Cantrell, Rita Baker, and Jennifer McNew for years of support. I am especially grateful to my husband, Matthew Stanley, for his encouragement, patience, friendship, and love and to my late mother Mary H. Martin for a lifetime of support. Thanks also to *Studies in American Humor* and the University Press of Mississippi for permission to reprint material and to the wonderful editorial staff at the University Press of Mississippi, particularly Vijay Shah and Katie Keene for their patience, support, and guidance.

Martin, Gretchen, "Swallow Barn's Signifying Son: Trickster Wit & Subversive Hero." ©2009 by *Studies in American Humor* and the American Humor Studies Association. Reprinted with permission.

Martin, Gretchen, "'Bawn in a Brier-patch' and Frontier Bred: Joel Chandler Harris's Debt to the Humor of the Old South," in *Southern Frontier Humor: New Approaches*. Jackson: University Press of Mississippi, ©2013. Reprinted with permission.

Dancing on the Color Line

Introduction

"Live with your head in the lion's mouth. I want you to overcome 'em with yeses, undermine 'm with grins, agree 'em to death and destruction, let 'em swoller you till they vomit or bust wide open. . . . Learn it to the young'uns," he whispered fiercely; then he died.

—RALPH ELLISON[1]

To be black in America and survive necessitates being a trickster.

—H. NIGEL THOMAS[2]

In his characteristically bold, controversial, and brilliant style, comedian Chris Rock asks his audience: "Who are the most racist people in the world?" After a pause, Rock responds:

Old black men. A brother in his sixties hates everybody. He can't stand white people. Why? Because old black men went through *real racism*. He didn't go through that "I can't get a cab" shit. He *was* the cab. The white man would jump on his back and say, "Main Street." An old black man also hates young black people. To him, they've fucked up everything he's worked for. But when an old black man sees an old white man, the old black man always kisses the old white man's ass: "How you doing, sir? Pleased to meet you. Whatever I can getcha, you let me know." But as soon as the white man walks out of sight, the black man starts up: "Crack-ass cracker . . . put my foot in his cracker ass, crack-ass cracker. I wish that cracker would have said some shit to me . . . saltine cracker." But when the white man comes back, it's, "Howdy, sir." (24)

Rock's versatile comedic method is uniquely represented in this segment, but his aesthetic style does not simply demonstrate a talented individual but rather highlights an individual's intricate use of his cultural inheritance, specifically the black aesthetic technique of signifying (also commonly referred to as *Signifyin(g)* or *signifyin'*). For authors, performers, musicians, and scholars, signifying is a crucial element in African American culture and operates in a variety of linguistic and nonverbal devices. Rock's "most racist guy in the world" encompasses several examples. On a verbal level, the old black man signifies on the old white man by what is known as *double voice,* making a statement that carries dual meaning: he intends his statement to be understood by the white man literally but maintains a private understanding of his statement as figurative—specifically, rather intense irony. He also signifies nonverbally by performing an artificial image of black masculinity that the white man accepts as reality, which functions paradoxically to mask reality. The old black man's irritation with the younger generation is his anger that they are exposing centuries of carefully protected cultural information.

Rock also employs other aspects of signifying throughout his performances. His opening question to the audience draws from the tradition of "call and response," and his figurative play on language describing the old man as "the cab" signifies on the historical objectification of black Americans by using humor as an edgy satiric critique of the highly serious issue of American racism.[3] Thus, in spite of his apology to his audience for dropping out of high school, stating, "I guess I'm not the best role model," he has been "hailed as the 'smartest,' most 'dangerous,' most 'fearless' comic working in America" (21).[4] His formal education is limited to a GED and a black history course. He notes, "I figured since I'm black I already knew everything. I figured I'd pass just by showing up. Failed it. Isn't that sad, a black man failing black history? But I didn't know anything about Africa.... All I learned in school about being black was Martin Luther King. That's all they ever teach" (21). Yet Rock's material indicates that he is highly educated in the nontraditional school of black vernacular signifying that had its origins during slavery. Henry Louis Gates Jr. notes that "some black genius or community of witty and sensitive speakers emptied the signifier 'signification' of its received concepts and filled this empty signifier with their own concepts. By doing so, by supplanting the received, standard English concept associated by (white) convention with this particular signifier, they (un)wittingly disrupted the nature of the sign = signified/signifier equation itself . . . thereby marking its sense of difference from the rest of the English community of speakers. Their complex act of language Signifies upon both formal language use and its conventions" (*Signifying Monkey* 46).

Rock's frequent references to slavery do not simply function to shed a glaring light on the brutalities of black Americans' history of oppression; indeed, in his claim, "if I'm not mistaken, didn't black people work 200 years for free," he is mistaken—it was close to 250 years—yet Rock has mastered what Roger Abrahams calls the aesthetic legacy of "black talk as art."

Abrahams notes that for the black performer, which includes comedy, music, and literature, "the attention of the audience is gained through a willingness of the performer to involve himself *totally* in the performance and to call for the audience to do so as strongly. This the artful talker does by 'dancing' his talk" ("Rapping and Capping" 135). The performative dynamics of "black talk as art" derive from a style and practice that had its origins in American slave folk culture known as *call and response*, a "musical trope of tropes [that] functions in black music as Signifyin(g) functions in black literature" and depends on an audience open to the full aesthetic experience of the performer/performance (Floyd 147). Signifying is a crucial aspect of African American literature, as well as other art forms, but is also evident in the works of many white authors as well. However, similar dependence on the audience to engage willingly and fully in response to an African American aesthetic evident in the predominantly white literary canon of the nineteenth century has often been highly problematic because to do so *totally* risks inviting uncomfortable truths and has resulted in a reluctance to explore the full implications of black aesthetics in mainstream American literature and culture.

Many scholars have expressed a need for greater awareness of what W. E. B. DuBois calls the "three gifts" derived from slave culture that African Americans have given to America: the gift of sweat, the gift of the Spirit, and, most significant for this study, the "gift of story and song" (386). Yet until the late twentieth century, few studies attempted to explore the extent to which "an African American aesthetic not only survives but thrives and has often been the vanguard of American cultural expression. . . . At a conscious and institutional level most Americans refuse to acknowledge or do not recognize the African-derived aesthetic they have unconsciously adopted as their own" (Caponi 7). These concerns echo the perplexity Ralph Ellison expressed regarding white Americans' resistance to explore "the true interrelatedness of blackness and whiteness" (55).[5] In his essay "What America Would Be Like without Blacks," Ellison contends that

> the spoken idiom of Negro Americans . . . its flexibility, its musicality, its rhythms, freewheeling diction and metaphors, as projected in Negro

American folklore, were absorbed by the creators of our great nineteenth-century literature even when the majority of blacks were still enslaved. Mark Twain celebrated it in the prose of Huckleberry Finn; without the presence of blacks, the book could not have been written. No Huck and Jim, no American novel as we know it. For not only is the black man a co-creator of the language that Mark Twain raised to the level of literary eloquence, but Jim's condition as American and Huck's commitment to freedom are at the moral center of the novel. (109)

In an interview with Shelley Fisher Fishkin twenty years later, however, Fishkin sensed Ellison's "frustration that his critical arguments had had so little impact on the cultural conversation" ("Interrogating 'Whiteness'" 428). But as this 1995 essay so amply demonstrates, several scholarly projects were then under way and came to "mark the early 1990s as a defining moment in the study of American culture. For in the early 1990s, our ideas of 'whiteness' were interrogated, our ideas of 'blackness' were complicated, and the terrain we call 'American culture' began to be remapped" (429). Numerous studies began to address Toni Morrison's call for greater recognition of the "black presence," which is "central to any understanding of our national literature and should not be permitted to hover at the margins of the literary imagination" (*Playing in the Dark* 5). Although a number of scholars have explored a wide range of aspects regarding the interrelatedness of black and white aesthetics, an area of inquiry that remains on the critical margins is an examination of the impact of black folklore in the white literary imagination of the nineteenth century.

The extensive influence of the creative traditions that derived from slave culture, particularly black folklore, in the work of nineteenth- and twentieth-century black authors, such as Charles Chesnutt, Paul Laurence Dunbar, Ralph Ellison, Richard Wright, Zora Neale Hurston, Toni Morrison, and others, has been one of the hallmarks of African American scholarship, yet similar inquiries regarding white authors adopting black aesthetic techniques has been largely overlooked. I, therefore, examine several nineteenth-century works to explore the influence of black-authored (or narrated) works on well-known white-authored texts, particularly the impact of black oral culture evident by subversive trickster figures in John Pendleton Kennedy's *Swallow Barn; or, A Sojourn in the Old Dominion*, Harriet Beecher Stowe's *Uncle Tom's Cabin; or, Life among the Lowly*, Herman Melville's *Benito Cereno*, a variety of Joel Chandler Harris's short stories, and Mark Twain's *Adventures of Huckleberry Finn* and *Pudd'nhead Wilson*. The black characters created by these white authors are often dismissed as little more than limited and demeaning stereotypes of the minstrel tradition, which is how most black characters are portrayed in the works of white nineteenth-century authors; other white authors simply avoided addressing America's black population entirely. Washington Irving's brief depiction of a black character in "The Legend of Sleepy Hollow" is representative of the common literary treatment of African Americans. In this sketch, Ichabod Crane's class session is interrupted by "the appearance of a negro . . . with an invitation to Ichabod to attend a merry-making or 'quilting frolic,' to be held that evening at Mynheer Van Tassel's and having delivered his message with that air of importance, and effort at fine language, which a negro is apt to display on petty embassies of the kind, he dashed over the brook, and was seen scampering away up the hollow, full of the importance and hurry of his mission" (22-23). The black characters created by the authors examined in this project are often assumed to reflect similar stereotypical portraits, most commonly humorous minstrel types, yet by teasing out important distinctions between the wisdom and humor signified by trickery rather than minstrelsy, I explore an overlooked aspect of the nineteenth-century American literary canon and show the extensive influence of black aesthetics in the work of several important narratives by white authors.

Aesthetic exchanges across the color line are, however, often obscured by a variety of historical factors, and it is important to note shifts in ideologies regarding social, cultural, legal, and scientific categories of black and white identity during the early American, antebellum, Reconstruction, and post-Reconstruction periods. As many scholars have pointed out, racial essentialism is a fiction, but this fiction has had an incalculable impact on American history as well as American literary history. The terms *black* and *white* thus remain useful relative to their social, historical, and legal functions in order to "accentuate the persistent power these categories have continued to exert, a power that speaks to the recalcitrance of the Western imagination, its recondite refusal to heed demythologists of racial definition" (Gubar 42). My contention is that Kennedy, Stowe, Melville, Harris, and Twain drew from African American aesthetic techniques to create character portraits that covertly function to demythologize racial definitions. The narratives examined also reflect ideological shifts regarding racial categories and are thus important indicators of changing attitudes in a society that, as Eric Lott observes, "racially ranked human beings" (*Love and Theft* 6). Yet this racial ranking system was not static and indeed frequently shifted according to changes in political, cultural, scientific, and religious factors.

Through the first half of the seventeenth century, the intense demand for labor, particularly in the Southern colonies, "was largely color-blind" (Kolchin 7).[6] But by the 1660s, colonies began drafting laws that defined and regulated labor based on race. In 1662, Virginia was the first to pass slave codes that determined that children would follow the status of the mother, and during the 1690s, the colonies that had formally legalized slavery shared several similar codes, such as statutes prohibiting interracial marriages and defining slaves as property; as such, they could not own property or participate in a legal contract, including a marriage contract.[7] During the revolutionary era, the issue of slavery was beginning to come under more intense scrutiny by leaders such as Thomas Jefferson who, although he opposed social equality and endorsed colonization, felt England had imposed an immoral institution onto the British colonies and advocated for the abolition of the practice in the first draft of the Declaration of Independence.[8] Southern resistance, however, convinced Jefferson and other opponents that the problem would have to be worked out by a later generation.

After the war, as the new nation's northern states began drafting their constitutions, either immediately abolishing slavery or implementing gradual abolition, many Southern leaders began evaluating the practicality of the institution as well, particularly as a result of the decline in the tobacco market, which created a large surplus of slaves and caused their value to plummet, becoming an economic burden on large planters with mounting debts. But the invention of the cotton gin, the Louisiana Purchase, and the end of the international slave trade in 1808 created a new market for the domestic slave trade. In order to defend the continuation of slavery, politicians, social theorists, scientists, and religious leaders began to formulate and formalize more aggressive concepts that "would give credence to the notion that the blacks were, for unalterable reasons of race, morally and intellectually inferior to whites" (Fredrickson 2). By the 1830s, the Southern perspective of slavery transitioned from the notion of a highly questionable institutional practice to the firm claim of an ideal social arrangement. According to proslavery advocates, highly civilized, intellectually superior, and humane men would serve as paternalistic protectors and providers of an inferior race, inherently incapable of intellectually or psychologically progressing beyond the level of advanced childhood and thus in need of this highly structured institution.[9] In return, masters would receive the loyalty, affection, and obedience of their dependents.

Proslavery advocates also claimed that slaves would not only have the benefit of the protection and guidance of their masters but their proximity to this more highly evolved and civilized class would have an elevating effect on blacks as well. John W. Roberts notes that "white Americans had during the period of slavery defended black subjugation by promulgating the idea that, though innately inferior to whites, black acculturation 'under the discipline of slavery' had served to eradicate the more savage aspects of the African character, an effect reflected in their docile and childlike behavior as slaves" (18). Moreover, social and political theories were supported and reinforced by "science." Robert S. Levine notes that "the late 1830s and 1840s saw an upsurge of writing on human racial differences by highly regarded scientists of what came to be termed the 'American School' of ethnology. These ethnologists gained international stature for writings that seemed to offer scientific 'proof' of black inferiority and difference" ("Race, Slavery, Prejudice" 386). Race theorists, North and South, concluded that "Negroes comprised the lowest human link in the chain of being, closest to the apes, while Europeans were the highest, and other races were in between" (Jackson and Weidman 39). By the mid-nineteenth century, these views were widely held, and most whites took for granted an assumption of black inferiority, a perspective in which abolitionists and proslavery advocates tended to agree. For instance, in 1860, abolitionist Owen Lovejoy opines: "'We may concede it as a matter of fact that [the Negro race] is inferior; but does it follow, therefore, that it is right to enslave a man simply because he is inferior?'" (qtd. in Fredrickson 51).[10] The Southern response was an extensive and complex defense of slavery articulated as serving the duty of noblesse oblige.

Southern authors, politicians, scientists, social theorists, and religious leaders defended the institution as an exemplary social arrangement, mutually beneficial to both slaves and masters. But as Eugene Genovese points out, paternalism created a system of reciprocity that gave slaves much more agency than masters had intended or were typically willing to admit. Although slaves depended on their masters for food, shelter, and clothing, the master was also dependent on his slaves for their labor, reproduction, and maintenance of his personal sense of himself as a benevolent patriarch, which also bolstered his reputation in the community. Genovese notes that paternalism was intended to undermine "the slaves' sense of worth as black people and reinforced their dependence on white masters. But these were tendencies, not absolute laws, and the slaves forged weapons of defense, the most important of which was a religion that taught them to love and value each other, to take a critical view of their masters, and to reject the ideological rationales for their own enslavement" (6). Another important weapon used by slaves to mitigate oppressive circumstances, as Charles Joyner explains, came from "a rich legacy of folktales" (*Down by the Riverside* 172). Joyner notes that "one of the persistent delusions of the slaveholders, of visitors to the plantations, and of several generations of others was that the trickster tales told by plantation slaves were mere entertainment" (172). Joyner explains that the trickster tales served as a crucially important tool in the slave community "to create solidarity" and "to inspire and educate" (173). Further, because the tales highlight a trickster hero who "lives by his wits" pitted against characters who "are usually strong and powerful but not very bright, [and] they are constantly being duped by the less powerful trickster figures," slaveholders and other whites who may have been privy to these tales would have been inclined to simply dismiss these stories as entertainment rather than to identify themselves as the powerful yet "not very bright" characters featured in the tales (173).

Defending paternalistic slavery was also an important feature of the antebellum plantation tradition. In response to growing northern criticism, proslavery authors mounted an extensive defense of the institution in their literature. The romance novels of the plantation tradition are typically structured by featuring an outsider visiting distant relatives on a Southern plantation. Over the course of his visit, the narrator comes to realize his "flawed" abolitionist-influenced perspective after observing the slaves happily engaged in their daily tasks, the evident carefree nature of life in the quarters, the mutual love between the master and his slaves, and, most important, the unequivocal integrity and honor of his host. Throughout the genre, the majority of black characters (including men, women, and children) are obliterated in a vast synecdochic sweep, continuously referred to reductively as the "hands" or "field hands." The few featured characters are typically depicted in common "stereotypes of submission, complicity, and clownish behavior," such as the loyal, subservient, and asexual uncle role, particularly for older male characters; younger men are also described as subservient and loyal but often used as a vehicle for the humor of the minstrel tradition, serving not only as the butt of the joke, the black buffoon stereotype, but also feeding the cultural and political proslavery machine as well (Carpio 21). Shirley Moody-Turner explains that blackface minstrelsy's "representation of black folk life reflected and solidified public opinion. At best, it showed blacks as natural, primitive, and carefree juxtaposed to evolved, modern, and civilized society. At worst, it branded blacks as immoral, stupid, lazy, and inferior" (34). Black women were often culturally and socially stereotyped as highly sexualized Jezebels, particularly on the minstrel stage, but in the more restricted literary outlets of the mid-nineteenth century, this image is rarely evident.[11] The more common literary treatment of black women features simply loyal domestic servants or what is presented as the highest ideal of black feminine identity, the mammy figure. Kimberly Wallace-Sanders notes that proslavery authors exploited the image of the mammy figure, particularly depictions of her love for her white charges, to serve "as a symbol of racial harmony within the slave system" (13).

The location of the plantation is also a common feature of early African American literature, both oral and written, but with clear and important differences. Analytical issues are further complicated by the necessary abstraction of the notion of "author" throughout the antebellum period due to an oral tradition circulating under a number of oppressive conditions, such as laws throughout the South that prohibited teaching slaves to read and write, a physically demanding system of forced labor, limited and controlled mobility, and an ideological "panopticon" of surveillance and invasiveness that contributed to a culture compelled to encode communication, particularly of the collective cultural wisdom of their folktales. Several scholars have challenged the widely held assumption that the Middle Passage was so traumatic that it created a tabula rasa of African culture and demonstrate that many of the stories that circulated in slave communities utilized African narrative devices adapted to New World conditions.[12] Moreover, the restrictive nature of slave culture further contributed to the viability and necessity of the slave community's oral traditions, which produced two important literary and symbolic heroes: the trickster figure and the fugitive slave.

The trickster figures featured in black folklore operate in a variety of genres, such as the flying African cycle, the animal tales (most familiar being Brer Rabbit and Brer Fox stories), the slave trickster (typically the John and Old Master tales), and the Signifying Monkey narrative poems.[13] Although there are many distinct features among the various types of black folktales, trickster traits include adaptability, maneuverability, keen verbal dexterity, and a commitment to survival (both physical and psychological). At their most fundamental level is a version of the signifying trickster figure who survives by *intelligence*, by outthinking his or her foes. In the black vernacular tradition, signifying "has assumed the singular role as the black person's ultimate sign of difference, a blackness of the tongue. It is in the vernacular that, since slavery, the black person has encoded private yet communal cultural rituals" (Gates, *Signifying Monkey* xx). And, as Fishkin notes, "in an environment where slaveholders exercised total, absolute power, the ironic doubleness of 'signifying' speech and song became the source of the impunity with which slaves could voice the unspeakable. On the surface, nothing subversive may have been said. Below the surface, however, the speaker sketched a highly subversive critique of the strong by the weak. For 'signifying' speech can generate two meanings: one appears neutral and unobjectionable; the other may embody potentially dangerous information and ideas" (61).[14] In addition to the semantic complexities of verbal signifying, particularly the play on language that produces dual meanings, signifying is also used intertextually as well as nonverbally.

In the African American literary tradition, writers often employ signifying as an intertextual device. Theodore O. Mason Jr. explains that an author "signifies on a particular work, author, form, or tradition by copying central elements or practices, even while revising those in some significant way. The repetition implicit in this form of signifying criticizes or extends the previous and frequently (though not exclusively) white literary or cultural source by setting it within the context of African American expressive culture" (665). However, nonverbal signifying is most evident by performative strategies known as *masking*. Moody-Turner notes that "masking has played an important part in African American culture. As a result of slavery and segregation, African Americans historically have had to learn how to mask or conceal their true feelings. Realizing that laments of discontent, plans for freedom, or displays of self-assertion could bring swift retribution from white oppressors, masking became a vital social practice through which African Americans could conceal and protect their inner lives and desires" (111). Masking, thus, operates as a strategic manipulation of appearances and reflects an important distinction between black and white cultural communities. Gates notes that at "the most poignant level of black-white differences is that of meaning, of 'signification' in the most literal sense. The play of doubles here occurs precisely on the axes . . . where black and white semantic fields collide" (*Signifying Monkey* 49).

Ideologically, these fields collide by the duality of black identity described by W. E. B. DuBois in his theory of double-consciousness created by the metaphorical "veil." DuBois contends that "the history of the American Negro is a history of this strife" that "yields him no true self-consciousness, but only lets him see himself through the revelation of the other world. It is a peculiar sensation, this double-consciousness, this sense of always looking at one's self through the eyes of others" (215). But as Dorothy Hale points out, "Du Bois's metaphor of the veil suggests that a position of social oppression has its compensations: what the subaltern lack in social power, they gain in knowledge. What can the 'Negro' see that the white cannot? He can see that the white cannot see him; he is behind a veil that the white mistakes for him. . . . The 'Negro' alone knows that this ignorance is created by his socially imposed identity, his veil. He alone knows, that is, just how constitutive of identity, or rather deconstitutive, social positionality can be. And finally, he [or she] *knows that the white does not know he possesses this knowledge*" (my emphasis 450). This unique insight is a central feature of black folklife and is evident in the linguistic conventions of the slaves' folktales as well as the adage "'Got one mind for white folks to see, 'Nother for what I know is me; He don't know, he don't know my mind'" (qtd. in L. Levine xxvii). This distinctive insight is, moreover, not only a matter of black knowledge of white ignorance but, further, of black knowledge that white ignorance is shielded by active resistance to knowledge or information that threatens to alter that ignorance.

Because black insight as well as trickster devices are also evident throughout the slave narrative tradition, I contend that fugitives who made it out of slavery did so by drawing on the cultural wisdom of their folklore to empower their endeavors and show that they too are a unique type of trickster, which I will refer to as the *fugitive trickster hero.*[15] Gilbert Osofsky notes that "fugitive slaves honed the art of pretense into a sharp-edged tool of self-defense. There are innumerable stories of women who pretended to be men and men who made wigs of horses' manes to dress as women, or wore false beards. An amazing use of disguises permitted William and Ellen Craft to get to Boston, and their story became familiar throughout the North" (28). Indeed, the Crafts utilize trickster tactics at every stage of their flight. Ellen disguises herself as a white Southern gentleman traveling with "his" body servant, and the pair utilize double-voice discourse throughout their journey. Hale points out that scholars "to a quite extraordinary extent, that is, African Americanists, have glossed Du Bois by way of M. M. Bakhtin, and argued that double consciousness is most powerfully represented in African American literature by the Bakhtinian technique of 'double voice'" (445). For example, William Craft employs the language expected of a slave, referring to his wife using male pronouns and the phrase "my master" throughout the narrative, whereas Ellen utilizes the language of honor of a Southern gentleman. Another especially bold and ingenious escape was Henry "Box" Brown's flight from slavery by having himself shipped to Philadelphia.

Other escape attempts occurred on board ships in slave mutinies, such as the *Amistad* (led by Joseph Cinqué, or Sengbe Pieh) and the *Creole* revolts (led by Madison Washington), which indicates another merging of the literal hero with the figurative. In this preaviation age, flying was commonly used as a metaphor for sailing, particularly to denote great speed; thus, a slave mutiny ideologically fuses the literal (sailing) with the figurative (flying) to indicate a literal form of the figurative "flying African" tradition. Helen Lock contends that "in a slave mutiny, not only are the superior/inferior, rulers/ruled binaries disrupted, but also the more fundamental human/nonhuman distinction: the cargo, in effect, becomes captain and crew, and the world is turned upside down" (56). For captains Amasa Delano and Benito Cereno, this is certainly an accurate perspective, but as Jacques Derrida points out, these oppositions—for example, "superior/inferior" theories of race—are Western cultural constructions, which Derrida challenges not by inverting binaries but by "exploding" them (qtd. in Clegg 233). Similarly, rebellion for blacks overthrowing the authority of captains, masters, overseers, and fugitive slave hunters is not simply an inversion of their authority but also a total rejection of their worldview, or, as Houston Baker puts it, "repudiation." Baker explains that "repudiation is characteristic of black American folklore; and this is one of the most important factors in setting black American literature apart from white American literature" (*Long Black Song* 13). As Cinqué, Washington, the Crafts, Henry "Box" Brown, and the estimated six thousand published accounts of escape demonstrate, "black slaves, then, possessed their own form of racial ethnocentrism and were capable of viewing the white race as a degenerate form of the black" (Levine, *Black Culture* 85). Furthermore, African American linguistic techniques have consistently demonstrated a rather poststructural perspective by the play on language that informs not only African American literary traditions but African American culture as well, and it is the wit of the trickster equipped and empowered by his or her signifying methodology that strategically informs the success of fugitive slaves. Ultimately, every successful slave escape was an example of the tactical outwitting of an entire white community (often several white communities), which amounts to an enormous roster of fugitive trickster heroes.

The wisdom necessary in accomplishing these escapes is also a source of humor and indeed can be viewed as the black trickster's ultimate joke. In her book *Laughing Fit to Kill*, Glenda Carpio notes that the central role of African American humor functions as a "form of release, a medium of protest, and a source of artistic freedom" (20). And although the slave narratives are not traditionally associated with humor, Carpio points out that "despite the seriousness of the antislavery cause and the role of humor in the oppression of African Americans, black writers in the nineteenth century made intricate uses of humor, in its varied modalities, to critique slavery and racism" (31). In addition to critique, these customs can also serve as a declaration of identity and humanity and as a subversive form of instruction. Moreover, several white authors show themselves to be savvy observers of these traditions, and a wide range of texts suggests stylistic and aesthetic influences representative of the artistry, subversive wit, and subtle humor of black figures of ridicule, resistance, and repudiation.

When black authors signify on white literary and cultural forms of black stereotypes to challenge, subvert, or satirize, they take an exegetical risk, and as Carpio asks: "Can stereotypes be used to critique racism without solely fueling the racist imagination?"—a tricky question indeed, and when the question is asked of white authors employing black figures similarly, the inquiry moves into deeper and more troubling territory (15). The tendency of many interpretive perspectives regarding white authors creating black literary roles is an assumption that these writers are either engaging in common standards of humor for the purpose of entertainment or simply reinforcing the political and social status quo; however, by examining works that suggest that white authors have adopted black aesthetic techniques, more subversive possibilities emerge, particularly evident by black figures operating covertly and thus demonstrating characteristics of the trickster figure. Representative of the oppressed, Nancy D. Tolson notes that "tricksters are capable of making a way out of no way, escaping when there is no visible passage out" (75). Tricksters also often appear in the most unlikely places.

In the African American tradition, trickster tales function to pass along cultural wisdom and to teach lessons of survival, but the white authors studied in this project draw from this tradition to serve very different purposes. The black trickster figures featured in their works do not operate to reinforce but rather to debunk cultural wisdom, particularly widely accepted theories of black intellectual, cultural, and moral inferiority in order to covertly challenge what scholars have called the twin evils of the nineteenth century: slavery and racism. John Pendleton Kennedy addresses these issues satirically and subversively in his novel *Swallow Barn; or, A Sojourn in the Old Dominion*, the focus of chapter 1. While *Swallow Barn* is typically regarded as one of the earliest and most familiar novels in the proslavery genre, this perspective overlooks the novel's gentle but insistent position that slavery is an immoral institution and must be abolished, yet Kennedy is equally insistent that extreme abolitionists are interfering with a plan to put an end to the institution.[16] The narrative ultimately addresses two distinct audiences. For Kennedy's northern readers, the novel endorses a design to abolish the institution yet simultaneously sanctions the Southern perspective that abolitionists are doing more harm than good. Kennedy's depiction of the slave community, moreover, subversively undermines white racial theories of black inferiority and destabilizes the theoretical defenses used to support the institution. Kennedy's depiction of black characters is, however, often understood as a reflection of his conflicted views of slavery. Of the novel's forty-nine chapters, two chapters deal directly with this issue. In "The Quarters" and "A Negro Mother, Abe," Kennedy critiques aspects of slavery by creating a defiant slave through the character Abe. Most scholars regard Abe as a chivalric hero who sacrifices himself in an ill-advised rescue mission, but while Abe's heroism is certainly evident by his actions, elements of African American folktale traditions, as well as the trickster wisdom of the slave narratives, suggest that this character operates on a still more deeply subversive level than has been previously suggested. I assert that the slave community's elders pass their trickster wisdom on to Abe to enable him to emerge as a drastically different kind of hero, the type growing out of the slave narrative: the successfully escaped slave.

While Kennedy's novel was well-received and popular, *Swallow Barn*'s modest sales of 1,550 copies of the first edition pales in comparison to the unprecedented 300,000 copies sold in the first year of Harriet Beecher Stowe's *Uncle Tom's Cabin*. It is interesting to note that, as Sarah Meer points out, "ironically, Stowe had been turned down by the first publishers she approached on the grounds that books about slavery did not sell" (4). Stowe is much more overt than Kennedy in her condemnation of slavery in *Uncle Tom's Cabin*, the focus of chapter 2, but her critique of American racism is presented covertly through a number of unique trickster figures. *Uncle Tom's Cabin* has, moreover, drawn a wide range of vastly different interpretive perspectives regarding her depiction of black characters. These views range from her clear familiarity with the slave narrative tradition and, therefore, highly sensitive portraits of black life, to offensive stereotypes of essentialist racism as well as limited and demeaning minstrel types. In chapter 2, I contend that Stowe demonstrates keen insight into the interiority of the slave community's unique cultural mores and creates several black characters who also operate covertly and suggest characteristics of the trickster figure. Stowe's depictions are particularly unique because her most cunning characters are often women. Lewis Hyde points out that most tricksters are male but adds that "there may be female tricksters who have simply been ignored" (185). The potential for overlooked female tricksters is, I assert, more than likely, and while these oversights are clearly a matter of gender, they are also due to highly familiar characteristics that are easily dismissed as limited stereotypes, such as the role often employed for black female characters, the mammy figure. Several of Stowe's most subversive and intelligent characters are females who strategically manipulate racial and gender stereotypes to undermine oppressive circumstances. Another rather unique trickster figure is demonstrated in the character George, who draws on his mixed racial identity to escape slavery by passing.

Herman Melville's *Benito Cereno* also shows evidence of intertextual engagement with African American material, and indeed, as Wyn Kelley contends, Melville may have been writing for a black audience as well as a white audience. In chapter 3, I argue that Melville employs the black vernacular technique of signifying as an aesthetic device and creates characters by drawing from several genres of black folk traditions, specifically the flying African cycle, the slave narratives, and, most notably, the Signifying Monkey narrative poems. While most of the folktales function on a dual structure, with two characters pitted against each other and typically represent "the binary opposite between black and white," the Signifying Monkey cycle is unique because, as Gates explains, these narrative poems operate on a "trinary" involving "the Monkey, the Lion, and the Elephant" (*Signifying Monkey* 55). This trinary force is similarly reflected in Melville's characters, Babo, Benito Cereno, and Amasa Delano, as well as the linguistic dynamics between them, and the similarities between Babo and the Signifying Monkey suggest that the novella's most crafty character does not simply operate to expose white racism but further to ridicule racist ideology. These elements indicate that African American folktales were a rich resource for one of Melville's most highly regarded works of art.

During the post-Reconstruction period, black stereotypes begin to transform into often dangerous manifestations, particularly for men. James Kinney notes that the image of "the black rapist became a powerful symbol not only of the economic rape of the South during Reconstruction, but also of racial division and conflict. For southern writers, the pre-lapsarian Eden ended with Emancipation and defeat; after the war, the phallic snake, the black rapist, was loosed in the garden. 'Protecting white womanhood' became a mystification used to create group identity among whites of all classes and regions" (*Amalgamation!* 227).[17] Because the primary stereotype of black masculinity developing is not only destructive but deadly, in chapter 4, I contend that Joel Chandler Harris turns to a debunking of Southern myth by intertextualizing black signifying forms to sabotage the growing stereotypes of black masculinity that are operating to rationalize extralegal murder. Harris's Uncle Remus stories, however, became so popular (as well as controversial) that they have had a tendency to overshadow critical attention to Harris's non-Remus fiction, which also shows evidence of the influence of black folk culture as well as white antebellum folk material and indeed highlights many common features between these groups. Furthermore, Harris's black characters have often been dismissed as offensive examples of the minstrel tradition, but particularly in the context of post-Reconstruction America, these characters show many telltale signs of the trickster. In chapter 4, I examine several short stories and argue that Harris drew from both black and white antebellum folk traditions to demonstrate many common features between these communities and to highlight the artistry of storytelling traditions, black and white. Harris's work demonstrates a quintessential aspect of Southern literature, a literary hybridity committed to the artistry of the story, told from many angles, in many forms, with sensitivity for voice, perspective, humor, but above all, the dignity, humanity, and intelligence of his featured characters.

The influence of white folk culture, particularly the genre of frontier humor, in Mark Twain's work has been widely discussed, but similar inquiries regarding black folktale traditions have only been marginally explored. Like Harris, Twain draws on antebellum folk material to sabotage an increasingly dangerous racial ideology. In chapter 5, I argue that Twain's intertextual negotiation of black and white discourses in *Adventures of Huckleberry Finn* and *Pudd'nhead Wilson* suggests that Twain's most complex (as well as controversial) black characters, Jim and Roxy, also operate as tricksters of the African American signifying tradition. Furthermore, like Stowe, Twain also features a highly cunning female character, and in his novel *Pudd'nhead Wilson*, Roxy functions as mammy and antimammy, tragic mulatto figure and subversive operator, but more important, she is also the speaking subject of sexual exploitation, and through this character, Twain thus produces his most crafty trickster figure.

Roxy's deeply personal story, like the personal stories of Lucy, Abe, Babo, Jim, Cassy, and many others, is an important but often overlooked aspect of their larger narratives; these stories often dwell in the narrative margins, the gaps, the omissions—and because they are often funny, that their stories offer a scathing critique of American institutional practices, social mores, and a highly unflattering revisionist history often compels readers to pass over the potential for discomfort and notice only the antics, witty quips, and the humor of the characters rather than what this humor signifies. These white authors do not create black characters by utilizing traditional linguistic and narrative practices but, rather, depict black characters that signify on black literary and cultural sources, which, however, often signify on white sources. The complexity of these characters thus anticipates Toni Morrison's paradoxical note in the final pages of *Beloved*: "It was not a story to pass on." This statement carries multiple implications: as a literary caveat for the reader, coming, however, much too late; as a story too terrible, too unprintable, too historically accurate, and thus not a story at all; as a story that has been but cannot continue to be overlooked, ignored, put aside. However uncomfortable, difficult, or—according to many critics—unsuccessful the depictions of black characters might have been for these white authors, the narratives of Roxy, Blue Dave, Babo, Abe, and Lucy are also not stories to "pass" on, and fortunately, these authors did not.

Chapter 1

Swallow Barn's Signifying Son

Trickster Wit and Subversive Hero

Originally published in 1832 and revised and republished in 1851, John Pendleton Kennedy's novel *Swallow Barn; or, A Sojourn in the Old Dominion* has become well known to scholars of Southern literature as a foundational text of the antebellum plantation school and model for postbellum plantation authors.[1] The novel is also an early example of the frame narrative, which would become an important structural device in the genres of frontier humor and late nineteenth-century plantation fiction. Published only a year after the Nat Turner rebellion in 1831, Kennedy's novel reflects the judicious balance he maintained in his personal and professional life in a period growing increasingly "embroiled in sectional rivalry," and his depiction of slavery functions as a careful but complex negotiation of what was becoming the central issue of the nineteenth century (MacKethan, "Introduction" i).[2] In her introduction to the novel, Lucinda MacKethan notes that Kennedy's mother was "allied to a thriving planter clan of old Virginia, aristocratic gentleman and ladies whose plantations were spread throughout the Shenandoah Valley–Berkeley County regions of a state far more southern in its leanings than was Maryland. Through his father, John Kennedy, he belonged to the Baltimore merchant class" (xii). After the death of his first wife, Kennedy married Elizabeth Gray, daughter of Edward Gray, a wealthy textile manufacturer who "opposed slavery and distrusted southerners as idlers" (xiii). As MacKethan notes, Kennedy adopted the political and economic views of his father-in-law, "but his Virginia relatives and their plantations kept a strong hold on his sympathies" (xiii). Kennedy's treatment of the issue of slavery in *Swallow Barn* is often viewed as cautiously endorsing the perspective of the novel's planter patriarch, Frank Meriwether, who regards the institution as an inherited evil and social dilemma, a perception similar to the paradox Thomas Jefferson expressed in his claim: "'We have the wolf by the ears and we can neither hold him, nor safely let him go. Justice is in one scale, and self-preservation in the other'" (qtd. in Kolchin 89). As MacKethan notes, "never a defender of slavery, Kennedy in his treatment of blacks in *Swallow Barn* shows how ever more deeply even he became entangled in the pastoral mystique of the world he set out to satirize" (xxv).

The novel is typically considered one of the earliest and most well-known representatives of the proslavery plantation tradition, and many consider *Swallow Barn*, as Frankie Y. Bailey notes, to be "a book offering an idyllic picture of plantation slavery" (3); other scholars have argued that this view overlooks the text's subversive complexities. In *Unwelcomed Voices*, Paul Jones contends that the novel "ultimately refuses to commit itself to a single view of the South and, instead, struggles with several, including one that is sympathetic and romantic and one that is ironic and critical" (123). Scott Romine identifies a duality of discourses and contends that "mediating between the two master discourses of apologist rhetoric—slavery as 'a necessary evil' versus 'a positive good'—Kennedy refuses the teleology of the latter, which would involve a cultural narrative producing the pastoral icon of the plantation community" (86). Romine asserts that rather than endorsing slavery, Kennedy's agenda is expressed through his character Meriwether's view that slavery is "morally wrong" and will eventually be eradicated but that the responsibility to create a plan to abolish the institution is a Southern rather than Northern responsibility; consequently, "the authorial control of the emancipation plot must remain a southern prerogative" (87). In addition to the master discourses that dominate the narrative perspective throughout the novel, another distinct discourse is evident by the voices of the slaves, which often operate to undermine these master discourses. Kennedy thus grants the South the prerogative of writing "the emancipation plot," but his depictions of black characters throughout the novel often function subversively to apply pressure to this expectation. Of the novel's forty-nine chapters, two chapters deal directly with the issue of slavery, yet the racial theories employed in the debates regarding slavery are typically presented as a given by the white characters. Kennedy, however, also integrates black voices throughout the novel that operate subversively to destabilize the foundation of racial theories. The first chapter to focus directly on slavery, "The Quarter," broadly addresses the issue during a visit to the plantation's quarters while the following two-part chapter, "A Negro Mother, Abe," provides the personal stories of two individual slaves, Lucy and her rebellious son Abe. The section featuring the character Abe has proven a particularly compelling and often perplexing critical aspect of the novel.[3]

Most scholars view the character Abe as representative of Kennedy's conflicted view of slavery and as a type of chivalric hero who sacrifices himself in an ill-advised rescue mission. However, throughout the novel, Kennedy features two distinct cultures, the white master class and the black community held in bondage by the master class. While the members of these respective communities interact with each other, they also maintain important cultural features and social values that distinguish one from the other. Kennedy presents Frank Meriwether as a representative of the ideal Virginia gentleman as well as his nephew Ned Hazard, who is depicted as a younger version and thus in the social process of becoming this ideal, particularly because he is next in line to inherit Swallow Barn.[4] The language of chivalry is utilized throughout the novel, typically by Ned during his courtship, and while often humorous, functions to delineate the Southern man of honor's appropriate behavior, social responsibility, proper etiquette, dress, and indeed worldview. A very different type of language is depicted by the slaves in this plantation community and often suggests rather subversive elements, which indicates an independent community culture.

The language of the slaves is presented through dialogue, stories, and songs and demonstrates unifying elements of an autonomous community culture. Houston Baker claims that "the singing that wafted to John Pendleton Kennedy's ears on his visit to 'the quarters' was not the gentle outpouring of a contented slave. When black Americans sang their spirituals, Pharaoh was a very real person: he was the white master who sat on the porch, whip in hand. The River Jordan was not a mystical boundary between earth and heaven: it was the very real Ohio that marked the line between slave and free states. And to 'steal away' was not to go docilely home to God but to escape from the southern land of bondage" (*Long Black Song* 12–13). For African Americans, as Baker points out, "the world is not composed of white supermen producing culture and nonwhite underdogs and colonial subjects attempting to rival white culture," which is the perspective typically attributed to the assessment of Abe as a chivalric hero, but for the slave community, their stories, songs, and cultural wisdom demonstrate that they celebrated very different types of heroes (10).

Roger Abrahams notes that "the trickster figure has been the most identified hero in Negro lore" and is "one who triumphs or functions by means of his wits" (*Deep Down in the Jungle* 62). Jeanne Rosier Smith explains that "Br'er Rabbit's tremendous wit highlights an important aspect on African American cultural identity. Because the American slave system involved living with whites in daily power-based relationships, African American trickster tales strongly reflect the necessity for the trickster's subversive, masking, signifying skills. Maintaining any sort of cultural identity under slavery demanded an overt acceptance of, and covert resistance to, the dehumanizing racial myths of slavery" (113). Another hero celebrated in the slave community is the fugitive, who as numerous examples of the slave narratives demonstrate, also succeeds "by means of his wits." Lawrence Levine notes that in the slave community, "for all their stress on the need for caution, they seemed to take delight and pride in telling stories of relatives and friends who challenged the system by escaping" (88). While Abe's heroism is certainly evident by his actions, elements of African American folktale traditions, as well as the trickster wisdom of the slave narratives, suggest that this character operates on a still more deeply subversive level than has been previously suggested. I contend that the slave community's elders pass their trickster wisdom on to Abe to enable him to emerge as a drastically different kind of hero, the type growing out of the slave narrative: the successfully escaped slave.

Kennedy uses the epistolary form and a variety of framing techniques in structuring his novel; thus, it is important to point out the distinction between story and plot. Story is defined as a specific narrative event, whereas plot is created by the way in which the stories are arranged in the narrative. The novel opens with an "Introductory Epistle" addressed to "Zachary Huddlestone, Esq., Preston Ridge, New York" from Mark Littleton, and chapters often contain embedded narratives that feature specific characters telling a story or a story Littleton records after hearing. Gerald Prince explains that stories function on "the content plane of narrative as opposed to its expression plane or discourse; the 'what' of a narrative as opposed to its 'how'" (*Dictionary of Narratology* 91). While the content of the stories is provided by the narrator Mark Littleton, frequently as a result of his role as narratee, the discourse plane of the narratives often betrays his limitations. Prince notes that the "the portrait of the narratee emerges above all from the narrative addressed to him" ("Study of the Narratee" 219). The distinction regarding Littleton's negotiation between narrator and narratee is important because he often functions as a listener to the narrative accounts of others, repeating these stories in his lengthy "letter." The stories he recounts, however, often indicate that he lacks the ability or inclination to fully comprehend the discourse plane of many narratives, which often implicitly expose issues regarding race, slavery, and power functioning on a deeply subversive level.

The chapters are typically structured by Littleton's description of the events that lead to a particular character telling a story or engaging in a discussion with Littleton. Ken Egan points out that the novel "is indeed a highly dialogized narrative" and speaks in "multiple voices" (63). These multiple voices are often evidenced by Littleton interacting with and telling stories of the novel's black characters. For example, when Meriwether's sister Prudence begins her morning uncharacteristically playing the piano and singing, "the domestics" regard her strange behavior as a sign of "some impending disaster" (155). Littleton notes that, according to the house slaves: "Such a change in the lady's habits could import no good! They intimated that when people were going to give up the ghost, such marvels were the not unusual precursors of the event. 'It was as bad,' one of the servant maids remarked, 'as to hear a hen crow at night from the roost, and she shouldn't wonder if something was going to happen,—a burying, or a wedding, or some such dreadful thing'" (155). The dialogue Littleton engages in with black characters exposes him to elements of the discourse plane of black oral culture. It is important to point out, however, that when slaves are talking to whites or to each other in the presence of whites, the dynamic of power is a crucially important element in examining these scenes. In this exchange, Littleton overlooks the implicit critique of this white woman by the slaves regarding her cheery mood as so unusual, they characterize her behavior as a marvel.

Throughout the novel, the slaves demonstrate their keen awareness of audience, routinely utilizing the terms *sir* and *master* when addressing white men, even toward those who are not their owners. Their behavior with whites also demonstrates their savvy insight regarding the appropriate behavior whites expected, which could be manipulated to influence white opinion and exploited to blacks' advantage. For example, when Scipio accompanies Littleton to Swallow Barn, according to Littleton, he conducted himself "with such a deferential courtesy and formal politeness, as greatly to enhance my opinion of his breeding" (22). Other characters Littleton records interaction with include Carey, Old Jupiter, and Uncle Jeff. Lewis P. Simpson regards Old Jupiter as "a parody of Meriwether," while Romine asserts that Carey, Meriwether's personal servant, also "intends to parody his master" (45; 71). Romine contends that Carey is "fundamentally different because his imitation is not, as it were, overtly slavish" and argues that "surely it is possible to read beneath Littleton's ignorant slave to one who cagily acts the fool perfectly aware of the performative demands being made of him" (71–72). Read in this light, Carey emerges as "one who consciously and cagily accommodates himself to his audience's expectations" (72). Furthermore, Simpson and MacKethan also detect performative strategies operating in the character Scipio as well; as MacKethan notes, "we can also see stirrings of the sentiment that produced Paul Laurence Dunbar's poem 'We Wear the Mask' and Ellison's devious grandfather figure in *Invisible Man* when Scipio, 'laughing till the tears came into his eyes,' says that 'people think old Scipio a fool, because he's got sense'" (xxv). The performative nature of these characters, which Egan describes as "active, energetic, even manipulative," suggests that they operate by drawing on trickster wisdom (67).

Characters functioning subversively and their strategic manipulation of appearances provide evidence of the influence of black oral culture in the novel. Romine notes that "Kennedy had ample opportunity to observe slaves at The Bower, the Pendleton plantation that provided the model for Swallow Barn, and if we cast him in a sheerly mimetic role as the recorder of actual slave behavior, his portrayal of this imaginary slave might well register a level of resistance of which he may not and probably could not have been aware" (73). Several scenes depict the activities of the black community independent of the white community, which indicates a distinct cultural identity. For example, after Carey entertains Ned Hazard and his guests in the main house with his banjo and songs, he then heads to the quarters, and as Littleton notes, "after I had got to bed, I could hear the negroes dancing jigs to Carey's banjo" (103). Similarly, during the Fourth of July celebration,[5] Carey serves as the carriage driver to conduct Hazard's guests to a party at "the Landing" and while "some thirty or forty [white] persons" entertain themselves dancing at the main house, Littleton observes that "a group of negroes, outside of the house were enjoying themselves in the same way, shuffling through the odd contortions of a jig, with two sticks lying crosswise upon the ground, over which they danced" (160). Another feature of black folklife is depicted after Carey is relieved of his duties, and he is free to spend time with his peers. Littleton observes that "Carey had collected about him a set of his old cronies, to whom he was delivering a kind of solemn harangue, of which we could only observe the energy of his gesticulations" (161). Carey's association with slaves from other plantations demonstrates that the black community is not limited to members of a specific household but indicates a much more extensive social group.

Other significant elements of slave life include keeping themselves well informed of the activities and conversations of the master class. Charles Joyner notes that

> at the center of the slave community was a communications network known as the "grapevine." The grapevine was a crucial element of slave

> resistance. "We used to carry news from one plantation to the other I recon, 'cause mammy would tell about things going on some other plantation and I know she never been there," recalled Phyllis Petite, a former slave. How did slaves learn what was going on in the larger world? According to Benjamin Russell, who had been a slave in South Carolina, "many plantations were strict about this, but the greater the precaution the alerter they became for outside information. Among the sources were girls that waited on the tables, the ladies' maids, and the drivers; they would pick up everything they heard and pass it on to the other slaves." (*Shared Traditions* 82)

During several social events, the slaves are depicted "gathered about the doorway, or peeped in at the window," and during one rainy afternoon while Hazard and his guests put on a play for their entertainment, Littleton overhears the "sundry distinct giggles from a group of servants on the outside of the door" (97, 99). Walter Johnson points out that "as much as slaveholders liked to think that their affairs were their own business, they could not stop their property from listening in on their conversations or gossiping with their associates or neighbors" (31). Scenes of black interest in white activities indicate that Swallow Barn's black community was keenly intent to keep themselves well informed of what was going on in the master's house, which could be exploited to their advantage. For example, although Carey is Meriwether's personal servant, he is constantly able to manipulate circumstances in order to accompany Hazard and Littleton on a variety of excursions, visits, and other activities, which benefits him by allowing him to gain information and relieves him of more arduous duties.

The language and behavior that slaves used with whites or between each other in the presence of whites, moreover, introduces a signifying system that Meriwether and Littleton are exposed to but unable to decipher because it is built on a network of communication designed to mask and protect the slaves' opinions, intentions, emotions, sense of self, and the intricacies of black vernacular. The complexity inherent in this language is that it is a form of communication overtly spoken but covertly understood, communicating different messages for distinct audiences. Julia Sun-Joo Lee points out that in the black vernacular tradition, "the signifier is emptied out—or opened up—to include a multiplicity of rhetorical figures. Thus, standard English signifying is transmuted into black vernacular Signifyin(g), a multivalent and multivocal trope that is skillfully wielded by the folkloric trickster" (462). Several scenes regarding black characters are described by Littleton and often suggest activities and communication operating subversively.

It is during a visit to the slave quarters that Kennedy provides Meriwether's explicit perspective regarding slavery and implicit view of race, which begins to indicate Meriwether's hermeneutic limitations. Meriwether's view of slavery reflects the notion of noblesse oblige built on a racially oriented hierarchy.[6] In her book *Race in North America*, Audrey Smedley notes that by the eighteenth century, "the word 'race' was transformed in the English language from a mere classificatory term to a folk idea that expressed certain attitudes toward human differences and prejudgments about the nature and social value of these differences" (5). Furthermore, these theories functioned

> as a way of imposing order and understanding on complex realities in which one group asserted dominance over others, "race" was the option that some Europeans chose. Those Europeans who came to dominate the colonial world of seventeenth- and eighteenth-century America created a world in which the status of "whiteness" achieved supremacy, while inferior or lower-status identities were imposed on those populations encountered and exploited.... Race conveyed a model of the world as being divided into exclusive groups that were naturally unequal and had to be ranked vis-à-vis one another. (6)

And, as Gates notes, "ideas about race were received from the Enlightenment, if not from the Renaissance. By midpoint in the nineteenth century, ideas of irresistible racial differences were commonly held" ("Editor's Introduction: 'Race'" 3). Although Meriwether and Littleton agree that slavery is "morally wrong" and that "the injustices of slavery must and will be removed by the southerner," their racially oriented view of the great chain of being is presented as a given (Romine 87). Littleton, for example, characterizes race in generalizations, noting "their predominant love of sunshine, and their lazy, listless postures, and apparent content to be silently looking abroad" (451). Littleton claims that before arriving at Swallow Barn, he was inclined to disapprove of the institution of slavery and notes: "I came here a stranger, in great degree, to the negro character. Knowing but little of the domestic history of these people, their duties, habits or temper, and somewhat disposed, indeed, from prepossessions, to look upon them as severely dealt with, and expecting to have my sympathies excited towards them as objects of commiseration" (452). His observations and discussions with Meriwether lead him to a different understanding of slavery, and he concludes that "they never could become a happier people than I find them here" (453). His view of race, however, remains unquestioned.

Kennedy then shifts the role of narrator to Meriwether, who acknowledges the polemical nature of slavery, which evidences his familiarity with and animosity toward abolitionist rhetoric. Meriwether concedes that he believes that "'slavery, as an original question, is wholly without justification or defense. It is theoretically and morally wrong'" (456). But, he complains, outsiders irresponsibly inflame "'the passions of these untutored and unreckoning people, our black population, with this subject'" (458). Meriwether's comments, however, fail to acknowledge Southern state laws that prohibit teaching slaves to read and write, and therefore, Meriwether ignores his complicity in their "untutored" condition.[7] Furthermore, the use of the word *unreckoning* as a racial generalization draws on widely held theories of intellectual inferiority touted by eighteenth-century philosophers such as David Hume and Immanuel Kant who theorized "with the authority of philosophy, the fundamental identity of complexion, character, and intellectual capacity" (Gates, "Editor's Introduction: 'Race'" 10). As Gates notes, Hume deems "[the negro] naturally inferior to the whites"; whereas Kant "was one of the earliest major European philosophers to conflate 'color' with 'intelligence,'" and, as Gates notes, "the correlation of 'blackness' and 'stupidity' Kant posited as if self-evident" (11). By the nineteenth century, these views were widely accepted. While Meriwether demonstrates a conflicted view regarding the morality of the institution of slavery and characterizes his role as serving "the great duty that is left to us," he clearly regards racial inferiority, much like Kant, as self-evident (456).

Meriwether's paternalistic perspective also demonstrates that his sense of identity is inextricably bound to his role as a master, and in many ways, he is dependent on his slaves to maintain his sense of self as well as his image in the community. William Tynes Cowan notes that "the planter wished to be the panoptic power that sees and controls all, but his simultaneous desire not to see his slaves as they performed services for him may have provided more freedom of cultural self-determination than the planter might have known or could have imagined" (12). Meriwether's daily routine demonstrates his role as master but also exposes his many vulnerabilities relative to his self-image as result of his dependence on that role. His morning custom involves rising early "to make a circuit on horseback, to inspect the progress of his farms," which is the extent of his involvement with the management of his business. The labor in the fields is regulated by his overseer, "Mr. Tongue," which allows Meriwether to keep his hands literally and figuratively clean (75).[8] He does not have to dirty his hands with field labor or the physical discipline necessary to command the labor of men and women working for life without compensation. While Meriwether contends that "no overseer is entirely to be trusted," which necessitate his morning inspections, employing an overseer is crucial to allow Meriwether to maintain his sense of himself as benevolent patriarch responsible for the guidance and care of his "dependents" and to protect his belief that in return, he receives their loyal devotion (451).

In spite of Littleton's depiction of Meriwether as a model of patriarchal benevolence, however, several aspects of slave life undermine this perspective. Littleton describes "the numerous herd of little negroes about the estate" and notes that his attempts to chat with them are met with "a suspicious gaze," and they run from him "very much frightened" (307–9). Littleton then describes their clothing: "They are almost all clad in a long coarse shirt which reaches below the knee, without any other garment . . . exposing their bare, black, and meager shanks" (309). Frederick Douglass notes that slave children were typically given "two coarse linen shirts a year" but were not provided with "shoes, stockings, jackets, or trousers" (*My Bondage* 10). Booker T. Washington, however, was permitted only one coarse shirt a year, which he hated. He recalls: "The most trying ordeal that I was forced to endure as a slave boy, however, was the wearing of a flax shirt. In the portion of Virginia where I lived it was common to use flax as part of the clothing for the slaves. That part of the flax from which our clothing was made was largely the refuse, which of course was the cheapest and roughest part" (34). A new flax shirt was so uncomfortable that Washington notes with immense gratitude the kindness of his older brother John's routine of wearing his brother's new shirt for him for "several days, till it was 'broken in'" (35).[9] Littleton's description of the slave children as a "numerous herd" that "sometimes afford us a new diversion" demonstrates his resistance to acknowledge signs that indicate children clearly deprived of adequate clothing, shelter, and, as their "meager shanks" suggest, proper nutrition (308–9).

During his visit to the quarters, Littleton describes the layout of the slave cabins and provides further details of their living conditions. He observes a large number of "lowly" structures of "plain log-cabins, compacted pretty much on the model by which boys build partridge-traps; being composed of the trunks of trees, still clothed with their bark, and knit together at the corners with so little regard to neatness that the timbers, being of unequal lengths, jutted beyond each other, sometimes to the length of a foot. Perhaps, none of these latter sort were more than twelve feet square, and not above seven in height" (448). Because the visit occurs in the middle of the day, the field hands are absent, but there are a number of "prolific mothers," "swarms of little negroes," and "a few reverend, wrinkled, decrepit old men" present. Littleton notes that these cabins "illustrate a whole species of habitations very common in Virginia, it will be seen, that on the score of accommodation, the inmates of these dwellings were furnished according to a very primitive notion of comfort" (450).[10] Littleton's comment implies that the "primitive notion of comfort" reflects the inhabitants' perspective, but it is the master's decision to determine how and in what conditions he chose to provide for his slaves, which as Littleton's account indicates, are cramped, crowded, cheap, and insufficient as protection from the elements. Furthermore, the cabins also have "little garden-patches attached to each, where cymblings, cucumbers, sweet potatoes, water-melons and cabbages flourished," which Littleton suggests indicate that the slaves are well provided for with a range of healthy foods but overlooks the fact that these gardens, which several historians demonstrate were common in the quarters, required slaves to toil in their gardens during the limited times they are not in the fields, yet these patches would not have been necessary had they not needed to supplement meager and often insufficient diets (45).[11]

In spite of these physical signs of deplorable living conditions, however, Littleton considers Meriwether "a kind and considerate master" and notes that "it is his custom frequently to visit his slaves, in order to inspect their condition" (451). During these visits, Meriwether is depicted fielding various requests, and "the petitioner was either gratified or refused in such a tone as left no occasion or disposition to murmur," which allows Meriwether to maintain his sense of himself as "kind and considerate" (451). One character in particular, Old Jupiter, seems especially insightful regarding Meriwether's vulnerabilities and rather adept at manipulating his master, managing to "extort" a horse, and as Meriwether good-naturedly complains, "'I seldom come here without finding myself involved in some new demand, as a consequence of my donation. Now he wants a pair of spurs which, I suppose, I must give him'" (452). During this visit, Meriwether is cajoled by Jupiter into parting with "a little money," which suggests that this "old fellow" possesses sharp insight into his master's weaknesses and is routinely able to manipulate him for his benefit.

The chapter that follows in *Swallow Barn* features the stories of two black characters, Lucy and her rebellious and discontented son Abe. MacKethan contends that "the issue of slavery dominates in ways that Kennedy scarcely intended. The story of Abe, which takes over the last part of the novel, indicates that Kennedy was quite as trapped by slavery's contradictions as was his character Frank Meriwether" ("Introduction" xxvi). While the novel maintains a "tone gently satirical of the foibles of provincial characters," this section suggests a much more complex critique of not only Meriwether but indeed the Southern power structure (xv). Jones contends that "the institution of slavery is treated with the double focus with which Kennedy views the larger South, that within this text, which is often dismissed as proslavery propaganda, a serious dialogue takes place that interrogates many of the region's assertions about the black race and the slave system" (137). A point of interrogation in the novel occurs in the contrast between the depiction of Meriwether as "a very model of landed gentleman" and the intersection of the "figure of resistance," which Romine explains was "virtually absent from proslavery rhetoric: the slave himself who exerted a tenacious pressure against the narrative that presumed to contain him" (33, 67). Kennedy grants the Southern elite the prerogative of creating the "emancipation plot," but his contradictory portrait of Meriwether, particularly his difficulty in dealing with "figures of resistance," also registers a sense of doubt regarding whether such trust is warranted.

In one of the novel's early chapters, Kennedy describes Meriwether as "a very model of landed gentlemen" (33). He is depicted as "hospitable, thinks lightly of the mercantile interest, . . . is apt to be impatient of contradiction, and is always very touchy on the point of honor. There is nothing more conclusive than a rich man's logic anywhere, but in the country, amongst his dependents, it flows with the smooth and unresisted course" (35). Toward his "dependents" he is "kind and considerate," and Littleton claims that "his slaves appreciate this, and hold him in most affectionate reverence, and therefore, are not only contented, but happy under his dominion" (34). Cowan notes that "not only did [the master's] ownership of slaves signify his class status, but signs of happiness among his slaves were indicative of his quality as a patriarch: a good master would have happy slaves" (22). This perspective reiterates the era's proslavery rhetoric of an ideal social arrangement mutually beneficial to both black and white; however, one of Meriwether's dependents is Abe, a character clearly not "happy under his dominion," and as Alan Henry Rose asserts, there is "a good deal of unconscious force involved in the image of the Negro in *Swallow Barn*" (220).

This "unconscious force" grows more direct as Abe develops into manhood and becomes increasingly uncontrollable, and as Abe matures, he hardens "into the most irreclaimable of culprits" (467). Abe has "been trained to the work of a blacksmith, and was, when *he chose* to be so, a useful auxiliary at the anvil. But a habit of associating with the most profligate menials belonging to the extensive community of Swallow Barn, and the neighboring estates, had corrupted his character, and, at the time of life which he had now reached, had rendered him offensive to the whole plantation" (my emphasis 467). These "profligate menials," belonging to Meriwether and other "neighboring estates," also indicate that Abe is not the only slave who is not "happy" under the authority of his master.

Abe expresses his discontent most overtly when he joins "a band of out-lying negroes, who had secured themselves, for some weeks, in fastnesses of the low-country swamps, from whence they annoyed the vicinity by nocturnal incursions of the most lawless character" (468). Cowan notes that "slaves using, running away to, or living in swamps suggested that all was not well on the plantation and, perhaps even more disturbing, that the world did not revolve around the planter and his well-being" (13). Meriwether's "refractionary bondsman" ultimately functions as a threat to Meriwether's authority and undermines his view of himself as benevolent and beloved patriarch, an image crucial to his sense of self as well as his reputation in the community. Peter Kolchin points out that rebellious slaves were a constant problem throughout the antebellum period, particularly as a challenge to the image of power because "masters could not tolerate public assaults on their authority" (161). The move to hire him out is not, as has been argued, Meriwether's reluctance to separate families because although Abe is not sold, mother and son are indeed separated, and Lucy's emotional reaction highlights "the unutterable anguish" Meriwether's decision causes this "poor, unlearned, negro mother" (468). Meriwether's solution to this problem consequently exposes his weakness and suggests a much more serious critique of this character than what is commonly considered light satire. Unable to endure a challenge to his authority or opinion, particularly an expressed perspective regarding the natural dependence on his "beneficent guardianship" of these "good-natured, careless, light-hearted, and happily-constructed human beings," Meriwether thus removes rather than confronts the problem (453–54).

The narrative then moves into the embedded story of Abe told to Littleton by Meriwether. Repeating the story from the perspective of Meriwether introduces evidence that it is indeed a story Meriwether is familiar with but one that has been provided to him through a discourse with which he is not and thus introduces an implication of questionable reliability. In the trickster tradition, Gates notes that "the Signifying Monkey is able to signify upon the Lion because the Lion does not understand the Monkey's discourse.... The Monkey speaks figuratively, in a symbolic code; the Lion interprets or reads literally and suffers the consequences of his folly" (*Figures in Black* 241). As the story unfolds, it becomes increasingly apparent that Meriwether also interprets literally and thus functions as an Amasa Delano–type of narrator unable to read the signifying system operating in his presence, largely due to his active resistance. Furthermore, Meriwether's inability to understand the full hermeneutic possibilities of the information he hears, sees, and describes to Littleton is not simply a lack of training in decoding a signifying system but rather resistance to knowledge that would contradict a worldview that enables him to exploit the labor and lives of others while simultaneously allowing him to view himself as serving a social duty. Such information would not only compromise but overturn his worldview and render his place on the great chain of being as barbaric and savage exploiter of others rather than benevolent patriarch. Mel Watkins notes that "accepting the Negro's humanity would have meant acknowledging their own callousness and barbarity—an admission of venality and hypocrisy belying nearly all democratic principles on which the nation was founded" (*On the Real Side* 30). Meriwether shares Abe's story, but the subversive content embedded in the tale he himself relates escapes his own recognition and comprehension.

As Meriwether explains to Littleton, after he informs Abe of his decision, Abe becomes moody, sullen, silent, and clearly angry about his master's decision. Abe then secludes himself in his mother's cabin but has a steady stream of visitors, particularly the older slaves, which suggests that they take advantage of this opportunity for privacy. Because of the invasive nature of slave life due to the constant supervision and relentless scrutiny of their labor in the fields and the master's house, the slave cabins, the kitchen, and often the woods and swamps afforded slaves the few places they could procure privacy; in these spaces, as Gates notes, "free of the white person's gaze, black people created their own unique vernacular structures and relished in the double play that these forms bore to white forms" (*Signifying Monkey* xxiv).[12] While Meriwether, as the narrator in this story, has no access to these private discussions, the change in Abe's behavior and his comments before he leaves indicate that the older members of the plantation community have utilized the occasion to equip Abe with information: "As the little community in which he had always lived gathered around him, with some signs of unusual interest, to talk over the nature of his employments, a great deal reached his ears from the older negroes, that opened upon his mind a train of perceptions highly congenial to the latent properties of his character. His imagination was awakened by the attractions of this field of adventure; by the free roving of the sailor . . . as they were pictured to him in story" (471). Joyner notes the importance of storytelling in the slave community and contends:

> To attempt to delineate the nature of power relations on the slave plantation without taking into consideration the evidence of the slaves' folktales is to ignore the medium through which they spoke from their very souls. Such questions as to what extent the slaves "accepted" the authority of the masters as legitimate will remain egregious speculation until careful analysis is made of the storytelling engaged in by the slaves when the master was not around . . . [storytelling] had cultural meaning for the slaves who told and for the slaves who listened . . . storytelling sessions thus functioned as both inspiration and education. (*Shared Traditions* 98)

In addition to storytelling as a subversive form of education, young slaves were also provided with important training and advice by community elders. Marie Jenkins Schwartz points out that

> grandparents or other older adults often played an important role in communicating folkways to a new generation. . . . Slave children grew up in a particularly dangerous world in which owners and overseers might construe even small offenses, a word or a look, as challenging their authority and deserving harsh punishment. Thus, lessons of survival went beyond the usual admonitions offered by parents everywhere not to play near the creek or tease dogs and included instructions on how to avoid trouble with owners and overseers. Guidance in this area began early and continued unrelentingly, as parents and other adults sought to inculcate behavior that would avert retaliations against children, their parents, or other slaves. (124–25)[13]

The older slaves' visits to Lucy's cabin and the stories shared have an observable influence on Abe, and shortly after hearing their tales, Abe's "person grew erect, his limbs expanded to their natural motion, and he once more walked with the light step and buoyant feelings of his young and wayward nature" (471).

The return to Abe's characteristic self-confident and "wayward nature" indicates the sway of the community's elders as well as Abe's trust in their guidance rather than his master. While Meriwether regards the change in Abe's behavior as the positive influence of the community's elders convincing Abe of the advantages of his master's decision, his conduct also suggests a more enigmatic optimism. The change in Abe's attitude as a result of the time he spends with these more experienced individuals suggests that he emerges from the cabin as their chosen signifying son, beneficiary of the wisdom of his trickster fathers.

The notable shift from sullen rebel to cooperative slave suggests that Abe has received information that alters his outlook. Abe's statements just before his departure are described to Littleton by Meriwether, which indicates that he was most likely present during this event, but elements in Meriwether's account suggest a number of signifying techniques operating in this scene that are lost on Meriwether. As Gates points out, signifying is "the slave's trope, the trope of tropes" (*Figures in Black* 236), which is particularly important given Meriwether's view that slaves needed "that constant supervision which the race seems to require" (453). Thus, Abe is performing for a white audience as much as he is communicating with his mother and the other slaves present, which suggests that Abe possesses black insight of white ignorance regarding black individuality and also implies the slave community's cultural interiority. Slaves, however, had to be supremely cautious regarding who could be trusted, particularly with potentially dangerous information. While gossip, critique, or ridicule of masters and mistresses (a common theme of the folktales), and other day-to-day information circulated fairly freely throughout the slave community, discussions of flight or other more risky endeavors was information that was much more carefully guarded. Indeed, several highly risky plots were undermined by black informants, such as Douglass's first escape attempt and the well-known betrayal by slave informants in the Denmark Vesey plot.[14] The scene regarding Abe's departure indicates that several slaves were not privy to or involved with the secretive discussion going on with the older slaves present. While Uncle Jeff and the other older slaves are depicted "conversing with each other in smothered tones," several of the younger slaves watch the scene "in ignorant and wondering silence" (472).

Abe is, moreover, tactically aware of audience, and his statements just before his departure communicate a message to Meriwether that is quite different from the communication to the older slaves as well as his mother, which suggests the trickster's characteristic double voice. Abe tells his mother, "'I never cared about the best silver my master ever had: no, nor for freedom neither. I thought I was always going to stay here on the plantation. I would rather have the handkerchief you wear around your neck, than all the silver you ever owned'" (474). These statements operate on a number of signifying levels. Meriwether takes his statements literally, understanding Abe to mean that he does not want freedom, whereas the communication to his mother is that he values her handkerchief above freedom or silver. Abe's statements also operate to satirize Meriwether's claims regarding slave families. During their visit to the quarters, Meriwether had explained to Littleton, in the presence of several slaves, particularly the older slaves, that he highly disapproves of the practice of separating black families and asserts that there should be laws established that would "respect and secure the bonds of husband and wife, and parent and child" (459). Abe's comment that he assumed he would always "'stay here on the plantation'" functions to ridicule the integrity of Meriwether's word by his removal from the plantation and thus his family. A more subversive communication to the older slaves present is also suggested by their secretive behavior, depicted as they are whispering together "in smothered tones" (472).

Abe's comment regarding liberty also operates on dual levels. Abe overtly refuses the idea of freedom but covertly suggests repudiation of a definition of freedom granted by white authority empowered to give and take his legal and social identity. Harriet Jacobs takes a similar stance when Mrs. Bruce offers to purchase her freedom. Jacobs writes, "I felt grateful for the kindness that prompted this offer, but the idea was not so pleasant to me as might have been expected. The more my mind had become enlightened, the more difficult it was for me to consider myself an article of property" (205). In spite of Jacobs's refusal, Mrs. Bruce purchases her freedom and sends word that the official "bill of sale" has been completed. Jacobs recalls, "I well know the value of that bit of paper; but much as I love freedom, I do not like to look upon it" (206). To Jacobs, the document represents "payment for what never rightfully belonged to him or his" family (206). The complexity of language relative to the notion of freedom, moreover, imparts a subtle distinction in terminology. In *Liberty and Freedom*, David Hackett Fischer explains that during the revolutionary and early national eras, liberty referred to "ideas of independence, separation, and autonomy for individuals or groups" whereas freedom was understood as "belonging and full membership in a community of free people" (10). Thus, Abe does not reject "freedom" in terms of liberty but repudiates an authority empowered to legally and socially define him, and as a result, rejects membership within that community entirely. It is interesting to note that, as MacKethan points out, Kennedy often visited his Virginia relatives at a plantation that, according to Kennedy's cousin, "'was merrily [and I would add ironically] nicknamed Liberty Hall'" (xxi).

The role of Abe's father, Luke, also functions to demonstrate another example of Meriwether's limited and flawed hermeneutic abilities, again misunderstanding the meaning of the word *freedom.* He explains to Littleton, with great satisfaction, that after the Revolutionary War, Luke's master, Captain Hazard, offers "Luke his freedom; but the domestic desired no greater liberty than he then enjoyed, and would not entertain the idea of any possible separation from the family" (465). Meriwether's account suggests that "the family" refers to the master's family, but a few sentences later, he notes that during the war, "Luke had married Lucy, a slave who had been reared in the family, as a lady's maid, and, occasionally, as a nurse to the children at Swallow Barn" (465). Over the course of their marriage, they have "eight or nine children," yet it does not seem to occur to Meriwether that Luke's rejection of manumission is a refusal to leave his own wife and children rather than his master's family (466). As Kolchin points out, most Southern states passed laws that "required that those who were freed to leave their borders" (128). In 1806, Virginia passed legislation requiring manumitted slaves to leave the state within one year. The statute reads: "And be it further enacted, That if any slave hereafter emancipated shall remain within this commonwealth more than twelve months after his or her right to freedom shall have accrued, he or she shall forfeit all such right, and may be apprehended and sold by the overseers of the poor of any county or corporation in which he or she shall be found, for the benefit of the poor of such county or corporation" (Guild 72).[15]

Early in the novel, Littleton is accompanied by a free black, Scipio, but he is depicted as very old and may have been manumitted as a way to eliminate the cost of his care after his labor is no longer productive, which was a common and rather heartless practice. Douglass notes that this was the fate of his grandmother and explains that after having "served my old master faithfully from youth to old age," she was sold, but her new owners "finding she was of but little value, her frame already racked with the pains of old age, and complete helplessness fast stealing over her once active limbs, they took her to the woods, built her a little hut, put up a little mud-chimney, and then made her welcome to the privilege of supporting herself there in perfect loneliness, thus virtually turning her out to die!" (180).[16] Scipio is also dependent on himself in his old age for his support and is tolerated in the community due to his advanced age and his rather convincing performance of deference and servility.

With a young family, however, Luke's manumission would have put him at much greater risk of being forced to leave had he had any trouble with the white community, and he would have been constantly vulnerable to being "apprehended and sold" (251). Luke's decision, thus, reflects what was a common dilemma for many slaves. As Douglass explains in his "Narrative": "It is my opinion that thousands would escape from slavery, who now remain, but for the strong cords of affection that bind them to their friends" (319). Meriwether's account of Luke's intention and perspective again suggests a narrator who doesn't fully understand the complexities of the stories he tells.

The years Abe spends as a sailor can be viewed as various types of training and preparation. Although William L. Andrews suggests that Abe functions as a "rebel without a cause," the dramatic change in Abe's behavior indicates that he has likely learned how to more productively channel his rebellious nature, which suggests that he is operating as a rebel with a rather covert cause (308–9). Within a few years, "great changes had been wrought upon him; he had grown into a sturdy manhood, invigorated by the hardy discipline of his calling. The fearless qualities of his mind, no less than the activity and strength of his body, had been greatly developed to the advantage of his character; and, what does not unfrequently happen, the peculiar adaptation of his new pursuits to the temper and cast of his constitution, had operated favorably upon his morals" (479). It is clear that Abe is well suited in his role as a sailor and that his mother benefits from the glowing reports by "his employers," which "had worked wonders in his favor at Swallow Barn," and he is permitted visits with his family (474). Yet the most dramatic change in Abe occurs before he leaves Swallow Barn, which suggests that his years at sea serve to help prepare him to carry out a plan that likely originated in the quarters during visits in which "a great deal reached his ears from the older negroes . . . pictured to him in story" (471). The stories of the oral tradition reflect the collective and creative wisdom of the black community and feature heroes very different from either the heroes lauded in white romance novels or the historical record of white men. The heroes celebrated in the black community were the tricksters featured in their folklore and the fugitive whose success required the trickster's characteristic wit.

What equips the trickster with power is not gaining access to legal authority, state power (in an overtly corporeal sense), or state control (in an ideological sense), but the sheer intellectual wit of the individual maneuvering within, under, and around official forms of power. In the animal tales of the oral tradition, Brer Rabbit's advantage is not simply his ability to escape danger and survive but also his aptitude for subverting power and undermining authority using intelligence as his only weapon. Riggins R. Earl Jr. explains that the stories of the trickster "show the creative way that the slave community responded to the oppressor's failure to address them as human beings created in the image of God. The stories reflect the genius of the oppressed community to create its own symbols in defiance of the perverted logic of the oppressor" (131). And, as Lawrence Levine explains: "The slaves' animal and human trickster tales shared a number of common elements: They placed the same emphasis upon the tactics of trickery and indirection, took the same delight in seeing the weak outwit and humiliate the strong, manifested the same lack of idealization, and served the same dual function which included the expression of repressed feelings and the inculcation of the tactics of survival. . . . He could outwit his master again and again, but his primary satisfaction would be in making his master look foolish and thus exposing the myth of white omniscience and omnipotence" (131–32). The trickster's ability to dupe, deceive, and often render his foe the fool has cast this figure into enduring heroic status.

Abe's actions and comments on the night of the storm insinuate trickster tactics representative of the trickster hero, and in particular, the fugitive trickster hero. Years of training at sea have equipped Abe with skill, introduced him to the black community of sailors, and diminished the threat to his family that his resistance to authority exposes them. However, while Abe enjoys many privileges as a sailor, he remains the legal property of Meriwether, and as such, he is always vulnerable to sale or Meriwether's decision to hire him anywhere he chooses. The storm and distressed ship, however, provides Abe and his "associates" an opportunity to become, not heroes of the chivalric code but of the tropolocial code. Littleton notes that in spite of an appeal "made to the most experienced mariners in port to undertake this voyage," in addition to rewards offered, these experienced white sailors "either evaded the duty, by suggesting doubts of its utility, or cast their eyes towards the heavens and significantly shook their heads, as they affirmed that there would be more certainty of loss to the deliverers than to the people of the stranded vessel" (480). Abe, however, "heard attentively, all that was said in disparagement of the projected enterprise; and it was with some emotion of *secret pleasure* that he learned that several seamen of established reputation had declined to undertake the venture. . . . He went immediately to those who had interested themselves in concerting the measure of relief, and tendered his services for the proposed exploit" (my emphasis 481). Littleton implies that Abe's secret pleasure is his sense of superior courage, but the emotion of secret pleasure may also be read as Abe's exhilaration in cagily recognizing a unique and perhaps long-awaited opportunity. While some slave escapes required immediate action after gaining dangerous information regarding a pending sale, other fugitives developed plots over the course of months and often years, requiring careful planning as well as patience in waiting for the right opportunity.[17]

Several scholars, however, contend that Abe volunteers for a "suicide" mission. Susan Tracy claims that Abe "died a hero's death" in his attempt "to rescue white sailors run aground in a storm" (147). Similarly, Michael Grimwood asserts that Abe sacrifices "himself in attempting to save white lives" (240).[18] But Abe does not embark on this mission alone, and moreover, it is unlikely he would put his fellow sailors at the same level of risk he would accept for himself, particularly with no indication of a discussion, which begins to insinuate a very different type of mission. Abe immediately "tendered his services" and established his "conditions," which include "the choice of his boat, and the selection of his crew" (481). Significantly, Abe chooses his crew "entirely from the number of negro seamen then in Norfolk. They amounted to four or five of the most daring and robust of Abe's associates" (481). Littleton claims that Abe's "associates" are "lured by the hope of reward, as well as impelled by that spirit of rivalry that belongs to even the lowest classes of human beings" (481). However, there is no discussion, no hesitation, and Abe's confidence in his selection of men implies knowledge of his crew rather than assumption. Further, Abe's associates immediately "placed themselves under the orders of their gallant and venturous captain" (481). In contrast to the refusal of every white sailor to accept the mission, as well as the "disheartening auguries of wise and disciplined veterans of the sea," the unquestioned acceptance of Abe's all-black crew suggests that they are carrying out a plan rather than accepting an offer. Jones points out that "the narrator ignores the very real possibility that the entire gesture had been nothing more than an opportunistic escape attempt on the part of Abe and his all-black crew, thus allowing Littleton to maintain his romantic view of the episode" (147). Ignoring the possibility of escape certainly enables Littleton to maintain his romantic view of the event, particularly the perspective of chivalric heroism, but the details of the account also suggest that Littleton once again provides narrative information that he fails to analyze and thus does not entirely understand.

Fully aware of the danger, the plan is not "the endeavor of a fool-hardy madman who was rushing on his fate" as Littleton claims because there is nothing in Abe's history or behavior to suggest foolishness, madness, or that he undervalues his life but rather suggests a mission that Abe and his associates are willing to risk their lives to attempt (482). Their determination intimates an agenda and commitment similar to what Douglass describes in his "Narrative": "In coming to a fixed determination to run away, we did more than Patrick Henry, when he resolved upon liberty or death. With us it was a doubtful liberty at most, and almost certain death if we failed. For my part, I should prefer death to hopeless bondage" (306). In addition to the evident commitment of the crew to their leader's plan, they also display bravery characteristic of traditional heroes, which, however, functions as a mask to conceal another type of heroism, the type featured in the genre of the slave narrative. Dickson Bruce explains that fugitives "emphasized their willingness to take risks for freedom. Every narrative documented a fight for freedom and did so in a manner that fit into larger contexts of ideas that had been pervasive in America since the era of the Revolution. These ideas were built on the notion that the people who most deserved freedom were those who were willing to risk their lives for it" (41). Another crucial element featured throughout the slave narrative tradition, as Bruce points out, was the "ingenuity" necessary in constructing a viable plan. The conduct of Abe and his crew overtly demonstrates bravery but covertly suggests ingenuity in carrying out a plan of escape rather than rescue, which is further suggested in the story by the symbolic name in Abe's choice of boat.

The name of the vessel Abe chooses, "the Flying Fish," functions emblematically to signify on an important legend of the black oral tradition, "the Flying African."[19] Indeed, the tale has proven a rich resource for a wide range of authors, such as Toni Morrison in *Song of Solomon* and Ishmael Reed in his novel *Flight to Canada*.[20] Wendy W. Walters explains that "the legend of the Flying Africans is a canonical tale which resonated throughout the expressive traditions of that part of the African diaspora which has known slavery in the New World" (3). Walters cites Esteban Montejo's account of the legend: "'Some people said that when a Negro died he went back to Africa, but this is a lie. How could a dead man go to Africa? It was living men who flew there, from a tribe the Spanish stopped importing as slaves because so many of them flew away that it was bad for business'" (3). The details of Abe's mission suggest that he operates in the role of the fugitive trickster to carry out the legend of the "Flying African" using the trickster's characteristic wit, which also functions as a signifying play on

Montejo's rhetorical question: "How could a dead man go to Africa?" While dead men can't, living men can signify on the "lie" by playing dead or "playing 'possum." The most well-known hero of the animal folktales is Brer Rabbit, yet the cycle also features a number of other weak animals pitted against stronger animals, including Brer Possum. In the tale "Why Mr. Possum Loves Peace," Brer Possum is pursued by Mr. Dog, and "de ve'y fus pass he [Mr. Dog] make Brer Possum fetch a grin frum year ter year, en keel over like he wuz dead" (Harris, *Complete Tales of Uncle Remus* 9). This strategy is alluded to earlier in the novel by Carey's subtle but important involvement after the discovery of "a large old 'possum" (397). In discussing plans to engage in a "'possum" hunt, Carey advises Harvey, Littleton, and Hazard to be aware that "'a 'possum was one of the cunningest things alive'" (399). As they corner the 'possum, "no sooner was pursuit threatened, or a cry raised, than he fell back into the same supine and deceitful resemblance of a lifeless body" (410). Because of Carey's insight regarding this animal's "cunning" nature, the strategy fails in this situation, but a similar tactic is suggested by Swallow Barn's signifying son with signs of greater success because this trickster's audience is less savvy regarding the performative nature of the trick.

Abe's role as a trickster equipped with black insight of his audience's ignorance is especially evident in the dialogue he engages in with the white sailors who caution against his plan. As Abe prepares to sail, one of the sailors chastises him and complains: "'It will be so dark to-night, you will not be able to see your jib'" (478). Abe replies: "'The little Flying Fish has ridden, summer and winter, over as heavy seas as ever rolled in the Chesapeake. I knows what she can do, you see'" (478). But the sailor offering the advice is resistant to fully contemplate what Abe "knows" and thus dismisses his comment as misguided chivalric bravery. Another sailor adds, "'Why, you couldn't find the brig if you were within a cable's length of her . . . if you were to see her I don't know how you are to get alongside'" (479). In Abe's response, he claims: "'I always obey orders!'" (479). However, Abe has *volunteered* for the mission. He is clearly not following his master's orders, and there is no evidence to suggest that he is following the orders of his "employers." Thus, his statement intimates that he obeys the orders of a higher authority, which again indicates use of double voice operating as a deceptive device.

Abe's responses suggest that he is not simply ignoring the sailors' caution regarding obscured visibility as a result of harsh weather but that he depends on poor visibility. As Abe heads out of port, he and his crew, as

Littleton notes, sail "into the profound, dark abyss of the ocean, when all his terrors were gathering in their most hideous forms" (483). As night falls, the spectators watch from shore as the "Flying Fish" sails "into the palpable obscure of the perspective" (480). The "perspective" is certainly obscured by the physical conditions of the storm but is also used to Abe's advantage. Once lost to view, the witnesses rely on the rather confusing "tale" of the "one seaman alone of the brig" to survive. MacKethan points out that this odd tale draws elements from "Coleridge's 'The Rime of the Ancient Mariner'" (xvii). But "various speculation" regarding "the destiny of Abe and his companions" introduces other possibilities, including the notion that "they might have luffed up close in the wind and ridden out the night, as the Flying Fish was stanch and true" and that "there was even a chance, that they had scudded before the gale, and, having good sea-room, had *escaped* into the middle of the Atlantic" (my emphasis 485). After three weeks with no sign of the vessel or the crew, "all doubts were abandoned, and the loss of the Flying Fish and her crew, ceased any longer to furnish topics of discussion" (485). The lack of any physical evidence of either the boat or the crew suggests that the mission of these experienced sailors was to depend on "the Flying Fish" to carry them through the storm rather than attempt to accomplish an objective the community's seasoned sailors have deemed impossible and regard as suicidal.

Further evidence that Abe's mission was very different from the white community's assumption is provided by what Littleton describes as an "unaccountable" fact and notes that when Lucy is informed of her son's death, "instead of giving herself up to such grief as might have been expected from her attachment to her son, received the intelligence even with composure" (485). In contrast to her emotional reaction when Abe leaves the plantation, fully aware of "the probabilities of future intercourse," her composure suggests that the news is not a surprise (471). Lucy "shed no tears, and scarcely deserted her customary occupations" (485). She does, however, demonstrate "an urgent and eager solicitude to hear whatever came from Norfolk, or from the Chesapeake" (485). Her uncharacteristic behavior, in addition to her refusal to wear the mourning dress Meriwether's wife prepares for her, suggests that her behavior demonstrates interest for news rather than confirmation of death. Indeed, when the dress is offered to her, she refuses it, claiming that "'it would be bad luck to Abe'" (487). Furthermore, her "unusual wanderings, by night, into the neighboring wood," while interpreted by Meriwether as "decay of reason," implies that she has access to information from a more covert source and, moreover, insinuates her complicity in Abe's flight as well as her own personal sacrifice for the best interest of her son. Lucy's loss also undermines proslavery theorists' claims that slaves inherently lacked the emotional sensitivity necessary to form deep attachments to their families that whites possessed. According to one proslavery theorist, "'the Negroes' natural affections are not strong, and consequently he is cruel to his offspring, and suffers little by separation from them'"; another claims that "'blacks are totally lacking in family feeling'" (qtd. in Fredrickson 58). Kennedy, however, offers a significant departure from these views by presenting a portrait of black family life united by deep familial bonds. Lucy is not only intensely committed to her son, demonstrating a mother's love for her child, but her daughter is also depicted taking great care of her elderly mother.

As the years pass, however, Lucy begins to show real signs of dementia, particularly evidenced by her confusion regarding the period of uncertainty just after Abe's disappearance and the types of questions she had posed, which threaten to expose information regarding the nature of Abe's mission. Lucy's progressive instability is most evident when she calls the "old negroes" to her cabin and announces Abe's return. When they arrive at her cabin, she addresses "an empty chair beside her, as if someone occupied it, [and] lavished upon the imaginary Abe a thousand expressions of solicitude and kindness" (489). The slaves leave her cabin in dismay but quickly form a plan to convince her of her son's death. The slaves return to Lucy's cabin "hoping to remove the illusion that Abe was still alive" and give her "a handkerchief resembling that which she had given to him on his first departure; and, in delivering it to her, reported a fabricated tale, that it had been taken from around the neck of Abe, by a sailor who had seen the body washed up by the tide upon the beach of the sea, and had sent this relic to Lucy as a token of her son's death" (489). While the "fabricated tale" is intended to comfort Lucy, it is also likely a way to protect dangerous and carefully concealed information, which is particularly evident given the many years that have passed since Abe's disappearance. The emotionally symbolic nature of the handkerchief finally convinces Lucy that Abe is indeed dead, yet Lucy continues to fluctuate between acceptance and confusion. The section ends with Lucy asking Meriwether and Littleton: "'How many years may a ship sail at sea without stopping?'" (490). Lucy's question demonstrates a very different perspective of her son's fate at the time of his disappearance, indicating that her concern was worry regarding the length of time Abe and his crew would need to sail without assistance rather than any expressed concern or interest in details of his demise. Meriwether and

Littleton, however, fail to analyze Lucy's question and simply dismiss her comments as evidence "of insanity" from the mind of a "crazed old menial" (489).

Meriwether's quick dismissal of Lucy's question also suggests resistance to consider information that would force into Meriwether's consciousness the notion that he and the entire white community have been outwitted by this slave. The idea of Abe's escape would also introduce additional unwelcomed details, indicating that not only has one of Meriwether's slaves escaped but further suggest that this slave has swindled the white community into allowing him to handpick his fellow fugitives, giving him the expensive vessel in which he makes his escape, watching as the fugitives embark on their flight from slavery, and deeming their ringleader bold, brave, and heroic. Furthermore, because all are presumed dead, the plan ensures that there will not be an extensive search for the men and that their families will not suffer retaliation for their actions. Abe and his crew are thus hailed as heroes of the chivalric code by Meriwether and Littleton, who resist deciphering the signifying techniques operating in the story they themselves present; for the slaves of Swallow Barn, Abe serves as a very different type of hero. Blassingame observes that the escaped slave became "a hero in the quarters. Symbolic of black resistance to slavery, the rebel and the runaway indicate that the black slave was often ungovernable" (131). Jones terms the discourses critical of slavery as "unwelcomed voices" and contends that "it might appear strange to include a writer who has long been considered as part of the foundation for the plantation ideals in southern literature as one of the 'unwelcome voices' of the antebellum period," but this reductive perspective "simply ignored the sections of *Swallow Barn* that were critical of its society and only saw it as a celebration of southern values and culture" (153). The novel's most urgent critique is ironically an indirect distrust of the planter elite to fulfill the promise to write the "emancipation plot" and ultimately figure out how to "let the wolf go." By including trickster figures empowered by wit, black insight, and community wisdom, Kennedy suggests that the emancipation plot is imperative as well as expected. Yet the novel's critique of Southern society also registers doubt regarding whether that plot would be written by the planter elite or for the planter elite.

The hermeneutic limitations of *Swallow Barn*'s narrators suggest stories they present but are ill-equipped to fully understand, largely due to active resistance regarding knowledge that would challenge their worldview. Furthermore, this type of active resistance is not limited to the interpretive deficiencies of *Swallow Barn*'s narrators but functions to foreshadow hermeneutic limitations and incompatibilities between black and white discourses that continue throughout the nineteenth century and well into the twentieth. As Gates points out, "Sterling Brown has summed up the relation of the black tradition to the Western critical tradition. In response to Robert Penn Warren's line from 'Pondy Woods': 'Nigger, your breed ain't metaphysical.' Brown replies: 'Cracker, your breed ain't exegetical'" (*Figures in Black* xix). The stories of the novel's black characters are provided by Meriwether and Littleton, but their inability to decode the narrative plane on which these stories operate shields them from understanding the type of hero they themselves describe. They characterize Abe's actions as chivalric rather than explore elements in the narrative that would compel them to, as Shoshana Felman notes, acknowledge their "own implication in the information" (417), which would reveal a character employing the wisdom of the black community to orchestrate a plan that utilizes trickster wit to become the subversive hero of the quarters, the successfully escaped slave, or, in other words, the fugitive trickster hero.

Chapter 2

Come Back to the Cabin Ag'in, Tom Honey![1]

Sparked to action by her disgust over the passage of the fugitive slave act in 1850, Harriet Beecher Stowe began work on what would eventually become the best-selling novel of the nineteenth century, *Uncle Tom's Cabin, or, Life among the Lowly*. Stowe drew inspiration from the death of her infant son Charley in 1849, which led her to contemplate similar losses suffered by slave mothers whose children were sold from them. Stowe's objective was not simply to depict the evils of the institution of slavery but further to "show the wrongheadedness of whites' contempt for blacks" (Reynolds 38). Much of her information regarding the lives of slaves, particularly women, came from firsthand accounts of former slaves who worked in her home during her years in Cincinnati, Ohio.[2] The house the Stowes lived in during this time was located on the outskirts of the city and rather isolated. The women Stowe hired provided not only welcomed help with the domestic duties of this financially struggling wife and mother of seven but much-needed company as well. Stowe drew from a wide range of literary and cultural sources in composing her novel, but these personal stories brought her emotionally and aesthetically into their world.

Uncle Tom's Cabin was originally published in weekly installments in the abolitionist paper the *National Era* from June to March in 1851. In 1852, the book was published in two volumes and sold more than 5,000 copies in its first week, "and from that point onward sales were astonishing—50,000 copies within eight weeks, 200,000 by January 1853, 300,000 after the first year" (Meer 4). Yet in spite of its unprecedented popularity, the novel generated an enormous amount of controversy and continues to do so well into the twenty-first century. While most nineteenth-century African American readers embraced the novel, Stowe's depiction of black characters was also a source of controversy. In a letter to Frederick Douglass in early April 1853, Martin Delany disdains *Uncle Tom's Cabin* and claims that Stowe "'*knows nothing about us*'" (qtd. in R. Levine, "*Uncle Tom's Cabin* in *Frederick Douglass' Paper*" 80; italics in original). In a later letter, however, Delany notes, "'I am of the opinion, that Mrs. Stowe has drafted largely on all the best fugitive slave narratives . . . but of this I am not competent to judge, not having as yet *read* 'Uncle Tom's Cabin,' my *wife* having *told* me the most I know about it'" (81; italics in original).[3]

Stowe's depictions of black characters and the narrative point of view regarding race (which is commonly assumed to reflect her personal views) continue to be contentious issues. When Henry Louis Gates Jr. was approached to edit an annotated edition of the novel, which he then invited Hollis Robbins to coedit with him, his interest in the project was piqued by these controversies. He explains in an interview:

> I wanted to figure out how a book that was so popular among African Americans, particularly African American intellectuals, in the nineteenth century—Frederick Douglass, William G. Allen in 1853 reviewed it—Frederick Douglass wrote about it between 1853 and 1855. Du Bois in 1903 talked about how beautifully rendered the book had been. And James Weldon Johnson said the two most important influences on the shaping of the African American literary tradition were *The Souls of Black Folk* and *Uncle Tom's Cabin*. And he wasn't being ironic or cynical or talking about it in a negative way. How a book that those gods of the black tradition could revere so thoroughly could become reviled for our generation, and the person who was the hero of that novel became the—or his name—the epithet for race betrayal, for the worst thing that you could possibly be in the African American tradition. ("*Uncle Tom's Cabin* Reconsidered")

As several scholars have observed, James Baldwin's essay, "Everybody's Protest Novel," generated a significant shift in the critical perspective of the narrative. Baldwin deems *Uncle Tom's Cabin* "a very bad novel" and claims that the hero, Tom, is a character who "has been robbed of his humanity and divested of his sex" (18).[4]

In response to Stowe's contemporary critics, like Delany who condemned the novel as sentimental propaganda that failed to accurately portray black life, Stowe published *A Key to Uncle Tom's Cabin* in 1853.[5] Stowe defends her motives for writing the novel as well as her character portraits, black and white, as deriving from personal experiences, published accounts, and stories shared by family members witnessing several events depicted in the narrative. It is also important to point out that Stowe's original audience was fairly limited. The predominantly white subscribers of the *National*

Era paper would have been open to her antislavery agenda but typically much less receptive to issues of social equality.[6] Stowe biographer David S. Reynolds notes that Stowe's husband and father were like most white abolitionists: conservatives who advocated for gradual abolition, supported colonization, opposed social equality, and tended to view more aggressive reform leaders like William Lloyd Garrison as extremists.[7] Stowe was also conscious of the potential for violent response to the more highly charged rhetoric calling for immediate abolition, such as the fate of her brother Edward's friend, the antislavery editor Elijah P. Lovejoy, who was shot and killed in 1837 at the warehouse "where the editor's printing press was stored" after it "was stormed by furious proslavery citizens" (Reynolds 95). A number of race riots in Cincinnati in 1829, 1836, 1841, and 1843 as well as Ohio's 1804 "Black Codes" further demonstrate the racial tensions of this segregated city, and Stowe was well aware of the hostility directed toward Cincinnati's black population.[8] Stowe's novel, thus, suggests a strategic negotiation of a wide range of cultural materials and sources to promote her overt antislavery agenda as well as more covertly generate greater sensitivity for America's black population, slave and free.[9]

In writing *Uncle Tom's Cabin*, Stowe took a much more complex, intertextual approach than in her earlier works. Debra J. Rosenthal asserts that as "an astute reader of literature and culture, Stowe borrowed and reworked numerous popular images and types. For example, *Uncle Tom's Cabin* incorporates popularly repeated figures such as the innocent dying child, the tragic mulatta, the fugitive mother with youngster, the minstrel performer, the evil slave owner, and the righteous matriarch" (238). The minstrel performer and other aspects of the minstrel tradition has generated a significant amount of critical commentary, most notably regarding the characters Tom, Sam, Andy, Topsy, and Chloe.[10] Yet these characters, and several others, also share another common feature, the trickster ethos of the slave community, which I contend is an important aspect of the novel and features a wide range of various trickster figures including men, women, and children. As H. Nigel Thomas points out, a crucial aspect of black folklife that developed from the slave community taught that "to be black in America and survive necessitates being a trickster" (81).

Stowe demonstrates unique insight into the cultural mores and social values of the slave community, and like John Pendleton Kennedy, features two distinct cultures, the white master class and the slave community, which is often depicted subversively pitted against the master class. A brief scene toward the end of the novel demonstrates that Stowe possessed unique understanding of black insight regarding white ignorance of black individuality and community identity. In chapter 32, "Dark Places," as Legree travels with his coffle of slaves, he calls on the "boys" to entertain him with a song. Tom begins to sing a hymn but is cut short by Legree who demands "something real rowdy" (429). Stowe writes,

> One of the other men struck up one of those unmeaning songs, common among the slaves. "Mas'r see'd me cotch a coon;
> High boys, high!
> He laughed to split,—d'ye see the moon,
> Ho! ho! ho! boys, ho!
> Ho! yo! hi—e! oh!"
> ... It was sung very boisterously, and with a forced attempt at merriment; but no wail of despair, no words of impassioned prayer, could have had such a depth of woe in them as the wild notes of the chorus. As if the poor, dumb heart, threatened,—prisoned,—took refuge in that inarticulate sanctuary of music, and found there *a language* in which to breathe its prayer to God! There was a prayer in it which Simon could not hear. (my emphasis 430)

Stowe's note that the singer began "one of those unmeaning songs, common among the slaves" but then providing clear insight regarding the subversive nature of these common songs demonstrates her keen perception of the complexities of black vernacular culture, and notably, Legree's inability to understand the dual nature of the musical discourse he hears. Moreover, Legree is not the only character who demonstrates white ignorance of black individuality and cultural interiority. Indeed, most of her white characters evince similar limitations, which provides an additional "key to Uncle Tom's Cabin."

Stowe opens the novel with a subtitle that also signifies a dual meaning. Gates points out that in this chapter, "Stowe begins signaling almost immediately that one of her primary concerns in the novel is the flexibility of language" (*Annotated Uncle Tom's Cabin* 5). In chapter 1, "In Which the Reader Is Introduced to a Man of Humanity," Stowe introduces "two gentlemen." One, however, "did not seem, strictly speaking, to come under the species," whereas the other, "Mr. Shelby, had the appearance of a gentleman" (14).[11] Shelby's etiquette, dress, and speech are representative of a Southern man of honor, and he is introduced as a traditional benevolent patriarch, "disposed to easy indulgence to those around him, and there had never been a lack of any thing which might contribute to the physical comfort of the negroes on his estate" (22). As the chapter develops, however, Shelby is revealed to be an antithesis of the Southern cultural ideal. He is an inept authority figure, a liar, a coward, and incompetent regarding the management of his business affairs. Indeed, it is his deficient business acumen that compels his distasteful involvement with a man he regards as his social inferior. Shelby demonstrates the weakness of his authority as the men negotiate terms, and Shelby asks that their affairs are conducted in a "quiet way." He tells Haley, "'You'd best not let your business in this neighborhood be known. It will get out among my boys, and it will not be a particularly quiet business getting away any of my fellows, if they know it, I'll promise you'" (21). The advice suggests that Shelby fears difficulties with his slaves as well as the public exposure that could jeopardize his reputation in "this neighborhood" as a result of the dangers of the "grapevine." In the slave narratives, as Osofsky notes, "references to a secret slave communications system appear in many narratives. Some, like Douglass, talk of double meaning in songs, but most just mention the fact that the system existed" (26). This communication network is first highlighted when slaves belonging to other "families hard by" attend a prayer meeting in Tom's cabin and share "various choice scraps of information, about the sayings and doings at the house and on the place" (47). Shelby's request to Haley to maintain privacy regarding their affairs indicates he fears the dangers the grapevine could pose to his reputation in the neighborhood.

Another character flaw is demonstrated by Shelby's cowardice after he consents to sell Tom and Harry, and he tells his wife, "'I'm going to get out my horse bright and early, and be off. I can't see Tom, that's a fact; and you had better arrange a drive somewhere, and carry Eliza off. Let the thing be done when she is out of sight'" (56). Mrs. Shelby reminds her husband that he has "'promised him his freedom'" and adds, "'You and I have spoken to him a hundred times of it,' yet as this scene demonstrates, Shelby's "word" is good only with another white man (52).[12] After Eliza's flight, Shelby is unable to leave as planned and is forced to face Tom. He attempts to maintain his image as a benevolent patriarch by telling Tom that he can have the day to himself as well as by addressing this man, who we learn is eight years his senior, with the pejorative term *boy* (81). Throughout this scene, Shelby's only genuine concern is that Eliza's flight, as he tells his wife, "'touches my honor'" (62). In these early chapters, Stowe consistently depicts not "a man of humanity" but rather of appearances.

In the opening chapter, Stowe also presents clear distinctions between the cultural features of the slaveholding class and the slave community.

Ezra Tawil contends that the slave community functions mimetically as an inferior imitation of the white community and asserts that "the novel's emphasis on the 'negro's' mimetic nature" indicates that "the trope of the 'imitative negro,' I argue, is in fact the linchpin of the novel's racial theory" (154). This perspective, however, overlooks numerous scenes that feature the black community covertly at odds with the white community. Marie Jenkins Schwartz notes that "extensive family networks among slaves formed the social basis for African-American communities and fostered the development and spread of an African-American culture with rules of conduct differing from those of owners" (11).[13] For instance, throughout the novel, slaves often gain important information by eavesdropping on their masters, which indicates a common lack of trust. The first example is when Eliza overhears Mr. Shelby and Haley talking in the parlor, and "she would gladly have stopped at the door to listen" further but "her mistress just then calling, she was obliged to hasten away" (22). She does, however, hear "enough of the conversation to know that a slave trader was making offers to her master for somebody" and brings her concerns to Mrs. Shelby (22).

Mrs. Shelby is commonly viewed as a model of virtue and compassion and representative of the nineteenth-century's ideal "of true womanhood."[14] Rosenthal identifies this character as the novel's "righteous matriarch," and Reynolds refers to her as an "anti-slavery woman" (238; 79). Stowe, however, provides several elements that undermine this characterization, particularly when she tells Eliza that Mr. Shelby "'never means to sell any of his servants as long as they behave well'" (23). While this comment is intended to alleviate Eliza's fears, the statement also contains a highly dangerous threat: "as long as they behave." Mrs. Shelby also implies irritation with Eliza's eavesdropping by her advice: "'Don't go listening at doors any more'" (23). Furthermore, Mrs. Shelby shows her own limited understanding of her family's slaves when she attempts to dissuade her husband from selling Tom and Harry and asks him, "'But why, of all others, choose these? . . . Why sell them, of all on the place, if you must sell at all?'" (53). Her initial reaction is not opposition to selling slaves but to the sale of particular family favorites. Based on this response, is it unlikely she would have shown similar resistance to the sale of Sam or Andy. She specifically opposes the sale of Tom because, as she tells her husband, the transaction would "'tear from him in a moment all we have taught him to love and value? I have taught them the duties of the family, of parent and child, and husband and wife. . . . I have talked with Eliza about her boy—her duty to him as a Christian mother, to watch over him, pray for him, and bring him up in a Christian way'"

(54). Numerous examples throughout the novel, however, demonstrate that slaves did not need to be "taught" to love their families, and Mrs. Shelby's comments to her husband are enormously revealing regarding her ignorance of these family bonds. Schwartz explains that family ties "served as conduits for cultural continuity between generations. Young slaves learned about marriage, family, and the limits of the owner's power in the slave cabin, not in the owner's house" (11). Furthermore, this "private" conversation is not as private as they assume. Eliza ignores Mrs. Shelby's instructions about "listening at doors," hides in a closet, and "with her ear pressed close against the crack of the door, had lost not a word of their conversation. When the voices died into silence, she rose and crept stealthily away" (56). Eliza's actions indicate that she does not entirely trust her master or her mistress. While Mrs. Shelby opposes her husband's decision to sell Tom and Harry and sanctions, although does not participate in, undermining the pursuit of Eliza and Harry, she takes no further action throughout the course of the novel to oppose slavery or make good on her pledge to redeem Tom. It is Chloe who maintains constant pressure throughout the novel to hold them to this promise.

The Aunt Chloe figure has been regarded as a character whose identity is a reflection of "her exposure to Mrs. Shelby as a model of domesticity" (Tawil 175). Kimberly Wallace-Sanders contends that Chloe functions as an example of "internalized racism" and as a classic although, she observes, complex "image of the mammy stereotype" (5). While Stowe drew from an established literary and cultural antecedent of the Aunt Chloe figure, Stowe's version is a much more savvy and subversive rendition and as such, I contend, more closely resembles what Wallace-Sanders calls an "antimammy" figure, a character she defines as "a mother that blacks could be proud of because she is most loyal to *her* children and therefore to the black community" (49).[15] Genuine loyalty, however, typically had to be concealed and masked by the performance of artificial loyalty, a characteristic tactic of the trickster, particularly in the John and Old Master cycle.

Most tricksters, as Lewis Hyde points out, "are male," but he notes that "there may be female tricksters who have simply been ignored" (185). The potential for overlooked female tricksters is, I contend, more than likely, and while these oversights are clearly a matter of gender, they are also due to highly familiar characteristics that are easily dismissed as limited stereotypes, such as the role often employed for black female characters, the mammy figure. Phil Patton describes the type: "Nurturing and protective, self-sacrificing, long-suffering, wise, often world weary but never bitter,

Mammy mixed kindness with sternness and wrapped her own identity inside that of her heartiness, her own sexuality inside her role as surrogate mother, teacher, and cook. Her outside life—especially her love life—is almost opaque. If she has children, they tend to be treated more brusquely than the white children in her charge. And she never escapes her sense of the limitations of being black" (5E).[16] Wallace-Sanders notes that "within the range of mammy characters Aunt Chloe is, however, a complex and fascinating character often ignored or misinterpreted by critics. She is a rare example of a fictional slave mother who is granted instances of deliberate influential action. The first and perhaps most important action comes when she purposely delays serving a meal so that Eliza can escape with her son Harry" (40). Wallace-Sanders explains that the slaves' plot to assist Eliza in her flight serves as "an example of the historical truth that fugitive slaves relied upon the cooperation of other slaves. Aunt Chloe's loyalty to the slave community is completely antithetical to prototypical mammy behavior and part of the complexity of Chloe's characterization" (41). Chloe's involvement in the scheme is certainly significant, but it is not her first nor most important act of covert resistance to white authority. Wallace-Sanders, however, claims that while Chloe is a complicated character, her relationship with George Shelby undermines her subversive potential, particularly in the scene in which George visits Tom's cabin and "Chloe makes her own children wait while she feeds a young white boy, allowing him to throw food at them and give her orders" (42). It is crucial to point out, however, that the family of this visitor (who may have been regarded as an intruder) to her domestic space *owns* her entire family and that she has no choice but to allow the "young master" to give her orders and is powerless to overtly interfere in his treatment of her children.

Furthermore, Chloe's gushing compliments to George can be viewed as manipulative flattery, which this young man is clearly susceptible to or he wouldn't spend time in a slave cabin rather than his own "easy, and even opulent" home (14). For instance, when George assures Chloe that he is well aware of his "'pie and pudding privileges'" and tells her, "'Ask Tom Lincoln if I don't crow over him every time I meet him,'" Chloe "sat back in her chair, and indulged in a hearty guffaw of laughter, at this witticism of young mas'r's, laughing till the tears rolled down her black, shining cheeks, varying the exercise with playfully slapping and poking Mas'r Georgey, and telling him to go way, and that he was a case—that he was fit to kill her, and that he sartin would kill her, one of these days . . . till George really began to think that he was a very dangerously witty fellow, and that it became him to be careful how he talked 'as funny as he could'" (42). Given Stowe's skills in constructing humorous scenes and depicting characters engaged in witty commentary and dialogue, she certainly could have given George a line that was actually funny.[17] She does not, which intimates that Chloe's extravagant response is intended to boost his ego and suggests that Chloe is signifying on George. Furthermore, Stowe repeatedly uses the term "young mas'r" in her description as well as Chloe's address to George throughout the visit, which reiterates the dynamics of power as well as Chloe's clear understanding of the power structure during this visit.

The scene in Tom's cabin begins by Stowe identifying Chloe's position as the head cook, and after completing her duties in the kitchen, she then heads to "her own snug territories, to 'get her ole man's supper'" (38). George explains his presence by telling Chloe that his family wanted him "'to come to supper in the house,'" but he claims, "'I knew what was what too well for that, Aunt Chloe'" (40). Chloe responds, "'You know'd your old aunty'd keep the best for you. O, let you alone for dat!'" (41). George's preference for supper in the cabin rather than his home, which would have been prepared by the same person, suggests an appetite for flattery as much as his evening meal. Furthermore, while Chloe cannot refuse to serve George and tells him that she has saved the best for him, Chloe returns to her cabin to prepare "her old man's supper," which suggests that she has reserved "the best" for her husband but has to accommodate this visitor. Indeed, the portraits of each member of Tom's family indicate that Chloe is routinely able to provide amply for her family. Chloe is described as having a "round, black, shining face" and a "plumb countenance," and the boys have "fat shining cheeks" (38–39). Tom is a "large, broad-chested, powerfully-made man" (39). In contrast to the "meager shanks" of the slave children described in Kennedy's novel, Chloe is able to use her position to feed her family much more substantially than the typical rations most slaves received.[18] Rather than showing "preference for George," it is more likely Chloe is performing for George and thus "putting on young mas'r."

Chloe's insight into the dynamics of power regarding this visitor is most evident when she tells her rambunctious young boys, "'Can't ye be decent when white folks comes to see ye? Stop dat ar, now, will ye? Better mind yerselves, or I'll take ye down a button-hole lower, when Mas'r George is gone'" (44). Referring to George as Mas'r George while addressing her children as well as noting his race demonstrates Chloe engaging in an important form of training. Schwartz explains that

> slaves needed to cooperate with masters and mistresses and to teach children the day-to-day deference owners considered their due while at the same time securing the youngster's loyalty to his or her family and the larger slave community. Life in the quarter was already precarious, and slaves relied on one another to keep secrets from their owners and to assist each other in times of trouble. Maintaining a cultural space within the family, defined separately from their owners' plantation households, gave slaves a means of creating identities for themselves other than those of master's field hand or mistress's seamstress. Parents wanted children to comply outwardly with owners' expectations concerning behavior; to do so otherwise would have invited disaster upon themselves and their youngsters. (78)

Chloe's interaction with her children in the presence of "young mas'r" highlights the complexities of the slaves' child-rearing practices. It is also important to note that the only instances in which Chloe uses the term *mammy* are when she addresses her *own* children, which further undermines the cultural stereotype.

Chloe also shows her ability to manipulate circumstances by signifying on her mistress when she is busy cooking an extensive dinner for "General Knox" but is continuously interrupted by Mrs. Shelby's advice and annoying "interferin'" (43). She cannot ask her mistress to leave, so she tells her, "'Now, missis, do jist look at dem beautiful white hands 'o yourn, with long fingers, and all a sparkling with rings like my white lilies when de dew's on 'em; and look at my great black stumpin' hands. Now, don't ye think dat de Lord must have meant me to make de pie crust, and you to stay in de parlor?'" (43). Chloe's flattery works to get her mistress out of her way.

Stowe provides much more revealing insight into this character when she is depicted in scenes free from white involvement. Indeed, like many of the novel's black characters, her conduct is notably different when she is in the presence of whites and when she is only with other blacks. A particularly insightful event is demonstrated by Chloe's reaction to the news of Tom's pending sale. Chloe is stunned by the information and states, "'The good Lord have pity on us. . . . O, it don't seem as if it was true! What has he done, that mas'r should sell him?'" (59). Chloe's question demonstrates that she too understands that the Shelbys' slaves are safe "as long as they behave" (23). Moreover, Chloe shows no hesitation when she advises her husband: "'Well, old man!' said Aunt Chloe, 'why don't you go, too? Will you wait to be toted down the river, where they kill niggers with hard work and starving? I'd a heap rather die than go there, any day! There's time for ye,—be off with Lizy,—you've got a pass to come and go any time. Come, bustle up, and I'll get your things together'" (59). Chloe's advice to her husband indicates that her loyalty is to her family and her husband's safety rather than her master's family, which further undermines the mammy stereotype. Moreover, as Peter Kolchin explains, "slaves in the upper South heard rumors of a far more brutal slavery in Alabama, Mississippi, and Louisiana, and being 'sold down the [Mississippi] river' was both a prevalent fear and a threat that masters used to keep their hands in line" (98). Aspects throughout the novel demonstrate that Stowe was also privy to these stories. Stowe notes that "selling to the south is set before the negro from childhood as the last severity of punishment. The threat that terrifies more than whipping or torture of any kind is the threat of being sent down river. We have ourselves heard this feeling expressed by them, and seen the unaffected horror with which they will sit in their gossiping hours, and tell frightful stories of that 'down the river'" (129). Chloe's comments regarding slave life in the Deep South and reference to "the river" indicate that the Shelbys' slaves are familiar with these stories, which additionally suggests that the threat of being sold "down the river" is implicitly embedded in their understanding of the consequences of violating the Shelbys' caveat: "as long as they behave."

The scene in the kitchen features Chloe free from the necessity to mask her opinion and highlights her role in the black community as a character "much revered" by the other slaves, and they are eager to "gossip with her, and to listen to her remarks" (79). Free from the restrictions imposed by white listeners, Chloe holds nothing back in expressing her "indignant" opinion regarding the business dealings between Shelby and Haley. When she is informed that Haley is growing "mightily uneasy" by the delay of the dinner, Chloe states, "'Sarves him right'" and adds, "'He'll get wus nor oneasy, one of these days, if he don't mend his ways. His master'll be sending for him, and then see how he'll look!'" (78). Little Jake opines, "'He'll go to torment, and no mistake,'" and Chloe replies, "'He deserves it! . . . he's broke a many, many, many hearts,—I tell ye all!' she said, stopping with a fork uplifted in her hand; 'it's like what Mas'r George reads in Ravelations,—souls a callin' under the alter! And a callin' on the Lord for vengeance on sich!—and by and by the Lord he'll hear 'em—so he will!'" (79). Tom enters and advises against such sentiments, which critics tend to regard as evidence of his submissive nature, but his advice is intended to protect their spiritual integrity, and he tells Chloe, "'—You oughter thank God that you ain't like him, Chloe. I'm sure I'd rather be sold, ten thousand times over, than to have all that ar poor critter's got to answer for'" (80).[19] Tom's advice, however, does not change Chloe's opinion and just before he is taken into Haley's custody, she expresses her anger and disgust with Mr. Shelby's lack of integrity, telling Tom, "'He owed ye yer freedom, and he ought ter gin't to yer years ago. . . . Them as sells heart's love and heart's blood, to get out thar scrapes, de Lord'll be up to 'em!'" (127–28). She also expresses her irritation with Mrs. Shelby when one of her boys announces that she is approaching. Chloe comments bitterly, "'She can't do no good; what's she comin' for?'" (130). Mrs. Shelby's emotional outburst as well as her pledge to redeem Tom "in a year or two" softens Chloe's anger, but when Haley arrives to take Tom, Stowe notes that she "looked gruffly on the trader, her tears seeming suddenly turned to sparks of fire" (131).

The chaos that ensues on the morning of Eliza's flight provides some of the novel's most humorous passages, and several scholars contend that Stowe drew heavily from the minstrel tradition in these scenes. Richard Yarborough claims that "the blacks she uses to supply much of the humor in *Uncle Tom's Cabin* owe a great deal to the darky figures who capered across minstrel stages and white imaginations in the antebellum years" (47). While Yarborough acknowledges Sam and Andy's "tricksterlike manipulation of Haley," he contends that they are motivated by a desire to "please their mistress" rather than "any real desire to help the fugitives to freedom" and regards the two as "little more than bumptious, giggling, outsized adolescents" (47). Reynolds, however, contends that

> Sam and Andy, who with their antics and clumsy language could come off as minstrel clowns. But they are *not* minstrel clowns. They are enslaved blacks who, along with an antislavery woman, use their wits to outsmart white males intent on enforcing an unjust, proslavery law. Besides stalling Haley through tricks like upsetting his horse, they delay him further with intentionally garbled words about which route Eliza may have taken. To make this potentially offensive scene more acceptable, Stowe has Sam seem comically wishy-washy, but his actions on behalf of the fleeing Eliza in fact support his boast that he is devoted to principles he would die to defend." (79–80)

Wit and trickery are, moreover, characteristics of the trickster hero of the slaves' folktales, which are traits that are evident in a number of black characters in the novel.

Sam's dialect is often cited as evidence of the type of exaggerated imitation of black vernacular featured on the minstrel stage, but his dialect also functions in contrast to the more privileged family favorites who have been educated, like Eliza. Furthermore, Blassingame points out that the Rabbit and other weaker animals featured in the slaves' folktales "are wise, patient, boastful, mischievous, roguish, guileful, cunning," and as Baker explains, "employ daring, resourcefulness, and a type of rude wit to gain personal benefits" (21; *Long Black Song* 12). Sam is a field hand with few privileges, yet like the trickster, uses what he has to his advantage; indeed, Stowe describes him as possessing "a native talent that might, undoubtedly, have raised him to eminence in political life,—a talent of making capital out of every thing that turned up" (102). Sam's potential is restricted by his social and legal status, but he uses his skills in more subversive ways, which suggests that he is primarily motivated by this unique opportunity to benefit himself and secondarily moved to please his mistress and defend his "principles" (80).

The scenes featuring Sam interacting with Haley also demonstrate that Haley is clearly no match for Sam's "native talent." When Sam brings Shelby's horses to begin the search, he notices that Haley's horse is "skeery," and "his black visage lighted up with a curious, mischievous gleam" (66). Sam approaches the "skittish young colt" and "on pretense of adjusting the saddle, he adroitly slipped under it a sharp little nut" (67). When Haley "touched the saddle, the mettlesome creature bounded from the earth with a sudden spring that threw his master sprawling, some feet oft" (69). Sam "attempts" to subdue the horse but "only succeeded in brushing the blazing palm leaf aforenamed into the horse's eyes, which by no means tended to allay the confusion of his nerves . . . and [he] was soon prancing away toward the lower end of the lawn, followed by Bill and Jerry, whom Andy had not failed to let loose, according to contract" (69). In spite of Sam's "heroic" exertions, no one is able to catch the horses until noon and by this time, the horses are exhausted and it is time for "dinner" (71). Stowe then features the two privately relishing the success of their schemes. Off to themselves, "Sam and Andy leaned up against the barn, and laughed to their hearts' content" (71).

Further trickster antics are evident in Sam's dialogue with Haley and reflect the performative nature of slave life. When Haley asks Sam if Shelby keeps any dogs, Sam responds, "'Heaps on 'em,' said Sam, triumphantly; 'thar's Bruno—he's a roarer! And, besides that, 'bout every nigger of us keep a pup of some natur or other'" (82). Stowe notes that "Sam knew exactly what he meant, but he kept on a look of earnest and desperate simplicity"

(82). Sam's most successful "trick" closely resembles Brer Rabbit's well-known tactic of escape from Brer Fox by pleading for what he is most intent to avoid. Sam dupes Haley similarly by drawing him into a verbal game of wit and offers deceptive information he intends Haley to accept as well. Haley informs Sam and Andy that they will "take the straight road to the river," and Sam replies, "'Sartin,' said Sam, 'dat's de idee. Mas'r Haley hits de thing right in the middle'" (83). Sam then introduces misleading information. He tells Haley, "'Now, der's two roads to de river,—de dirt road and der pike" and asks "which mas'r mean to take?'" (83). Sam advises, "'I'd rather be 'clined to 'magine that Lizy'd take de dirt road, bein' it's de least travelled'" (83). Haley becomes annoyed and confused while "Sam's face was immovably composed into the most doleful gravity," and he comments: "'Course,' said Sam, 'mas'r can do as he'd rather; go de straight road, if mas'r thinks best,—it's all one to us. Now when I study 'pon it, I think de straight road de best *deridedly*'" (83). Haley, assuming superior intelligence, takes the dirt road, and the group ends up at a barn that "stood conspicuously and plainly square across the road" (85). Haley accuses Sam of knowing "'all about this,'" and Sam replies quite honestly but with private satisfaction, "'Didn't I tell yer I *know'd?*'" (85). Stowe notes that "it was all too true to be disputed, and the unlucky man had to pocket his wrath" (85). The ploy buys more time, but as they approach the tavern, "Sam's quick eye caught a glimpse of" Eliza, and "at this crisis, Sam contrived to have his hat blown off, and uttered a loud and characteristic ejaculation, which startled her at once" (85). Sam's quick thinking alerts Eliza and enables her escape across the ice.[20]

The pair's ingenuity in duping Haley is, however, often obscured by Stowe's use of dialect, which many critics claim indicates limited intelligence. Meer contends that the humor in these scenes is "rooted in early minstrel themes" and that Sam's comments reflect "the way in which comically uneducated, self-serving, or cowardly characters can also serve to make digs at white slave-owning society" (33). But "digs at white slave-owning society" are much more representative of the slaves' folktales than the minstrel tradition. Another feature that is more indicative of the trickster than the minstrel is the trickster's linguistic skill. Meer deems Sam's verbal play "linguistic anarchy" adapted from "blackface convention" (33). The trickster is, however, a master of linguistic anarchy, and Sam's political scene indicates he is more representative of the trickster hero of the oral tradition than the minstrel fool, a figure Ralph Ellison characterizes as engaged in acts of "self-humiliation" and "symbolic self-maiming" (49).[21]

On the minstrel stage, the black buffoon functioned as the symbolic punch line, but in the trickster tradition, the strong are fooled by the weak and are thus the butt of the joke in this tradition. Stowe notes,

> It must be observed that one of Sam's especial delights had been to ride in attendance on his master to all kinds of political gatherings, where, roosted on some rail fence, or perched aloft in some tree, he would sit watching the orators, with the greatest apparent gusto, and then, descending among the various brethren of his own color, assembled on the same errand, he would edify and delight them with the most ludicrous burlesques and imitations, all delivered with the most imperturbable earnestness and solemnity; and though the auditors immediately about him were generally of his own color, it not unfrequently happened that they were fringed pretty deeply with those of a fairer complexion, who listened, laughing and winking, to Sam's great self-congratulation. (103)

Stowe does not offer a depiction of Sam's imitation of these speeches, but the reference provides context to his later "speechifying." This scene also implies his ability to manipulate Mr. Shelby into joining him on these trips, which yields many benefits. These excursions relieve him of fieldwork, allow him to spend time with his peers, and give him the content and opportunity to ridicule white politicians, which in the antebellum South, were typically men from the planter class. Sam also benefits from the rewards of the kitchen for his clever assistance in helping to undermine the search for Eliza and, indeed, procuring food is often the driving force of many of the John and Old Master as well as Brer Rabbit tales.

A particularly ingenious and bold act of trickery is orchestrated by Eliza's husband George Harris. Mel Watkins notes that Harlem Renaissance author Rudolph Fisher's character Fred Merrit is "one of the first trickster mulattos to emerge in American fiction," yet Stowe's George Harris suggests a trickster mulatto that precedes Fisher's by close to a century (*African American Humor* 116). Stowe introduces the character by describing him sarcastically as "intelligent chattel" and notes that "this young man was in the eye of the law not a man, but a thing, all these superior qualifications were subject to the control of a vulgar, narrow-minded, tyrannical master" (26). George's master's hostility toward him is fueled by his "uneasy consciousness of inferiority," and he determines to subdue his slave by putting "him to hoeing and digging, and 'see if he'd step about so smart'" (26). In this scene, Stowe demonstrates the personal hatred many slaves felt toward their masters but had to conceal, yet as Bernard Wolfe points out, an important aspect of folk culture was the way in which the oral tradition helped slaves cope psychologically with what might otherwise grow into uncontrollable and dangerous rage. He notes that "the function of such folk symbols as Brer Rabbit is precisely to prevent inner explosions by siphoning off these hatreds before they can completely possess consciousness. Folk tales, like so much of folk culture, are part of an elaborate psychic drainage system" (535). Stowe notes that when George's master abruptly demands his wages and "announced his intention of taking him home," George "folded his arms, tightly pressed in his lips, but a whole volcano of bitter feelings burned in his bosom, and sent streams of fire through his veins. . . . He had been able to repress every disrespectful word; but the flashing eye, the gloomy and troubled brow, were part of a natural language that could not be repressed—indubitable signs, which showed too plainly that the man could not become a thing" (27). George's master is not, however, equipped to read the signs that constitute this "natural language" and foolishly believes himself capable of breaking this man's will.

While George is a highly intelligent individual, he also possesses the wisdom of the quarters, which he draws on to form a strategic course of action. Lawrence Levine notes that "in the individual tale the rabbit begins as weak and vulnerable; he's assaulted by strong animals, and through his wits he generally thwarts their plans, defeats them, and emerges as the victor, or at least the survivor" (xviii). George also thwarts his master's plan by using his wits to covertly rather than overtly repudiate his authority. George visits his wife to inform her of his decision to attempt an escape, and as he departs, he tells her, "'I'm going home quite resigned, you understand, as if all was over. I've got some preparations made,—and there are those that will help me; and, in the course of a week or so, I shall be among the missing some day'" (35). Osofsky notes that a common aspect of many slave escapes "required [the] strategic appearance of obedience to their masters, like seeming most satisfied at the moment they were most discontented" (21).

Several critics claim that Stowe's highly intelligent black characters are, as Baldwin puts it, "as white as she can make them" (16). This perspective, however, overlooks George's partner, Jim Selden, who is described as a "black fellow" as well as "a giant in strength, and brave as death and despair" (241).[22] He is also bold, intelligent, and committed to freeing his mother as well as helping another slave escape. George and Jim engage in a rather ingenious and dangerous ruse and operate as a trickster duo; indeed, their plan shows many similarities with the Crafts' brilliant escape. Their strategy requires confidence, bravery, and ingenuity, which are common features in the slave narrative tradition. Osofsky notes that a number "of light-skinned slaves passed for whites, some audaciously stopping at the best restaurants and hotels to exchange gossip on the price of land, cotton, and slaves" (28). George's plan is also rather "audacious." He travels through Kentucky in a "small one-horse buggy" and stops at an inn with his "colored servant" (144). George "walked easily in among the company, and with a nod indicated to his waiter where to place his trunk, bowed to the company, and with his hat in his hand, walked up leisurely to the bar, and gave in his name as Henry Butler, Oaklands, Shelby County" (144). George then boldly picks up and reads the advertisement for his capture and asks his "servant" Jim, "'Seems to me we met a boy something like this up at Bernam's, didn't we?'" Jim responds, "'Yes, mas'r'" and adds, "'only I an't sure about the hand'" (144). Referring to the fugitive advertised as "boy" and Jim's address to George as "mas'r" reinforces their charade as a wealthy Southern gentleman traveling with his body servant, and consequently, the "landlord was all obsequious" (144).

Their scheme is threatened, however, when George recognizes Mr. Wilson, but he maintains his composure and casually requests a private conversation. Although Wilson highly respects George, he cautions against this "dangerous, very dangerous" plan, but George is committed to defend his escape with deadly force if necessary (152). The conversation also allows Stowe to include the highly controversial issue of the sexual violation of black women by white men. George explains that his father was his master, and after his death, his mother and her seven children were put up for sale "with his dogs and horses to satisfy the estate" (149). George and his beautiful older sister are purchased by the same master. George notes that he was initially grateful to be sold with his sibling but explains, "'I was soon sorry for it. Sir, I have stood at the door and heard her whipped, when it seemed as if every blow cut into my naked heart, and I couldn't do any thing to help her; and she was whipped, sir, for wanting to live a decent Christian life, such as your laws give no slave girl a right to live; and the last I saw her chained with a trader's gang, to be sent to market in Orleans,—sent there for nothing else but that'" (149).[23] For white mothers, particularly in the nineteenth century, a daughter's beauty was typically a source of pride and could provide young women with many advantages, but for slave mothers, early signs of budding beauty in their young daughters was often a soul-chilling moment of recognition, foreshadowing a lifetime of sexual vulnerability that far too often became the brutal reality of routine sexual exploitation and violation. Stowe also demonstrates in this scene that black sons, fathers, husbands, and brothers were typically powerless to protect female family members from these abuses, and as a result, were also victimized by this contemptible but much too common practice (471).

Their conversation also highlights many admirable qualities in the character Jim. Wilson asks George who he is traveling with, and he responds, "'A true fellow, who went to Canada more than a year ago. He heard, after he got there, that his master was so angry at him for going off that he had whipped his poor old mother; and he has come all the way back to comfort her, and get a chance to get her away'" (151). Wilson asks if he "'has got her,'" and George replies, "'Not yet; he has been hanging about the place, and found no chance yet. Meanwhile, he is going with me as far as Ohio, to put me among friends that helped him, and then he will come back after her'" (152). This information indicates that Jim has been protected by the black community "about the place" and further demonstrates that he is willing to risk his own freedom to help a fellow bondsman escape as well. Both men are brave, highly intelligent, and successfully carry out a brilliant and audacious escape as they "travel by day, stop at the best hotels, go to the dinner tables with the lords of the land," and by doing so, cleverly outwit "the lords of the land" (153).

The most controversial character in the novel is the hero Tom. While several scholars acknowledge the sacrifice Tom makes for the Shelbys' slaves, noting they could all be sold, many contend that when Tom is sold to St. Clare, he shifts his loyalty from the black community to his new master.[24] Tawil asserts that "Stowe places her negro characters in changing circumstances so that we can observe what alterations of character, if any, will result" (162). Tawil claims that "Tom has imbibed his 'tastes and feeling'" from "the Shelby household" and that when he is sold to St. Clare, he functions as a "case study of the proverbially 'sympathetic and assimilative' negro" (172). Throughout the course of the novel, which chronologically spans five years, Tom has three masters, but his character remains consistent throughout the narrative. Furthermore, were Tom a reflection of Shelby, he would be, as noted, a liar, a coward, and an incompetent businessman, but as we learn in the earlier chapters, Tom's management skill is the primary reason Mr. Shelby does not want to part with him because, as he tells Haley, Tom "'manages my whole farm like a clock,'" which includes traveling and conducting business on Shelby's behalf (14). Furthermore, Tom is also fully aware that he is superior to Shelby regarding business matters, which is evident by his concern that the Shelby farm "will be kinder goin' to rack, when I'm gone" (80).

Tom also bears no resemblance to his second master, St. Clare, most notably St. Clare's role as a husband, his self-proclaimed hypocrisy, and his spiritual apathy. Baldwin claims that Tom has been "divested of his sex" (17), and many scholars also view Tom as sexless, including Gates and Robbins; however, Tom and Chloe have three children and the youngest is less than a year old, which indicates that Chloe certainly does not regard her husband as sexless. In contrast to the Shelby and St. Clare families, with only one child, Tom is depicted as more sexual than his masters. He is not, however, the hypersexual stereotype of the minstrel tradition but a husband in an obviously loving, sexual, and monogamous relationship. Furthermore, unlike both Shelby and St. Clare, Tom is a man of his word as well as clearly morally and spiritually superior to both.

While a number of critics regard Tom as an allegorical Christ figure, other readers consider Tom's Christianity his greatest weakness. Historians, however, have noted that whites' "attempt to reduce Christianity to an ethic of pure submission was rejected and resented by the slaves" (L. Levine 45). Slaves maintained a point of view regarding Christianity that was very different from the white community's and, moreover, interpreted Jesus from the perspective of their oral traditions. Paul Harvey explains that "African Americans saw a distinct Jesus—one that whites could hear about but whom they would never understand. The white Jesus became a trickster of the trinity, able to enter the world of whiteness, defy it, and sometimes dismantle it. Jesus as trickster profoundly unsettled the social order. . . . Slaves thus embraced a Jesus that the whites around them feared and tried to repress . . . for Jesus's own life and message were a trickster tale of how the powerless might overcome the powerful through parable and poetry" (36).[25] Throughout the novel, Tom consistently undermines the power of his legal masters by indicating that his "true" master is the Lord and thus his only authority, which suggests that Tom is not an allegorical Christ figure but rather functions as a trickster of the trinity.

Stowe provides the black community's perspective regarding Christianity early in the novel during the prayer meeting in Tom's cabin. Because most slaves were prohibited from learning to read or write, Osofsky notes that Bible stories were "put to memory, [and] passed on through oral tradition, through folklore and folktales or in the form of songs" (36). During the meeting, they take advantage of George's ability to read and request a number of specific passages, most notably "the last chapters of Revelation," which as Chloe's remarks in the kitchen demonstrate, provided slaves an important sense of retributive justice as well as belief in a higher authority far more powerful than their masters. Lawrence Levine notes that "not only did slaves believe that they would be chosen by the Lord, there is evidence that many of them felt their owners would be denied salvation" (34). The practice of call and response is also featured in this section with comments such as, "'Only hear that! . . . Jest think on't! . . . Is all that a commin' sure enough?'" (48).

After George reads several passages, "the singing commenced" and many of these "made incessant mention of 'Jordan's bank' and Canaan's fields, and the 'New Jerusalem'" (47). In the black community, slaves employed double entendres to create overt and covert meanings for biblical stories and songs.[26] Stowe references this duality when she depicts Eliza's arrival at the Ohio River and notes that "her first glance was at the river, which lay, like Jordan, between her and the Canaan of liberty on the other side" (76). Douglass explains that the song, "'O Canaan, sweet Canaan, / I am bound for the land of Canaan,' symbolized something more than a hope of reaching heaven. We meant to reach the North, and the North was our Canaan" (*My Bondage and My Freedom* 197). And, as Baker notes, "the river Jordan was not a mystical boundary between earth and heaven; it was the very real Ohio that marked the line between slave and free" (*Long Black Song* 13). The common knowledge of the dual nature of these songs in the black community is referenced when Sam tells Mr. and Mrs. Shelby about Eliza's flight "'clar 'cross Jordan. As a body may say, in the land o' Canaan'" (100). Mrs. Shelby, however, does not understand Sam's double entendres and asks, "'Why, Sam, what *do* you mean?'" (100). It is also likely that George Shelby was unaware of the dual nature of the songs he was exposed to during the meeting as well.

As a spiritual trickster, Tom also functions as a foil to expose the morality and integrity of each owner. While St. Clare is depicted as a benevolent and indulgent master and highly critical of the institution of slavery, indeed identifying himself as a hypocrite, he is, however, oblivious to the inner lives of his slaves. St. Clare's ignorance is most overtly evident by his irritation with Tom's reaction when he tells Tom he plans to free him. Stowe notes that "the sudden light of joy that shone in Tom's face as he raised his hands to heaven, his emphatic 'Bless the Lord!' rather discomposed St. Clare; he did not like it that Tom should be so ready to leave him" (384). Their dialogue further exposes St. Clare's ignorance. He asks Tom,

"You haven't had such very bad times here, that you need be in such a rapture, Tom," he said, dryly.

"No, no mas'r! 'tan't that,—it's being *a free man!* That's what I'm joyin' for."

"Why, Tom, don't you think, for your own part, you've been better off than to be free?" "No, indeed, Mas'r St. Clare," said Tom, with a flash of energy. "No, indeed!"

"Why, Tom, you couldn't possibly have earned, by your work, such clothes and such living as I have given you."

"Knows all that, Mas'r St. Clare; mas'r's been too good; but, mas'r, I'd rather have poor clothes, poor house, poor every thing, and have 'em *mine*, than have the best, and have 'em any man's else,—I had *so*, mas'r; I think it's nature, masr." (384)

To St. Clare's surprise, if not chagrin, Tom does not want to be a slave and is deeply committed to reuniting with his family, and indeed, he begins thinking "of his home, and that he should soon be a free man, and able to return to it at will. He thought how he should work to buy his wife and boys. He felt the muscles of his brawny arms with a sort of joy, as he thought they would soon belong to himself, and how much they would do to work out the freedom of his family" (395). Tom has, however, given his word to St. Clare and is committed to honoring his promises, unlike Shelby. Ultimately, Tom is morally superior to all his of masters, men with far greater life advantages due to wealth, race, and social position.

Stowe also provides other characters whose trickster traits have been overlooked, likely because they are female. In the St. Clare household, the craftiest character is Topsy, and through this character, Stowe creates another version of the trickster figure. As a "little negro girl, about eight or nine years of age," Topsy represents the weakest and most vulnerable character in the social hierarchy, and through this portrait, Stowe is able to subversively include highly controversial issues regarding child abuse, northern racism and hypocrisy, and trickster wit as a means of survival. Topsy bears keen resemblance to the most well-known hero of the trickster tales, Brer Rabbit, and as Osofsky notes, "the world, in Brer Rabbit's wary eyes, is a jungle. Life is a battle"; furthermore, it is "a battle without rules" (530). Life for this child must have also looked like a battle without rules. St. Clare tells Ophelia that he buys her because she "belonged to a couple of drunken creatures that keep a low restaurant that I have to pass by every day, and I was tired of hearing her screaming, and them beating and swearing at her" (302). Miss Ophelia accepts the responsibility to supervise Topsy, but as Stowe points out, "approached her new subject very much as a person might be supposed to approach a black spider" (302).

Aspects of her personal history are further revealed when she is given a bath, which exposes "the back and shoulders of the child" and reveals "great welts and calloused spots, ineffaceable marks of the system under which she had grown up thus far" (303). In addition to her brutal treatment, Stowe also provides a great deal of insight regarding the unique circumstances of being, as Schwartz puts it in her title, *Born in Bondage: Growing Up Enslaved in the Antebellum South*. She explains that "for slaves, as for other children, important milestones marked developmental categories. Weaning signaled the end of infancy. Early childhood concluded when the children grew old enough to obey and to serve. By the age of five or six, children were initiated into the world of work through education and training intended to enhance a slave's economic worth. During this stage of development, harsh punishments were introduced to prevent children from performing duties poorly. Another significant event was the assumption of adult work responsibilities, usually between the ages of ten and twelve" (14). As Stowe demonstrates, Topsy has been introduced to this world of work as well as the harsh disciplinary training that has, at this early age, already left many signs of abuse on her body. Furthermore, like many elements recounted in the slave narratives, Topsy does not know her age, who her parents are, or how long she has been with her master and mistress. Because Topsy has already had her bath, Ophelia poses a rather insensitive if not foolish question, asking the girl if her master and mistress were "'good to you?'" Topsy responds with obvious irony that is lost on Ophelia, "'Spect they was,' said the child, scanning Miss Ophelia cunningly" (304).

Further evidence of her brutal existence is depicted when Eva offers Topsy words of comfort, but Stowe notes, "it was the first word of kindness the child had ever heard in her life; and the sweet tone and manner struck strangely on the wild, rude heart, and a sparkle of something like a tear shone in the keen, round, glittering eye; but it was followed by the short laugh and habitual grin. No! the ear that has never heard any thing but abuse is strangely incredulous of any thing so heavenly as kindness; and Topsy only thought Eva's speech something funny and inexplicable,—she did not believe it" (309). As an eight- or nine-year-old, Stowe's note that it was "the first word of kindness" she has ever heard in her life indicates that her abuse was not only physical but psychological as well.

Like Brer Rabbit, Topsy is small, physically weak, and highly vulnerable yet also possesses the Rabbit's characteristic superior intelligence, but as Osofksy observes, "cunning and intelligence had to be concealed" (25). Osofsky notes that an important theme of the trickster tales was "to use wit, guile, and cunning, as real slaves did, to turn a situation to his [or her] own advantage" (46). Topsy has early learned, if not mastered, the art of signifying as a survival strategy. Stowe repeatedly refers to her "shrewdness and cunning," which she strategically conceals behind a performative "veil" (300). Topsy presents herself with "doleful gravity" as well as "a most sanctimonious expression of meekness and solemnity over her face" (300). Stowe demonstrates insight into the performative nature of this child by noting that in spite of Topsy's expression of meekness, she is regularly described as cunning, shrewd, and acute. Topsy's intelligence is highlighted when Ophelia begins to teach her to read and sew, and

> in the former art the child was quick enough. She learned her letters as if by magic, and was very soon able to read plain reading; but the sewing was a more difficult matter. The creature was as lithe as a cat, and as active as a monkey, and the confinement of sewing was her abomination; so she broke her needles, threw them slyly out of windows, or down in chinks of the walls; she tangled, broke, and dirtied her thread, or, with a sly movement, would throw a spool away altogether. Her motions were almost as quick as those of a practiced conjurer, and her command of her face quite as great; and though Miss Ophelia could not help feeling that so many accidents could not possibly happen in succession, yet she could not, without a watchfulness which would leave her no time for anything else, detect her. (311)

Nowatzki claims that Topsy's antics indicate that "of all the black characters in Stowe's fiction, Topsy most resembles the blackface clown" (162). But this perspective overlooks Topsy's intelligence, which she uses to engage in a clever type of common but highly subversive form of resistance to white authority. Kolchin explains: "The most common, but difficult to isolate, was a collection of acts that historians have labeled 'silent sabotage' or 'day-to-day resistance,' acts through which slaves, without threatening the security of the slave regime, caused considerable aggravation to individual slave owners. Throughout the South, slaves dragged their feet, pretended to misunderstand orders, feigned illness, 'accidentally' broke agricultural implements, and stole coveted items (especially food) from their owners, viewing such appropriation as 'taking what rightfully belonged to them'" (157). Indeed, Topsy is not the only character featured engaging in "silent sabotage;" Dinah also employs this tactic as well. She is annoyed with Ophelia's interference with her system and "mentally determined to oppose and ignore every new measure, without any actual and observable contest" (264).

Topsy also uses her wits to maneuver within this new household, particularly in dealing with the difficult "upper servants," and like Brer Rabbit who could be vindictive when provoked,

> it was very soon discovered that whoever cast an indignity on Topsy was sure to meet with some inconvenient accident shortly after;—either a pair of ear rings or some cherished trinket would be missing, or an article of dress would be suddenly found utterly ruined, or the person would stumble accidentally into a pail of hot water, or a libation of dirty slop would unaccountably deluge them from above . . . and on all these occasions, when investigation was made, there was nobody found to stand sponsor for the indignity. Topsy was cited, and had up before all the domestic judicatories, time and again; but always sustained her examinations with most edifying innocence and gravity of appearance. Nobody in the world ever doubted who did the things; but not a scrap of any direct evidence could be found to establish the suppositions, and Miss Ophelia was too just to feel at liberty to proceed to any lengths without it. (312)

Topsy's ingenuity "soon made the household understand the propriety of letting her alone; and she was let alone accordingly" (312).

While Topsy has difficulties with the "upper servants," she is revered by the slave children for her ongoing seditious battle of wills with Miss Ophelia, and Topsy routinely emerges as the victor. Lawrence Levine notes that "for all the limitations imposed upon slave tricksters and all the hazards they faced, it is not difficult to understand the pleasures slaves derived from their exploits. In spite of the role playing and subservience forced upon them and the defeats they often suffered, slave tricksters continually made the whites look foolish and always seemed one step ahead of them" (129). Topsy is also always one step ahead of Ophelia, and Ophelia's exasperation leads her to attempt to subdue Topsy with physical discipline, but this strategy also fails. Topsy, moreover, turns the event to her advantage and "roosted on some projection of the balcony, and surrounded by a flock of admiring 'young uns,' she would express the utmost contempt of the whole affair. 'Law, Miss Felly whip!—wouldn't kill a skeeter, her whippins. Oughter see how old mas'r made the flesh fly; old mas'r know'd how!' Topsy always made great capital of her own sins and enormities, evidently considering them as something peculiarly distinguishing" (313). Topsy's "peculiar" distinction is her ability to undermine, exasperate, and ridicule white authority, particularly adults, and the flock of "young uns" admire her skills and share her delight.

Another especially cunning character is Cassy and is, I contend, the novel's most crafty trickster figure. Although Gates makes a brief reference to Cassy as a trickster during her escape, noting "Cassy's role as a trickster recollects the antics of Sam and Andy in chapter six," her trickster traits are suggested when she is first introduced in the novel by the dynamics of the weak pitted against the strong (*Annotated Uncle Tom's Cabin* 421). Stowe demonstrates the antagonism between Cassy and Legree when he arrives with his new slaves, and Cassy "said something" that angers him. Legree responds, "'You may hold your tongue! I'll do as I please, for all you'" (433). Cassy's dealings with Legree's henchmen Sambo and Quimbo are also highly antagonistic. Indeed, the three are arguably the most despicable characters in the novel; although the term *Uncle Tom* became, as Gates puts it, "the worst thing you could possibly be in the African American tradition," Sambo and Quimbo are much more representative of the characteristics that define the pejorative insult. Their loyalty to their master rather than the slave community results in their rejection from its society, and "the plantation hands, one and all, cordially hated them" (432). They, rather than Tom, are traitors to their race, but these literary images became distorted by various minstrel renditions, and *Uncle Tom* came to represent slavish devotion to whites, whereas *Sambo* became synonymous with the black buffoon.[27] Another reworking of Stowe's characters also appears in Robert Alexander's 1991 play, *I Ain't Yo' Uncle: The New Jack Revisionist Uncle Tom's Cabin*. In this drama, the characters "put Stowe on trial for creating damaging racist stereotypes," yet Stowe does not *create* these damaging stereotypes but rather signifies on existing stereotypes (Rosenthal 251). Furthermore, Alexander creates Cassy as a much more overtly hostile character who ultimately shoots Legree and then turns to the fictitious Stowe and states, "'You wrote every word of the rage that's in me! You just didn't give me a gun'" (88). Stowe does, however, empower this character with a weapon that proves equally deadly but actually much more brutal to Legree than the quick death by gunshot featured in the play.

The introduction of the novel's villain also functions to further demonstrate white ignorance of black individuality and community interiority. In spite of Legree's opinion of slaves, which is similar to Haley's, that "'niggers never gets round me, neither with squalling nor soft soap,—that's a fact,'" Stowe creates several scenes featuring slaves strategically getting "round" Legree and thus repudiating his authority (424). Tom's first rejection of Legree's authority, although private, occurs when Legree tells him, "'I'm your church now! You understand,—you've got to be as I say'" (422). While Tom remains silent, Stowe notes that "something within the silent black man answered, No! and, as if repeated by an invisible voice, came the words of an old prophetic scroll, as Eva had often read them to him,—'Fear not! For I have redeemed thee. I have called thee by my name Thou art MINE!' But Simon Legree heard no voice. That voice is one he never shall hear" (422). Stowe's use of the word *redeemed* in the context of the novel functions to reinforce the Shelbys' failure to honor their promise and simultaneously reiterates the strength of Tom's faith, which helps him maneuver within this dangerous environment. Furthermore, while "he saw enough of abuse and misery to make him sick and weary; but he determined to toil on, with religious patience, committing himself to Him that judgeth righteously, not without hope that some way of escape might yet be opened to him" (439). Legree is unable to comprehend signs of the private rejection of his authority as well as Tom's secret desire to escape.

Tom's introduction to Cassy unites the two quickly, and indeed, throughout the chapters featuring Legree's plantation, suggest that Tom and Cassy also operate as a trickster duo. When Tom helps Lucy by putting cotton in her sack, Cassy, "taking a quantity of cotton from her basket, she placed it in his" and tells him, "'You know nothing about this place,' she said, 'or you wouldn't have done that. When you've been here a month, you'll be done helping any body; you'll find it hard enough to take care of your own skin!'" (422). Tom responds, "'The Lord forbid, missis!'" (422). Cassy's advice suggests that she has been reduced to a purely self-serving existence; however, after Tom refuses Legree's orders to flog Lucy and receives a brutal beating, Cassy slips out to minister to his injuries. She brings him water and tells him, "'Drink all ye want,' she said; 'I knew how it would be. It isn't the first time I've been out in the night, carrying water to such as you'" (449). Cassy then administers "cooling application to his wounds," and Stowe notes, "the woman, whom long practice with the victims of brutality had made familiar with many healing arts, went on to make many applications to Tom's wounds, by means of which he was soon somewhat relieved" (449). Cassy's assistance indicates that she engages in subversive activities that Legree is unaware of, but she is moved to take further action "when Legree brought Emmeline to the house" and "all the smouldering embers of womanly feeling flashed up in the worn heart of Cassy, and she took part with the girl" (463).

Cassy often rather boldly defies Legree's authority, but the task of helping Emmeline will require a much more strategic approach. Cassy is, however, uniquely skilled at manipulating Legree. For example, when Tom refuses to get on his knees and beg Legree's pardon, Cassy "with woman's tact, touched the only string that could be made to vibrate"—Legree's greed (473). She reminds him that he has paid twelve hundred dollars for this field hand and is damaging his productivity "'in the press of the season'" and has, furthermore, made a bet with "Tomkins" he is sure to lose if his "'crop comes shorter in the market'" (473). Cassy asks him, "'Will you be a fool? . . . Let me alone to get him fit to be in the field again'" (476). Legree relents, which highlights Cassy's ability to manipulate Legree and, further, implicitly signifies an answer to Cassy's rhetorical question.

In spite of Cassy's physical weakness and legal powerlessness, she is brave, compassionate, and highly intelligent. She has also learned to trust Tom and consults his opinion. His loyalty to the black community rather than his master is clearly evident in the advice he offers, telling Cassy, "'If ye could get away from here,—if the thing was possible,—I'd 'vise ye and Emmeline to do it'" (496). Cassy asks Tom to join them, but he replies, "'No, time was when I would; but the Lord's given me a work among these yer poor souls, and I'll stay with 'em and bear my cross with 'em till the end'" (496). Tom's decision to forgo another opportunity to escape indicates a dual sacrifice; it improves the women's chances because fugitives were more successful in small numbers or alone rather than in groups, and his decision also demonstrates that he sacrifices this opportunity to continue to provide physical and spiritual help for the black community.[28]

Well aware of the difficulties of escape on this plantation but intent to protect Emmeline, Cassy draws on her intelligence and begins to work on a plan. Cassy had "often revolved, for hours, all possible or probable schemes of escape, and dismissed them all, as hopeless and impracticable; but at this moment there flashed through her mind a plan, so simple and feasible in all its details, as to awaken an instant hope" (497). Although Anna Brickhouse regards Cassy's influence over Legree as stemming from "magical powers associated with vodun," Cassy's power derives from her superior intelligence, which she utilizes to signify on rather than draw from supernatural elements, which are elements that cause Legree considerable uneasiness (430).[29] Stowe also refers to a number of dangerous animals in this section to indicate Legree's physical and legal power, specifically the alligator, rhinoceros, the lion, and the dog, but as Stowe notes, each "have a spot where they are vulnerable" (476). Like these animals, Legree also has a point of vulnerability, which is his "superstitious dread" (476). Stowe identifies superstition as Legree's personal weakness but also undermines common cultural assumptions that African Americans are inherently superstitious.[30] Cassy, however, strategically exploits this spot of vulnerability to facilitate her plan.

The subtitle of the escape chapter is titled "The Stratagem," and Stowe characterizes the plan as "a game that Cassy played with Legree" (504). This game is a contest between the weak pitted against the strong, like the trickster tales, and superior intelligence is the trickster's only weapon. Alan Dundes points out that in the oral tradition, "cunning though the fox may be, he is no match for the ingenious rabbit!" (525). Cassy draws on the power of the slaves' oral culture to initiate her scheme by reviving "stories" and "legends" that "the negroes used to whisper darkly to each other" regarding "a negro woman, who had incurred Legree's displeasure," and he confined her to the garret of the house for "several weeks" (499). Eventually, "the body of the unfortunate creature was one day taken down from there, and buried" (499). The garret was subsequently "avoided by every one in the house, from every one fearing to speak of it; and the legend was gradually falling into desuetude" (499). Cassy's first move in the game is a request to change rooms. Legree asks why, and she tells him, "'I suppose it wouldn't disturb *you!* Only groans, and people scuffling, and rolling round on the garret floor, half the night from twelve to morning" (500). Legree forces a laugh and inquires, "'Who are they, Cassy?'" She replies, "'To be sure, Simon, who are they? I'd like to have you tell me. You don't know, I suppose'" (500). Stowe notes that "Cassy perceived that her shaft had struck home; and from that hour, with the most exquisite address, she never ceased to continue the train of influences she had begun" (500). She next inserts the neck of a bottle in a knothole in the garret, causing the "most doleful and lugubrious wailing sounds" (500).

Cassy then baits Legree by leaving a book on a table he had "noticed Cassy reading" and "took it up, and began to turn it over. It was one of those collections of stories of bloody murders, ghostly legends, and supernatural visitations, which, coarsely got up and illustrated, have a strange fascination for one who once begins to read them" (502). Legree becomes uneasy by the disturbing material and asks Cassy, "'You don't believe in ghosts, do you, Cass?'" (502). Knowing she has him on the hook, Cassy draws him further into her game by responding ambiguously, "'No matter what I believe'" (502).

Legree then attempts to dismiss her complaints about noises in the garret by claiming it must be rats, but Cassy asks, "'Can rats walk down stairs; and come walking through the entry, and open a door when you've locked it and set a chair against it . . . and come walk, walk, walking right up to your bed, and put out their hand, so?'" (502). Cassy further fuels Legree's fear by keeping "her glittering eyes fixed on Legree, as she spoke, and he stared at her like a man in the nightmare, till, when she finished by laying her hand, icy cold, on his, he sprung back, with an oath. 'Woman! What do you mean? Nobody did'" (502). Cassy replies, "'O, no—of course not,—did I say they did?" (502). Her question, however, sends a dual message because she didn't say that they did but implies that they did, and the subsequent "vague horror" that "fell on" Legree indicates that her insinuation was highly effective. Cassy's manipulation is ultimately so successful that Legree "would sooner have put his head into a lion's mouth than to have explored that garret" (504). Cassy then stocks the garret with food, clothing, and other provisions while also appearing "unusually gracious and accommodating in her humors; and Legree and she had been, apparently on the best of terms" (505). Like George and other slaves planning an escape, Cassy *appears* "most satisfied at the moment" she is "most discontented" (Osofsky 21).

When the preparations are complete, Cassy then explains the plan to Emmeline, and the two flee into the swamp in plain sight of the fieldworkers, which appears to be a rather foolish endeavor. A search party is quickly formed, and they head out after the women. Cassy's "stratagem" is, how ever, highly successful and as the pursuit advances, Cassy and Emmeline circle back and casually "glide" into the house and watch the chaos ensue. After hours of futile searching, the unsuccessful pursuers return, and Cassy physically and symbolically looks down on the "crestfallen" Legree and quips with satisfaction: "Ah, my good sir, you'll have to try the race again and again,—the game isn't there'" (509). Cassy's play on words (referring to Legree ironically as "good sir" and the dual nature of "the game," indicating their role as the subject of the hunt as well as the game Cassy plays with Legree) further highlights her intelligence as well as her gratification in making a fool out of Legree.

Legree returns from the chase "baffled and disappointed" and over the course of weeks, he becomes consumed by his wrath at failing to capture the women. His psychological turmoil is compounded by "footsteps, in the dead of night . . . descending the garret stairs, and patrolling the house," and his sleep is disturbed by "screams and groaning" coming from the garret as well as "a shadow, a horror, an apprehension of something dreadful hanging over him" (527, 529). Cassy's tactics lead Legree to become "a harder drinker than ever before. He no longer drank cautiously, prudently, but imprudently and recklessly" (529). As Legree sinks into madness that proves fatal, Stowe depicts a rather brutal and drawn-out demise. On his deathbed, Legree "raved, and screamed, and spoke of sights which almost stopped the blood of those who heard him; and at his dying bed stood a stern, white, inexorable figure, saying, 'Come! Come! Come!'" (530). Stowe notes ironically, "By a singular coincidence, on the very night that this vision appeared to Legree, the house door was found open in the morning, and some of the negroes had seen two white figures gliding down the avenue towards the high road" (530). Cassy's ingenuity not only results in their successful escape but also gives her a unique opportunity to retaliate for years of abuse.

Cassy is clearly a highly intelligent woman, but Stowe also indicates that Tom was involved with the plan. When Legree announces that the women have escaped, Stowe notes that "Tom heard the message with a forewarning heart; for he knew all the plan of the fugitives' escape, and the place of their present concealment;—he also knew the deadly character of the man he had to deal with, and his despotic power" (514). When Legree confronts Tom and asks what he knows, "Tom stood silent" (514). Legree then "stamping, with a roar like that of an incensed lion," demands that he "'Speak!'" Tom replies, "'I han't got nothing to tell, mas'r,'" which indicates, however, that he has nothing to tell to "mas'r" (515). Legree asks if he knows anything, and Tom responds, "'I know, mas'r; but I can't tell any thing. I can die!'" (515). Tom receives a beating that leads to his death but maintains the same tenacious faith he is first introduced with, and his refusal to betray Cassy and Emmeline directly repudiates the authority of his legal master while reiterating his dedication to a higher power. The appearance of Tom's former master, George Shelby, during Tom's final moments reiterates the consistency of his character. His comment that "'heaven is better than Kintuck'" also suggests a reproach for the actions of this family who is ultimately responsible for his death. Furthermore, Tom's only request is that George not tell Chloe "'how ye found me;—'twould be so dredful to her. Only tell her ye found me going into glory, and that I couldn't stay for no one. And tell her the Lord's stood by me every where and al'ays, and made every thing light and easy. And O, the poor chil'en, and the baby!—my old heart's been most broke for 'em, time and again!'" (523). It is interesting to note that Tom does not request that Mrs. Shelby be spared the terrible details of his final moments.

When Chloe is informed of her husband's death, she is so upset that she briefly drops her mask and offers her unguarded opinion. Chloe gathers the money she has worked for years to earn for her husband's redemption, boldly hands it to Mrs. Shelby, and states "'Don't never want to see nor hear on't again. Jist as I knew 'twoud be,—sold and murderen on dem ar' old plantations!'" (547). Chloe's expression of anger and comment about the money she has earned implies that she blames the Shelbys for Tom's death, but Chloe realizes that such open honesty is unwise and quickly resumes her careful masking, telling Mrs. Shelby, "'O missis! 'scuse me, my heart's broke,—dat's all!'" (547). The guilt George Shelby suffers as a result of his family's responsibility for the death of Tom compels him to free his slaves. Although Baldwin claims that all the black characters are shipped off to Africa, the Shelbys' slaves are free in the end and will be paid for their work. Tom's wife and most important his children ultimately receive the freedom he had hoped to provide for them, which is, however, made possible by the many virtues of their father.

While the issue of colonization is a highly controversial subject, it is important to note that Stowe's characters choose to go to Africa and by doing so, repudiate white authority, including "benevolent societies" that supported colonization. Meer points out that George's actions "could be taken as an endorsement of the American Colonization Society's scheme to send freed slaves to Liberia. However, in a passage that is often overlooked, Stowe refutes this interpretation in her concluding remarks, stating that 'to fill up Liberia with an ignorant, inexperienced, half-barbarized race, just escaped from the chains of slavery, would be only to prolong, for ages, the period of struggle and conflict which attends the inception of new enterprises'" (69). Another critique of the issue of colonization is made by St. Clare regarding Ophelia's representative northern racism. After Ophelia expresses her disgust with Eva's interaction with the servants, St. Clare ridicules her hypocrisy: "'You would think no harm in a child's caressing a large dog, even if he was black; but a creature that can think, and reason, and feel, and is immortal, you shudder at; confess it, cousin. I know the feeling among some of you northerners well enough. . . . I have often noticed, in my travels north, how much stronger this was with you than with us. You loathe them as you would a snake or a toad, yet you are indignant at their wrongs. You would not have them abused; but you don't want to have any thing to do with them yourselves. You would send them to Africa, out of your sight'" (229). Stowe's depiction of the issue of colonization in this scene is highly critical of white Americans who are motivated by a desire to rid America of its black population because of racism rather than benevolence.

The final chapter, "Concluding Remarks," is written in a much more overt style than the main narrative, and Stowe shifts the point of view from third person to the perspective of "the author." In this chapter, Stowe is much more direct in challenging many commonplace racial theories, particularly the notion that blacks are inherently intellectually limited. Stowe notes that "the first desire of the emancipated slave, generally, is for education. There is nothing that they are not willing to give or do to have their children instructed; and, so far as the writer has observed herself, or taken the testimony of teachers among them, they are remarkably intelligent and quick to learn" (558). Stowe then provides a list of several former slaves who have become productive members of Cincinnati society and notes that "in all states of the Union we see men, but yesterday burst from the shackles of slavery, who, by self-educating force, which cannot be too much admired, have risen to highly respectable stations in society" (559). Ultimately, the subtext of the concluding remarks is an appeal for "man's freedom and equality" (560). Because white Americans are free indicates that the line references only black Americans and suggests that the novel not only opposes slavery but also supports equal rights. Were Stowe as racist as she has often been charged, it is unlikely she would have highlighted the values of the Quaker community. Indeed, the most admirable white characters in the novel are members of "The Society of Friends," a community of staunch advocates of both abolition and social equality. While George, his family, and Topsy choose colonization, the novel ends with Tom's family free, and as such, likely to avail themselves of the opportunity to add to the list of those who have "risen to highly respectable stations in society" the names of Uncle Tom's children (559).[31]

Chapter 3

Melville's Signifying Monkey "Starts Some Shit"

"Deep down in the jungle so they say
There's a Signifying Monkey down the way
There hadn't been no disturbin' in the jungle for quite a bit,
For up jumped the Monkey in the tree one day and laughed
'I guess I'll start some shit'"[1]

With sporadic education due to the death of his father and his brother's bankruptcy, Herman Melville sought employment in several unrewarding endeavors. He worked as a farm laborer, a schoolteacher in Massachusetts and New York, and a bank clerk, and briefly studied surveying. In 1839, Melville determined to, as his biographer Andrew Delbanco notes, "make an escape, or at least an experiment. Following the example of one of his cousins, he arranged to sail as a cabin boy aboard a merchant ship that plied the route between New York and Liverpool carrying cotton and a few passengers" (37).[2] His decision to head to sea would have a profound impact on his life, introducing him to various international and intranational cultures that would drastically alter his worldview. During visits home, his family was so captivated by his tales of life at sea that they encouraged him to begin to write about his adventures. Although his first endeavor, *Typee: A Peep at Polynesian Life*, published in 1846 by New York–based Wiley and Putnam, was well received and highly successful, Melville's experiences with editors critical of his frank narrative style and unapologetic critique of Western values became increasingly exasperating. His well-known letter to Nathanial Hawthorne in 1851 captures his frustration. He writes, "'Try to get a living by the Truth—and go to the Soup Societies. Heavens! Let any clergyman try to preach the Truth from its very stronghold, the pulpit, and they would ridicule him out of his church on his own pulpit bannister. It can hardly be doubted that all Reformers are bottomed upon the truth, more or less; and to the world at large are not reformers almost universally laughing-stocks? Why so? Truth is ridiculous to men'" (qtd. in Horth 191).[3] Carolyn L. Karcher explains that Melville then "started experimenting with increasingly elaborate strategies for subverting his readers' prejudices and conveying unwelcome truths" ("Herman Melville" 2622). His exposure to people of various backgrounds, cultures, races, and nationalities was an important influence in forming more strategic means to get at the truth, and no cultural community was more adept at subversive techniques than African slaves maneuvering within the oppressive white world governed by the Spanish, British, French, and the Americans. As Karcher notes, Melville experimented with allegory, satire, and symbol, and created a "daring mixture of genres and forms" (2622), yet an important element of this mixture that has been largely overlooked is Melville's use of the black aesthetic technique of signifying, which I contend is most evident in his novella *Benito Cereno*.

Benito Cereno was first published in *Putnam's Monthly* in 1855 and included in the collection *The Piazza Tales* the following year.[4] Melville drew from the historic 1805 slave insurrection on board the Spanish ship *Tryal,* recounted in American captain Amasa Delano's 1817 *Narrative of Voyages and Travels, in the Northern and Southern Hemispheres* as well as a wide range of other sources. Wyn Kelley describes the novella as a "mélange of genres and styles" and regards *Benito Cereno* "as a historical tale, a slave narrative, and a form of popular theater" (11). Other scholars have explored Melville's use of African and African American sources, with which he became familiar during his travels as a sailor.[5] For example, Bruce Bickley notes similarities between Babo and African American trickster figures Brer Rabbit and the slave trickster John, and Sterling Stuckey examines evidence of African cultural practices, specifically regarding dance and music, as well as also addressing the "striking similarities between Babo" and "Brer Rabbit, the supreme hero of African American folklore" (*Going through the Storm* 165). These sources are particularly important because Melville was likely "aware of having African American readers and could conceivably have been writing for and to them, anticipating a response in very different publications from the white-owned venues he had worked in before. This fact makes *Benito Cereno* conceivably one of the first American slave narratives to be written for two races" (Kelley 22). Melville's narrative, moreover, suggests further evidence of his creative engagement with African American sources in terms of style, structure, and aesthetic methodology. In this chapter, I argue that Melville adopts the black aesthetic technique of signifying and creates characters by engaging several genres of black literary and oral traditions, specifically the flying African cycle, the trickster wisdom evident in the slave narratives, and, most notably, the Signifying Monkey narrative poems. Indeed, the similarities between Babo and the Signifying Monkey suggest that the novella's most crafty character does not simply operate to expose white racism but further to ridicule its tenets.[6]

There are many distinct features among various types of black folktales but what they share in common at their most elemental level is a version of the trickster figure whose main weapon is intelligence used to outwit his or her foes, which Roger Abrahams defines as "the clever hero" (*Deep Down in the Jungle* 63). The Signifying Monkey cycle is unique in the extensive genre of black folktales because this cycle features characters that derive more directly from African oral traditions than other animal tales. In their introduction to *The Book of Negro Folklore*, Langston Hughes and Arna Bontemps explain that "in the African prototypes of the American Negro tales the heroes were generally the jackal, the hare, the tortoise, and the spider. The African jackal survived as the American fox, the African hare as the American rabbit, and the African tortoise as the American dry-land turtle or terrapin. The spider came only as near as the West Indies, where it reappeared in the Anansi tales of Jamaica. As a villain the African hyena was replaced by the American wolf, but that role is sometimes assigned to the fox or the bear in the American tale. The rest of the cast of characters, the lions, leopards, tigers, and monkeys, was safely transported" (xiii). As the reigning king of the jungle, the Lion functions as a dangerous symbol of physical power and pride, but the Elephant is also supremely physically powerful as well and thus a threat to the Lion's status, particularly because the Elephant is also renowned for intelligence and memory. The Monkey lacks the physical power of these much larger animals but is also known for his supreme intelligence, which the Monkey utilizes to maneuver within the dangerous environment of the jungle. Kermit E. Campbell notes that "signifying as derived from the Signifying Monkey tales means the use of certain discourse forms not only to put down or poke fun at someone but categorically to debunk an individual's or community's self-imposed status of power" (465). Furthermore, while most of the folktales function on a dual structure and feature two characters pitted against each other, representing "the binary opposite between black and white," the Signifying Monkey cycle is unique because, as Gates explains, these narrative poems operate on a "trinary" and involve "the Monkey, the Lion, and the Elephant" (*Signifying Monkey* 55). Gates notes that "to read the Monkey tales as a simple allegory of the black's political oppression is to ignore the hulking presence of the Elephant, the crucial third term for the depicted action" (55). This trinary force is similarly reflected in Melville's characters, Babo, Benito Cereno, and Amasa Delano, as well as the verbal and nonverbal dynamics between them, which strongly suggests that African American folktales were a rich resource for one of Melville's most highly regarded works of art.

In terms of structure, the narrative encompasses five distinct sections. Chronologically, they are: the mutiny, the staging, Delano's "visit," the voyage to Lima, and, finally, the deposition; however, details of the first and second sections are not provided until the deposition, yet all of the narrative events generate out of these omissions. Karcher contends that the main narrative, the visit, is "an exploration of the white racist mind and how it reacts in the face of a slave insurrection" (*Shadow over the Promised Land* 128). But Babo's insight into the workings of the white racist imagination suggests that the story is as much a tale of this character's cunning intelligence as it is a story of those duped by him.[7] Melville begins the novella in third person focalized by Captain Amasa Delano, who serves as the novella's "focal character," which functions as "the character in terms of whose point of view the narrative situations and actions are presented" (Prince, *Dictionary of Narratology* 31). The novella opens in 1799 on the second day that the *Bachelor's Delight* is anchored in the "harbor of St. Maria—a small, desert, uninhabited island toward the southern extremity of the long coast of Chili" (35). At dawn, Captain Delano is informed by a "mate" that "a strange sail was coming into the bay" (35). Over the course of a few hours, Delano prepares to offer assistance to what he perceives to be "a ship in distress" (37). His assumption is confirmed when he boards the *San Dominick* and is greeted "at once surrounded by a clamorous throng of whites and blacks, but the latter outnumbering the former more than could have been expected, negro transportation-ship as the stranger in port was. But, in one language, and as with one voice, all poured out a common tale of suffering" (39). The reference to their "tale," however, signifies on the activities that occurred on board the *San Dominick* in the hours prior to Delano boarding, and upon his arrival, he is "thus made the mark of all eager tongues," which situates him in the role of the signified, their tale operating to signify distress (39).

When Delano is "made the mark," Melville begins to shift from third-person point of view to a more ambiguous perspective. Critics have struggled to clearly define the narrative's point of view; for example, Sarah Robbins contends that Melville "did not, strictly speaking, provide a point of view. Delano was not relaying facts to the reader directly. Some unseen, unnamed, depersonalized narrator recorded what happened to Delano, as Melville made frequent use of indirect constructions (with phrases like 'was seen' recurring) to emphasize the American's essentially passive role while inviting audience critique of it" (553). These indirect constructions indicate, as Paul Downes observes, "Melville's relentlessly ambiguous deployment of free indirect discourse" (467)—a technique that reports a character's "thought and preconscious feeling in the language of third-person storytelling; but while maintaining the third-person reference, the narrative also suggests a simulation of the character's own mental discourse" (Reilly 45). It is important to point out, however, that the omitted events of the mutiny and staging that occurs while the ship is being watched inform this perspective, and as the orchestrator of these events, Babo is ironically "directing" the direction of free indirect discourse and in this respect can be viewed as creating or controlling the narrative point of view.

Although Melville drew heavily from Delano's 1817 *Narrative*, there are several important distinctions between the historical account and Melville's novella, such as backdating events, "fusing Babo and his son Muri"[8] into one main character, the disposal of Don Alexandro Aranda's body (which was thrown overboard), Cereno greeting Delano when he boards the ship, and, perhaps most significant, the single reference in the historical account of Delano interpreting Cereno's behavior as offensive. In his *Narrative*, Delano writes: "After the Spanish ship was anchored, I invited the captain to go on board my ship and take tea or coffee with me. His answer was short and seemingly reserved; and his air very different from that with which he had received my assistance. As I was at a loss to account for this change in his demeanor, and knew he had seen nothing in my conduct to justify it, and as I felt certain that he had treated me with intentional neglect; in return I became less sociable, and said little to him" (117).

In Melville's account, however, Delano is routinely duped by the clever hero Babo into feeling animosity, suspicion, insult, distrust, and fear of Benito Cereno. Indeed, Delano repeatedly suspects Cereno of "maturing some plot" and at one point fears that "at the signal of the Spaniard, he was about to be massacred" (64, 69). Delano also surmises that Cereno may be "simulating mortal disease, the craft of some tricksters had been known to attain. To think that, under the aspect of infantile weakness, the most savage energies might be couched—those velvets of the Spaniard but the silky paw to his fangs" (54). Delano's mistake, however, is his failure to consider that it is not the Spaniard's "loose Chili jacket of dark velvet" that conceals the threat but rather Babo's humble attire, consisting of simply "wide trousers, apparently, from their coarseness and patches, made out of some old topsail; they were clean, and confined at the waist by a bit of unstranded rope"

(46–47). Delano is thus duped by reading the "contrast in dress" as "denoting their relative positions," which he assumes reflects the ship's hierarchy of authority (46). This assumption leads him to suspect Cereno of trickster craft rather than Babo.

Several scholars have noted Babo's resemblance to another "clever hero," the trickster Brer Rabbit. Stuckey points out that "in no sense does the success of Brer Rabbit or Babo depend on physical strength, for both are too small to confront their enemies physically. Babo's mastery of his world, like Brer Rabbit's mastery of his, depends upon superior intellectual powers. Not surprisingly, Melville takes the liberty of stressing Babo's slight stature when there is no mention of it in the historical document" (*Going through the Storm* 165). While Stuckey makes a number of excellent observations regarding Brer Rabbit and Babo, the characteristics of physical weakness and intellectual superiority are also reprehensive traits of the Signifying Monkey as well, yet the comparison of dual opponents overlooks the crucial third element in the Babo-Delano-Cereno triangle, an oversight that, as Gates notes, is also commonly made regarding the Signifying Monkey tales. Furthermore, Abrahams notes that while the Signifying Monkey and Brer Rabbit can both be vindictive and aggressive, "the two tricksters are working with different dupes. Rabbit is contesting for his life against those not only much bigger than he but who desire to eat him. His reasons for tricking others in most of the stories are defensive in the broadest sense of the term. . . . The Monkey, on the other hand, has no apparent motive for his trickery beyond a purely sadistic one, wanting to see another (and bigger) get beaten" (*Deep Down in the Jungle* 69–70). Although Abrahams indicates that the Monkey's antics have "no apparent motive," Gates points out that "the Monkey—a trickster figure, like Esu, who is full of guile, who tells lies, and who is a rhetorical genius—is intent on demystifying the Lion's self-imposed status as King of the Jungle" (*Signifying Monkey* 56). The Monkey accomplishes his goal by pitting one powerful figure against another equally powerful opponent. Gates notes that "the Monkey, clearly, is no match for the Lion's physical prowess; the Elephant is, however. The Monkey's task, then, is to trick the Lion into tangling with the Elephant" (56).

The third element is crucial in the Signifying Monkey cycle and functions similarly in the Babo-Cereno-Delano triad because the Monkey's trick is to create conflict between two powerful forces while simultaneously deflecting suspicion of his own involvement as the instigator. Similarly, Babo's task is to "trick" Delano into tangling with Cereno, yet Melville establishes a more specific motive for creating conflict between the captains by signifying on Western social and scientific theories of race, specifically the binary of white superiority and black inferiority, in order to deflect information that could jeopardize the rebels' plot of attaining liberty. Another less laudatory feature that distinguishes the Monkey from the Rabbit is the Monkey's penchant for simply "starting some shit," a characteristic Babo possesses as well. For example, as noted in the deposition, when the rebels spot the *Bachelor's Delight,* Atufal cautions against unnecessary risk and advises that they sail away, "but the negro Babo would not, and, by himself, cast about what to do; that at last he came to the deponent, proposing to him to say and do all that the deponent declares to have said and done to the American captain" (99). Not content with his domination on board the *San Dominick* and against the advice of the more cautious Atufal, Babo sets his sights on yet another powerful figure to further his scheme as well as stir up trouble in this allegorical jungle.

Babo's agenda is important because it pivots on one of the most controversial interpretive issues over which "critics have deadlocked . . .—whether Melville champions or condemns the rebels" (Karcher, *Shadow over the Promised Land* 127). Given Melville's involvement in the 1842 mutiny on board the *Lucy Ann,* he clearly felt there were circumstances that justified rebellion, and, as Sundquist contends, by backdating "Delano's encounter with Benito Cereno from 1805 to 1799," Melville "accentuated the fact that his tale belonged to the Age of Revolution, in particular the period of violent struggle leading to Haitian independence presided over by the heroic black general Toussaint L'Ouverture" (*To Wake the Nations* 140). Furthermore, Stuckey observes the "link between Benito Cereno and the Highlander, the ship in *Redburn,*" and points out that the character Jackson "used to tell of the middle passage, where the slaves were stowed, heel and point, like logs, and the suffocated and dead were unmanacled, and weeded out from the living every morning" (*African Culture and Melville's Art* 37). The narrator of the novel, Redburn, also notes that at the base of the London statue of Lord Nelson are featured "four naked figures in chains . . . in various attitudes of humiliation and despair," which brings to mind "four African slaves in the market-place," and Redburn muses, "my thoughts would revert to Virginia and Carolina" (Melville, *Redburn* 8). The rather brutal depiction of the Middle Passage and recollections of Southern slaves evoked by "attitudes of humiliation and despair" provide compelling evidence that Melville intended the novella to serve in support of the slaves' liberation. In this respect, Melville also signifies on a common theme of both the flying African tales as well as the slave narratives, which is a belief in the rebels' unalienable right to freedom and, particularly evident in the slave narrative genre, a commitment to risk their lives to attain their liberty, which Melville strongly implies they are as entitled to as were those who fought for American independence.

Babo's actions throughout the narrative are thus motivated by the main objective of attaining liberty, which are advanced by his savvy understanding of the limitations of his audience. Like Abe, Babo also draws on black insight of white ignorance to manipulate what Delano hears and sees by performing the socially imposed identity of the humble and loyal slave and thus influences what Delano thinks and feels. Captain Delano is able to note a variety of events that occur on the Spanish ship but is unable to interpret these events and, therefore, incapable of fully comprehending the various signs throughout the ship that suggest slave rebellion, nor is he able to understand the linguistic complexities of Babo's double voice. Like the Signifying Monkey, Babo also "speaks in double-entendres" (A. Smith 182). This form of signifying, as Claudia Mitchell-Kernan notes, "incorporates essentially a folk notion that dictionary entries for words are not always sufficient for interpreting meanings or messages, or that meaning goes beyond such interpretations" (311). Babo's verbal dexterity and his insight regarding the limitations of his audience allow him to signify on Delano, which is similar to the ways in which the Monkey signifies on the Lion. As Gates notes, "the Signifying Monkey is able to signify upon the Lion because the Lion does not understand the Monkey's discourse.... The Monkey speaks figuratively, in a symbolic code; the Lion interprets literally and thus suffers from the consequences of his folly" (*Figures in Black* 241). Babo's double voice is evidenced, for example, by his consistent reference to Cereno as "my master," which functions to dupe Delano into regarding the relationship between Babo and Cereno as master and slave and additionally functions as a signifying pun on Cereno's authority. Gates explains that "by supplanting the received term's associated concept, the black vernacular tradition created a homonymic pun of the profoundest sort . . . their complex act of language Signifies upon both formal language use and its conventions" (47). Babo's routine use of the address of *master* rather than *captain* or *sir* implies a rather profound pun on the dynamics of power between Babo and Cereno as well as repudiation of white authority. Babo's use of the term also operates as a device to dupe Delano, which is particularly effective given Melville's description of Delano as "a man of such native simplicity as to be incapable of satire or irony" (52).

Babo's double voice, moreover, often operates in three ways and in many scenes suggests that he utilizes triple voice to communicate with Delano, Cereno, and his fellow mutineers. For example, in order to deflect suspicion, particularly signs of a physical threat, Atufal plays the role of a slave punished for his alleged resistance to authority. When he initially approaches the trio, Babo is the first to speak, stating: "'How like a mute Atufal moves'" (51). And before Delano can ask a question or Cereno comment, Babo addresses Cereno: "'See, he waits your question, master'" (51). Babo's comments demonstrate that these roles have been rehearsed and function to mislead Delano, instruct Cereno, and serve as periodic confirmation between Babo and Atufal that events are proceeding according to plan. On a nonverbal level, Atufal's "colossal form" appears contained and controlled by Cereno, who carries around his neck a symbol of his presumed authority, a key that can release the chains secured by the padlock around Atufal's waist. Delano regards the "padlock and key" as "significant symbols" but assumes, as Babo intends, that they represent Cereno's "lordship over the black" (52). Cereno's nervous response to Delano's "playful allusion" to these symbols leads Delano to believe that Cereno "seemed in some way to have taken it as a malicious reflection upon his confessed inability thus far to break down, at least, on a verbal summons, the entrenched will of the slave" (52). But, more important, Delano fails to notice the "verbal summons" that Babo issues to Cereno and is again duped into an unflattering opinion of Cereno. Delano subsequently "became less talkative, oppressed, against his own will, by what seemed the secret vindictiveness of the morbidly sensitive Spaniard" (53). The performance works to direct suspicion away from Babo and Atufal and onto Cereno, reinforcing Delano's opinion of him as emotionally erratic, oversensitive, and stubborn.

Babo's comments and behavior are, moreover, particularly effective in duping Delano because Delano's ignorance is not simply a matter of lack of intelligence nor training in decoding a particular signifying system but rather active resistance to information or knowledge that threatens to alter his worldview. Addressing issues of teaching and learning, Shoshana Felman contends that ignorance is not "simply opposed to knowledge: it is itself a radical condition, an integral part of the very structure of knowledge," and argues that "teaching, like analysis, has to deal not so much with lack of knowledge as with resistances to knowledge" (417). Ignorance is "nothing other than a desire to ignore . . . not a simple lack of information but the incapacity—or the refusal—to acknowledge one's own implication in the information" (417). Delano's resistance is conspicuously evident on the few occasions that he harbors misgivings regarding the blacks, and at one point feels that "the hatchets had anything but an attractive look, and the handlers of them still less so" (48). His suspicions are, however, limited to an assumption that if the blacks are involved, they are led by the whites, particularly by the Spanish captain whom Delano considers the "central hobgoblin" (59). In another instance, recalling Atufal's physical power, Delano wonders fearfully: "Was the negro now lying in wait . . . the Spaniard behind—his creature before" (85). Delano takes for granted that if a dangerous plot were in the works, it would be led by the whites and merely supported by the blacks because the blacks "were too stupid" (65). This perspective reflects widely held beliefs that associate color with intelligence. Gates notes that eighteenth-century philosophers Hume and Kant theorized "with dictatorial surety" the "correlation of 'black' and 'stupid,'" which influenced early nineteenth-century philosophers such as Hegel ("Editor's Introduction: 'Race'" 10). Kant, for example, refers to a "fellow" who was "quite black from head to foot," which he takes as "clear proof that what he said was stupid"; according to Hume, "'there are Negroe slaves dispersed all over Europe, of which none ever discovered any symptoms of ingenuity'" (qtd. in Gates, 10-11). Hume, it would seem, had not been exposed to the ingenuity of the slaves' trickster tales; it is much more likely that Melville had, "given [his] close contact . . . with African-American sailors" (Karcher, "Riddle of the Sphinx" 197). Melville was also familiar with the theories of these philosophers as verified through the "appearance of the Melville *Journals* in 1989," in particular his 1849 note dated Monday, October 22, regarding talking with Adler and Taylor of "'metaphysics continually, and Hegel, Schlegel, Kant and others were discussed'" (Stuckey, *African Culture and Melville's Art* 36). Melville, thus, creates a black character who not only undermines theories of racial inferiority but indeed cleverly exploits this perspective to his advantage.[9]

Babo consistently draws on common assumptions of his intellectual limitations to outwit those who take black intellectual inferiority as a given. Melville also depicts white characters resistant to admit signs of black intelligence because such information threatens to jeopardize the assumption of white intellectual superiority as well as, as Susan Ryan puts it, the "fantasy of benevolent white supremacy" (71). Ryan notes that "Delano can be taken to represent an obtuse brand of northern humanitarianism, one whose proponents have drained sympathy for the oppressed of its critical content. He provides the 'slaves' with food and water but cannot fathom giving them their freedom or altering their circumstances in any other way" (70).

Delano also cannot fathom the ingenuity necessary in crafting a highly sophisticated plot of insurrection deriving from a black source.

The plot that paved the way for the rebellion indicates a successful intellectual victory prior to the physical contest and demonstrates that Delano is not the only character who evidences white ignorance of black intelligence. Both Benito Cereno and Alexandro Aranda are duped by this limitation as well. Walter Johnson notes that slave revolts on ships depended on an "'infrapolitics' of the slave community in the trade—the generally invisible processes by which a group of strangers formed themselves into a resistance collective" (75). In addition to the historic account of Amasa Delano, several scholars have pointed out similar elements of other slave revolts in the novella as well, in particular the *Amistad* in 1839 and the 1841 *Creole* revolt led by Madison Washington.[10] Johnson notes that in the *Creole* event,

> it is ultimately unclear whether the nineteen rebels had tried to keep their plans secret from the others, tried unsuccessfully to convince them to join, or even, as the mate suspected, "been appointed by the others as chief." It is clear that their eventual action emerged, one way or another, out of a negotiation with all the slaves in the hold. Indeed, it is hard to imagine that some among the 115 or so other slaves on the boat did not notice and help hide the fact that nineteen of the slaves were planning a revolt. Nor were the other slaves on the *Creole* the only slaves who might have been complicit with the nineteen slaves who took over the ship. The plan those nineteen men put into action was shaped around their broader knowledge of the Atlantic world—of the African colony of Liberia and the fate of a specific shipment of slaves that had run aground in the Caribbean the year before—a knowledge that must have been the product of the same underground network used by Charles Ball in plotting his escape. (76)

An underground network of intelligence is also alluded to throughout the deposition. In his testimony, Cereno reports that when the voyage began, "all the negroes slept upon deck, as is customary in this navigation, and none wore fetters, because the owner, his friend Aranda, told him that they were all tractable" (93-94). Melville notes that the ship set sail with "one hundred and sixty blacks, of both sexes, mostly belonging to Don Alexandro Aranda" and adds that "one, from about eighteen to nineteen years, named Jose" served as the personal servant of Aranda for "four or five years" (93). Jose takes advantage of his proximity to the ship's authorities to provide "information to the negro Babo, about the state of things in the cabin, before the revolt," which demonstrates Aranda's ignorance about the slaves' tractability and, in particular, his flawed assessment of the slave who served as his personal servant for several years (101). Furthermore, until "the negroes revolted suddenly" at "three o'clock in the morning," Cereno saw no signs that would lead him to question Aranda's opinion that "fetters" were unnecessary. The result of these misjudgments is that Cereno loses command of his ship and Aranda and several crew members lost their lives.

Like the Signifying Monkey, Babo's main weapon is the intelligence he conceals behind his performative mask, which demonstrates another form of signifying. Abrahams notes that this strategy is used "in recurrent black-white encounters as masking behavior" (*Talking Black* 19).[11] Throughout Delano's visit, Babo is shown to be an expert of this technique and functions, like the Signifying Monkey, as the novella's "great Signifier" (Gates, *Signifying Monkey* 54). As the ringleader, Babo stages the performance and takes on the leading role of master signifier—ironically, by drawing on the stereotype of devoted slave faithfully serving his beloved master. Babo's role is a particularly brilliant casting decision because it gives him a number of advantages, most notably direct access to the most significant threat to the plan, the captain, who is the person the visiting captain would customarily seek out for information. He thus occupies the position of security guard and has, furthermore, assigned the other blacks similar security and supervisory duties, yet the blacks' security system is strategically concealed behind their performance of menial tasks, which Delano regards as natural and, therefore, not suspicious. Babo orchestrates a plan of constant surveillance, positioning his fellow mutineers throughout the ship in places that allow extensive points of visibility, which provides the blacks surveillance of a wide range of the ship, command of the whites, and the ability to communicate with each other nonverbally.

When Delano first boards the ship, he is greeted by a "throng of whites and blacks" on the main deck (39). He then observes "four elderly grizzled negroes, their heads like black, doddered willow tops, who, in venerable contrast to the tumult below them, were couched sphinx-like" (39). These men are strategically arranged with "one on the starboard cat-head, another on the larboard, and the remaining pair face to face on the opposite bulwarks above the mainchains" (39). Delano observes that "they each had bits of unstranded old junk in their hands, and, with a sort of stoical self-content, were picking the junk into oakum, a small heap of which lay by their sides. They accompanied the task with a continuous, low, monotonous chant" (39). While Delano dismisses their chanting as "droning and druling away," the oakum pickers are more than likely communicating with each other as well as with Babo because he has assigned these roles and duties. Delano next notices "the cross-legged figures of six other blacks; each with a rusty hatchet in his hand, which, with a bit of brick and a rag, he was engaged like a scullion in scouring" (40). These men are stationed on "an ample elevated poop" and also "lifted, like the oakum-pickers, some eight feet above the general throng" on the main deck (40). Melville notes that, unlike the oakum pickers, these men "neither spoke to others, nor breathed a whisper among themselves, but sat intent upon their task, except at intervals, when, with the peculiar love in negroes of uniting industry with pastime, two and two they sideways clashed their hatchets together, like cymbals" (40). Because the ten men are engaged in menial tasks, Delano fails to suspect that they have been carefully positioned throughout the ship for the purpose of surveillance, nor does he consider that the six hatchet polishers are handling weapons rather than performing the routine maintenance of tools. Delano is also oblivious to the possibility that the clashing is a form of communication because he dismisses the practice as simply "the peculiar love in negroes of uniting industry with pastime" (40). Sundquist points out that "like the 'monotonous chant' of the oakum pickers, the language of the hatchets, which is a 'barbarous din' to Delano's uncomprehending ears, has the pragmatic value of regulation and signal. Arising at crucial moments in the enactment of Babo's masquerade, the percussive sounds are, in fact, the language in which the Africans' communication occurs during the suspended duration of Delano's presence. Such sounds are nothing less than a kind of speech" (*To Wake the Nations* 166). Babo's orchestration of these events, moreover, shows his savvy understanding of racial generalizations and stereotypes, particularly the perspective of the "antebellum era's scientific racism" that Africans are "naturally servile," which Babo cleverly exploits to facilitate his plan (Ryan 70).

Delano then "turned in quest of whomsoever it might be that commanded the ship" and observes Cereno "leaning against the main-mast" (40). This scene deviates significantly from the historic account because in the historic record, Cereno immediately greets Delano and offers a version of their hardships. Melville shifts this perspective, and Delano is given "the tale" by the general throng of black and white before meeting or talking to Cereno. The distinction emphasizes the commitment of all the blacks in following Babo's plan for their collective liberty, which blasts the myth of the contented slave and highlights Babo's brilliance in crafting and carrying out a highly sophisticated scheme. Babo's role is, moreover, a performance intended to conceal his intelligence, which he also carries out brilliantly.

Babo's masquerade as body servant and the "services" he renders allow him to scrutinize, interpret, and, when necessary, intervene. Delano first observes Babo standing beside Cereno and reads Babo's face as equally blended "sorrow and affection" for what Delano assumes to be "his master" (40–41). Delano interprets Babo giving "his master his arm" or "taking his handkerchief out of his pocket for him" as an expression of "that affectionate zeal which transmutes into something filial or fraternal acts in themselves but menial; and which has gained for the negro the repute of making the most pleasing body servant in the world" (42). In addition to misleading Delano regarding the rebellion, Babo's proximity to Cereno allows him to know what is said between the two captains and continue to command the ship by feigning the subordinate role as the captain's assistant. Any orders issued by the captain were "delegated to his body-servant, who in turn transferred them to their ultimate destination, through runners" (42).

Babo's role also enables him to intervene on a number of potentially threatening occasions. For example, when Delano presses Cereno to explain "'the particulars of the ship's misfortunes'" and asks that Cereno "'favor him with the whole story,'" Cereno "faltered; then, like some somnambulist suddenly interfered with, vacantly stared at his visitor, and ended by looking down on the deck" (44). Delano reads Cereno's behavior as "rude" and walks away, but "he had hardly gone five paces, when with a sort of eagerness Don Benito invited him back" (44). Because there is no one "near but the servant," it is clear that Babo intervenes and compels Cereno to call Delano back. Under Babo's watchful eye and the threat of death, Cereno struggles to provide Delano with the requested information.

As Cereno continues with the tale, his fear and the memory of Aranda's demise physically unsettles him, which threatens to jeopardize the plot; Babo is thus obliged to act carefully, quickly, and strategically. He must behave in a way that will deflect Delano's suspicion while simultaneously reinforcing the physical threat to Cereno. Babo then draws "a cordial from his pocket [and] placed it to his lips. He a little revived. But unwilling to leave him unsupported while yet imperfectly restored, the black with one arm still encircled his master, at the same time keeping his eye fixed on his face, as if to watch for the first sign of complete restoration, or relapse, as the event might prove" (45). Babo's quick thinking works to simultaneously caution Cereno and pacify Delano. By presenting himself as a loyal and devoted servant, Babo reinforces Delano's view of the *social roles* of black serving white as natural. Ryan explains that "antebellum Americans generally believed that their racial attributions recurred to some natural and unalterable truth" (66). Ryan notes that "the assertion of a caring, familial relationship between master and slave, long a staple of proslavery rhetoric, became a central preoccupation of slaveholders and their allies. . . . Delano's credulous response to that performance suggests the extent to which proslavery representations conditioned non-slaveholders' beliefs about interracial benevolence" (70). In this instance, as Delano views the image of "the black upholding the white," he "could not but bethink him of the beauty of that relationship which could present such a spectacle of fidelity on the one hand and confidence on the other" (46). The spectacle has, however, been manufactured by Babo and demonstrates his careful control of appearances in order to maintain his command.

Babo again intervenes when Cereno's "cough returned," and he "fell heavily against his supporter" (45). Babo does not wait for or give Cereno an opportunity to account for these fits and not only speaks for Cereno but claims to understand the inner workings of Cereno's mind as well. Babo tells Delano, "'His mind wanders. He was thinking of the plague that followed the gales" and assures Delano that "'these fits do not last long; master will soon be himself'" (45). Babo's comments imply that his bond with his master is so profound that he is able to understand his master's thoughts and, therefore, speak on his behalf. The result is that Babo is able to pacify Delano while simultaneously communicating caution and instruction to Cereno, which has the desired effect of "reviving" Cereno (45).

Babo's tactic of proximity and intervention is again utilized as Delano continues his questioning after the supply boat departs from the *San Dominick*, particularly when Delano points out an inconsistency in Cereno's story. When Delano makes note of Cape Horn, Cereno asks: "'Cape Horn?—who spoke of Cape Horn?'" (70). Delano responds, "'Yourself did'" (70). Babo intervenes and interrupts the conversation by informing Cereno: "'Master told me never mind where he was, or how engaged, always to remind him, to a minute, when shaving-time comes'" (71). Babo suggests to Cereno, "'Why not let Don Amasa sit by master in the cuddy, and master can talk, and Don Amasa can listen, while Babo here lathers and strops?'" (71). Babo's "timely interruption served to rally his master from the mood which had evidently been coming upon him" (71). Babo's strategy works to distract Delano from his line of questioning and to direct Cereno's relocation to the cuddy. Cereno then proceeds with his story while Babo prepares to shave him. Babo's manipulation of appearances during this scene enables him to threaten Cereno with a deadly weapon while simultaneously presenting to Delano the appearance of performing the commonplace duties of a servant. To Delano, the spectacle is particularly "pleasing to behold" and reinforces for Delano the widespread belief of "something in the negro which, in a peculiar way, fits him for avocations about one's person. Most negroes are natural valets and hairdressers; taking to the comb and brush congenially as to the castanets, and flourishing them apparently with almost equal satisfaction. . . . And above all is the great gift of good humor. Not the mere grin or laugh is here meant. Those were unsuitable. But a certain easy cheerfulness, harmonious in every glance and gesture; as though God had set the whole negro to some pleasant tune" (73). Melville's use of free indirect discourse indicates that this perspective regarding race, while focalized by Delano, reflects commonly held views rather than simply Delano's personal opinions. Indeed, before the mutiny, Aranda also likely regarded the slaves' "easy cheerfulness" as well as "the docility arising from the unaspiring contentment of a limited mind, and that susceptibility of blind attachment sometimes inhering in indisputable inferiors" as convincing evidence that "fetters" were unnecessary (73, 93). Babo's crafty manipulation of the shaving materials, however, sends a very different message to Cereno.

During the shaving episode, Babo tucks "a great piece of bunting" under "his master's chin," leading Delano to regard the choice of material as a reflection of "the African love of bright colors and fine shows" (74). Babo's choice, however, is much more calculated. By using the flag of Spain, Babo shows his contempt for and total repudiation of Spanish authority, and his gesture of stropping the razor in "close sight" of Cereno's face functions as a deadly form of intimidation. The communication has the desired effect, but when Cereno begins to tremble, Babo strategically advises: "'You must not shake so, master'" and, turning to Delano, Babo explains: "'—See, Don Amasa, master always shakes when I shave him. And yet master knows I never yet have drawn blood, though it's true, if master will shake so, I may some of these times'" (75). Babo's double voice again works to threaten Cereno and pacify Delano. Babo's orchestration of appearances also operates to manipulate Delano's opinion of Cereno. After Delano's departure from the cuddy, Babo approaches him on deck, complaining that his master has cut him "'with the razor, because, only by accident, Babo had given master one little scratch'" (77). Delano regards the alleged discipline as further evidence of Cereno's "spite" (77).

During the lunch scene, Babo manipulates appearances similarly but shifts his tactics by signifying nonverbally throughout the course of the meal. Babo strategically "placed a rug under Don Benito's feet, and a cushion behind his back, and then stood behind, not his master's chair, but Captain Delano's. At first, this a little surprised the latter. But it was soon evident that, in taking his position, the black was still true to his master; since by facing him he could the more readily anticipate his slightest want" (79). Delano regards the scene as evidence of Babo's superior service-oriented skills and comments to Cereno, "'This is an uncommonly intelligent fellow of yours, Don Benito'" (79). Delano's opinion of Babo's intelligence is, however, restricted to his assumption that Babo's intellect is inherently limited to matters of service, which Babo consistently reinforces. For example, rather than interrupt verbally when the discussion between the captains becomes risky, Babo intervenes and signifies caution by "pushing the Canary over towards him. At length a few sips served partially to restore him" (79). After Delano requests a private conference with the Spanish captain, his resistance leads Delano to regard him as quarrelsome, and when Cereno grows more reserved, once again "the hand of his servant, mute as that on the wall, slowly pushed over the Canary" (80). Babo's subtle manipulation of the situation allows him to watch Cereno carefully, intervene nonverbally, and present to Delano the appearance of "the silent sight of fidelity" while simultaneously influencing Delano's feeling a "little tinge of irritation" toward Cereno as a result of his "querulousness" and "splenetic mood" (80).

Delano regularly fails to understand the complexity of Babo's comments, behavior, or his constant presence at the side of the captain. Delano also fails to suspect that throughout the ship, black and white are not haphazardly intermingled but rather have been strategically arranged, with the whites typically flanked by the blacks. Babo assigns the white crew to duties of routine ship maintenance and, again drawing on stereotypes of "docility," "unaspiring contentment," and "a limited mind," assigns the blacks menial tasks that give the appearance of service while covertly functioning as security regulation (18). For example, Delano "chanced to observe a sailor seated on the deck engaged in tarring the strap of a large block, with a circle of blacks squatted round him inquisitively eyeing the process . . . the tarpot held for him by a negro" (61). Delano then "advances to an old Barcelona tar, in ragged red breeches and dirty night-cap, cheeks trenched and bronzed, whiskers dense as thorn hedges. Seated between two sleepy-looking Africans, this mariner, like his younger shipmate, was employed upon some rigging—splicing a cable—the sleepy-looking blacks performing the inferior function of holding the outer parts of the ropes for him" (61). Seeing nothing out of the ordinary, Delano moves on to the Spanish seamen working at the pully-ends with each seaman flanked by a "subordinate black" (61). Delano fails to suspect that the whites are under the control of the rebels due to Babo's careful staging, assigning the blacks "subordinate" and "inferior functions," which Delano regards as natural and thus not suspicious; the odd behavior of the whites reiterates Cereno's scripted account of their bad behavior. To Delano, the old whiskerando's sheepishness plainly betrays "a consciousness of ill-desert" and hence accounts for his "furtive, diffident air" when Delano approaches him (62).

Delano misjudges similarly when he encounters "an aged sailor seated cross-legged near the main hatchway. . . . His hands were full of ropes, which he was working into a large knot. Some blacks were about him obligingly dipping the strands for him, here and there, as the exigencies of the operation demanded" (65). The old man desperately attempts to communicate with Delano in a symbolic nautical code as well as English, which the old man assumes are idioms that Delano should understand but that the "blacks about him" would not and "threw the knot towards him, saying in broken English,—the first heard in the ship,—something to this effect—'Undo it, cut it, quick!'" (65). But due to Babo's ingenuity in constructing multiple layers of signification, the old sailor is unable to break through Babo's signifying fortress, and the old man's attempt simply baffles Delano. He thus stood "for a moment, knot in hand, and knot in head," and quickly dismisses the puzzling scene as the "sailor rose, muttering, and, followed by his subordinate negroes, removed to the forward part of the ship" (66). He is then approached by "an elderly negro" and "with a good-natured, knowing wink, he informed him that the old knotter was simple-witted, but harmless; often playing his old tricks. The negro concluded by begging the knot, for of course the stranger would not care to be troubled with it. Unconsciously, it was handed to him. With a sort of congé, the negro received it, and turning his back, ferreted into it like a detective Custom House officer after smuggled laces. Soon, with some African word, equivalent to pshaw, he tossed the knot overboard" (66). Because the "elderly negro" feigns good-natured deference, Delano understands the old man's comments literally rather than figuratively and fails to consider that it is the elderly negro "playing his old tricks" rather than the old sailor. Furthermore, because Delano cannot imagine any reason other than innocent curiosity in examining the knot, he fails to suspect that the man is disposing of a dangerous attempt at communication by the old sailor. These scenes also demonstrate that the blacks are carrying out the carefully drilled details of Babo's instructions, demonstrating unity, bravery, and the implicit commitment to follow their leader.

Delano's most significant oversight is his failure to suspect that he is also under the command of the blacks. His movements about the ship are under constant scrutiny by the blacks, particularly the oakum pickers stationed as they are above the main deck, which allows them to watch over Delano and communicate nonverbally "as between the responsive posts of a telegraph, an unknown syllable ran from man to man among the perched oakum-pickers" (69). These men are especially alert during the few occasions Delano is not with Cereno and Babo. Early in his visit, during one of Cereno's fits, Babo "gently conducted his master below"; left on his own, Delano "made his way through the blacks, his movement drawing a queer cry from the oakum-pickers, prompted by whom, the negroes, twitching each other aside, divided before him; but, as if curious to see what was the object of this deliberate visit to their Ghetto, closing in behind, in tolerable order, followed the white stranger up. His progress thus proclaimed" (60–61). Delano is unaware that as he moves about the ship, "with sober curiosity peering down upon him was one of the old oakum-pickers, slipped from his perch to an outside boom" (64). On another occasion, after lunch, as Delano makes his way to the deck, he is startled "at the unexpected figure of Atufal. . . . Atufal's presence, singularly attesting docility even in sullenness, was contrasted with that of the hatchet-polishers, who in patience evinced their industry; while both spectacles showed, that lax as Don Benito's general authority might be, still, whenever he chose to exert it, no man so savage or colossal but must, more or less, bow" (81). Delano is repeatedly duped by the blacks' performance into regarding Cereno's authority as not only a given but indeed excessive, which functions to steer suspicion toward Cereno and away from the real danger. As a result, Delano does not suspect that he is under surveillance and thoughtlessly taking deadly risks.

Throughout Delano's visit, there is only one instance noted that depicts a black character unaware of Delano's whereabouts. While walking alone on deck, Delano's notices a

> slumbering negress, partly disclosed through the lace-work of some rigging, lying, with youthful limbs carelessly disposed, under the lee of the bulwark. . . . Sprawling at her lapped breasts was her wide-awake fawn, stark naked, its black little body half lifted from the deck, crosswise with its dam's; its hands, like two paws, clambering upon her. . . . The uncommon vigor of the child at length roused the mother. She started up, at distance facing Captain Delano. But as if not at all concerned at the attitude

which she had been caught, delightedly she caught the child up, with maternal transports, covering it with kisses. (63)

Because Delano is the focal character, Melville's use of free indirect discourse indicates Delano's assumption that the woman is "not at all concerned at the attitude which she had been caught," which implies that she was conscious of Delano watching her. However, because of the ambiguities of the narrative point of view, it is also possible that she may not have been aware of his presence at all. The woman's display of affection for her child thus indicates that she either does not feel restricted by Delano's presence or that she is unaware of an audience, yet both interpretive possibilities indicate her love for her child and the joy her maternal role gives her. The scene also features a woman free from the gender-specific stresses slave women routinely endured, which was the constant threat that their children could be taken from them as well as the common "practice of white male slaveholders using female slaves for their sexual gratification" (McLaurin 21). Karcher points out that "the women's presence and role in the revolt enabled Melville to expose an aspect of the slave trade generally veiled in silence—the routine raping of the captives" ("Riddle of the Sphinx" 212). Indeed, slave women were not only sexually vulnerable while imprisoned on a slave ship but throughout the duration of their time as slaves as well, which for most meant throughout their entire lives. It is important to note that Cereno testified in the deposition that Babo "and his companions" decide to kill Aranda because they "could not otherwise be sure of their liberty, and that, to keep the seamen in subjugation, he wanted to prepare a warning of what road they should be made to take did they or any of them oppose him; and that, by means of the death of Don Alexandro, that warning would best be given" (95). However, the "negresses, of age, were knowing to the revolt, and testified themselves satisfied at the death of their master, Don Alexandro; that, had the negroes not restrained them, they would have tortured to death, instead of simply killing, the Spaniards slain by the command of the negro Babo; that the negresses used their utmost influence to have the deponent made away with" (102). While the role of the women is comparatively brief, they too demonstrate their commitment to the common goal of liberty, but they also reveal an agenda that differentiates them from the men. The hostility they express toward Cereno and Aranda strongly insinuates that these men have committed or permitted gender-specific offenses that they want avenged.

As Delano's visit draws to a close, Babo cautiously maintains his delicate control, guiding Cereno by "placing his master's hand on his naked shoulder, and gently holding it there, formed himself into a sort of crutch," and as the captains shake hands, Babo, "still presenting himself as a crutch, and walking between the two captains, he advanced with them towards the gangway" (86–87). Babo maintains his judicious control over both captains as they part, but when Delano settles himself in the boat and Cereno unexpectedly "sprang over the bulwarks, falling at the feet of Captain Delano," Babo impulsively shifts his tactics (87). Babo reacts in an instant, abandoning his most powerful weapon for one far less effective due to events occurring "with such involutions of rapidity, that past, present, and future seemed one" (87). As Delano seizes "Don Benito by the throat he added, 'this plotting pirate means murder!'" (87). In this moment of crisis, Babo makes a physical rather than intellectual move and is quickly overpowered and captured. Babo's downfall is similar to the Monkey's because both abandon their most powerful weapon—their superior intelligence—in the heat of the moment. While most of the tales of the Signifying Monkey conclude with, as Gates notes, the hero's successful escape into a tree to "return to signify on another day," Abrahams points out that in others, "the Monkey's signifying leads him to get excited and he falls and is captured by the Lion . . . so in some versions the unusual situation occurs where the hero dies. This fact seems significant" (*Signifying Monkey* 58; *Deep Down in the Jungle* 68). Babo also becomes excited and reacts rather than reasons and is eventually defeated by his attempt to use physical power in a contest with opponents far more physically powerful.

Other similarities in the novella with the Signifying Monkey cycle reflect the awkward dynamics between the Lion and the Elephant as a result of the Monkey's signifying. Gates notes that when the Lion realizes that he has been duped by the Monkey, he "perceives his shaky, self-imposed status as having been challenged, rushes off in outrage to find the Elephant so that he might redress his grievances and preserve appearances" (*Signifying Monkey* 56). Similarly, during the voyage to Lima, Delano also demonstrates his need to redress his grievances and preserve appearances, telling Cereno: "'You have saved my life, Don Benito, more than I yours; saved it, too, against my knowledge and will'" (106). Delano rationalizes and, therefore, dismisses his misjudgments as owing to his "good nature, compassion, and charity" (106). Cereno, however, expresses his chagrin by reminding Delano: "'You were with me all day; stood with me, sat with me, talked with me, looked at me, ate with me, drank with me; and yet, your last act was to clutch for a monster, not only an innocent man, but the most pitiable of all men'" (106). Delano's response shows his need to save face by advising: "'You generalize, Don Benito; and mournfully enough. But the past is passed; why moralize upon it? Forget it" (106). Ryan observes that the experience "ultimately kills Cereno but leaves Delano, the more skilled at repression, unchanged" (74). Delano's repression is, moreover, motivated by his excessive pride, like the Lion, whereas Cereno's inability to "forget it" is a characteristic of the Elephant, renowned for his memory, which he is unable to escape. The scene is particularly interesting because during their dialogue, there is no mention of Babo at all and ends like one version of the Signifying Monkey tales, concluding with simply "the hapless Lion and the puzzled Elephant" (Gates, *Figures in Black* 241). Similarly, because Delano dismisses the incident as merely one of those unlucky (or hapless) events "owing to Providence," the experience has little effect on him; whereas, Cereno is, like the Elephant, left baffled.

Several scholars have characterized Babo's demise as a failure, his silence as defeat, and his capture as a return to slavery, which has had a tendency to overshadow his many accomplishments.[12] Although Babo is certainly physically overpowered and seized, he is taken into custody, tried, and convicted as a rebel, not as property. Indeed, from the moment the mutiny begins, Babo is never again a slave. From a financial perspective, he is no one's inventory, inheritance, or object of commercial value; Babo and the others executed for mutiny are a total financial loss to their "owners," which amounts to a rather successful repudiation of the master's authority. Furthermore, in spite of numerous "attempts to get him to talk," his silence further reiterates his repudiation of their authority as well as his commitment to his fellow bondsmen. By refusing to speak, Babo also refuses to risk implicating his comrades or to provide information that could jeopardize other slaves' escape attempts. This type of intentional omission of information is also commonly noted in many slave narratives. For example, Henry "Box" Brown notes that in designing a strategy of escape, he and a trusted friend consider several possibilities, but he notes "it may not be best to mention what these plans were, as some unfortunate slaves may thereby be prevented from availing themselves of these methods of escape" (134). Douglass takes a similar stance in his "Narrative," explaining: "I deem it proper to make known my intention not to state all the facts connected with the transaction. My reasons for pursuing this course may be understood from the following; First, were I to give a minute statement of all the facts, it is not only possible but quite probable, that others would thereby be involved in the most embarrassing difficulties. Secondly, such a statement would most undoubtedly induce greater vigilance on the part of slaveholders . . . which would, of course, be the means of guarding a door whereby some dear brother bondman might escape his galling chains" (385). Babo's silence similarly signifies on these principles of caution, protection, and a refusal to enlighten his oppressors with information, particularly carefully guarded black insight and highly private cultural wisdom.

The mutilation of Babo's body also ironically signifies success by announcing white barbarity by his "unabashed" gaze. While the whites who view this horrific spectacle would likely read this "sign" as appropriate justice, Babo's gaze "towards St. Bartholomew's church" operates as a reproach of Christian benevolence and self inflicted ignorance (107). But perhaps more important, for black spectators as well as black readers, Babo functions much like the clever hero of the folktales. Abrahams notes that an important characteristic is the hero's "ability to revolt in the face of authority and possible death. Death does not matter, just style of living. If dying results from this style, that is all right" (*Down in the Jungle* 74). Like the Signifying Monkey, as well as the heroes of the fugitive slave narratives, Babo demonstrates intelligence and courage and functions as a powerful symbol of commitment to the principle of liberty or death. As DuBois writes in *The Souls of Black Folk*, "throughout history, the powers of single black men flash here and there like falling stars, and die sometimes before the world has rightly gauged their brightness" (215). Babo represents one such flash of brilliance and subsequent blighting—a rather brutal and barbaric blighting at that. Yet in spite of Babo's demise, throughout the course of the novella, the white characters are regularly duped by this signifying genius and are, therefore, ultimately the butt of the joke, which implies a conclusion similar to another version of the Signifying Monkey cycle, ending with the Monkey boasting: "Tell yo' momma and yo' daddy, too, Signifying Monkey made a fool outta you" (Watkins, *African American Humor* 109).[13]

Chapter 4

Born in a Brier-Patch and Frontier Bred

Joel Chandler Harris in Black and White

Joel Chandler Harris's most well-known character, Uncle Remus, has been and continues to be a critically polarizing figure in American literature, and the Uncle Remus collections have dominated scholarly attention of Harris's work. According to Alice Walker, Harris "stole a good part of my cultural heritage" (637), whereas Ralph Ellison and James Weldon Johnson commend Harris for recognizing the aesthetic artistry of black folktales as well as his work collecting these stories.[1] Mel Watkins point out that

> since few Americans were interested in recording or collecting slave folktales before Emancipation, and even fewer slaves would have risked relating those tales to outsiders, nearly all examples of the period's humor were assembled after slaves had been freed. The animal tales collected by Joel Chandler Harris, a white journalist, are exceptions. As a teenager, Harris had lived on a Georgia plantation and had overheard and noted stories related by slaves. The publication of *Uncle Remus, His Songs and His Sayings* in 1880—although somewhat distorted by the fictitious "faithful darky" narrator, Uncle Remus—remains a crucial development in the preservation of black folk humor. Many of those tales portrayed slaves in the symbolic guise of the mischievous and cunning Brer Rabbit and cast slave owners in the role of the gullible and villainous Brer Fox who, although stronger, was nearly always outwitted. These animal stories, however, were only the tip of a much larger body of trickster tales. (*African American Humor* 1–2)

In addition to the slaves' folktales, Harris was also familiar with and indeed drew from another important antebellum literary tradition, Southern frontier humor, praising in particular Augustus Baldwin Longstreet's *Georgia Scenes* and William Tappan Thompson's *Major Jones's Sketches of Travel* in his book *Stories of Georgia* (250).[2] Throughout his work, including but not limited to his Uncle Remus collections, Harris employs a wide range of the literary and aesthetic techniques commonly featured in frontier humor as well as black folktales, such as the use of dialect, wit rather than formal education to demonstrate a character's exceptional intelligence, and tales that highlight the cultural and social values of nonelite communities. Indeed, a common theme of many frontier humor sketches and black folktales is featuring stories that are often quite critical of ruling-class planters, particularly those who abuse their power.

As a newspaper editor, fiction writer, avid reader, and, perhaps most important, attentive listener, Harris was uniquely knowledgeable about Southern culture and its discourses, which he often covertly criticized.[3] Several of his short stories are set prior to the war but often function to allegorize many of the problems of the post-Reconstruction period, particularly the shift from the paternalistic racism prevalent in the antebellum era toward a highly charged and often deadly radical racism. During the post-Reconstruction era, black stereotypes begin to transform into often dangerous manifestations. In her book *Race, Rape, and Lynching*, Sandra Gunning explores post-Reconstruction American culture "within the specific context of American literature's confrontation with the figure of the black as beast and the American tradition of lynching" (3). During this period, representations of blacks, in particular black males, transform into "the figure of the criminalized black male body—as well as the white violence through which that figure is produced" (3).[4] Because the primary image of black masculinity developing is not only destructive but deadly, I contend that Harris turns to a debunking of Southern myth by intertextualizing black signifying forms to sabotage the growing stereotypes of black masculinity that are operating to rationalize extralegal murder.

Harris's Uncle Remus stories, however, became so popular (as well as controversial) that they have had a tendency to overshadow critical attention to Harris's non-Remus fiction, which also shows evidence of the influence of black folk culture as well as white antebellum folk material and, indeed, highlights many common features between these groups. Eric Sundquist considers the Uncle Remus tales as "Harris's imaginative fusion of the postbellum and antebellum frames" (*To Wake the Nations* 350). Yet Harris's non-Remus fiction also suggests a similar fusion. Moreover, Harris's black characters have often been dismissed as offensive examples of the minstrel tradition, but particularly in the context of post-Reconstruction America, these characters show many telltale signs of the trickster. In this chapter, I examine several short stories and argue that Harris drew from both black and white antebellum folk traditions to demonstrate many common features between these groups and to highlight the artistry of storytelling traditions. Harris's work demonstrates a quintessential aspect of Southern literature: a literary hybridity committed to the artistry of the story, which is told from many angles, in many forms, and with sensitivity for voice, perspective, humor, and, above all, the dignity, humanity, and intelligence of his featured characters.

As several scholars have demonstrated, Harris was highly influenced by African American culture. Harris's biographer Bruce Bickley notes that Harris

> spent hundreds of hours in the "quarters" during his years at Turnwold, and he was often joined by Turner's son Joseph Sidney and by his two daughters. Joel felt less self-conscious around the patient and indulgent older slaves; and, as Jay B. Hubbell suggests, his own humble background probably gave him insight into the mind of the black field hand. Furthermore, his supersensitivity to people also found a new, and healthier, direction: he listened with a keen ear for inflection, and with an eye for gesture, to the dialectical and narrative rhythms, the humor, and the irony of the animal fables that Terrell and other Negroes shared with him. Harris learned to love these folk tales. (*Joel Chandler Harris* 23)

In addition to black folktales, Harris was also familiar with the antebellum plantation tradition, and his Uncle Remus tales have been regarded as a frame combining these seemingly incompatible literary genres. Hemenway contends that Harris utilized "a medium that he could mimic but never fully comprehend" (30); Ashleigh Harris claims that Harris "completely isolated the Brer Rabbit tales from their present African-American context as well as from the historical trajectory from which they originated. Through providing a depoliticized, decommunalised, deracialised and emasculated narrator, Harris's tales fundamentally changed the social and political significance of the Brer Rabbit tales. . . . Harris caricatures African-American plantation and slave identity and culture, and this in turn ridicules and distorts the significance of the characters and narratives of the stories" (66). These scholars suggest what Kenneth Lynn describes as the predominant narrative structure of the frontier humor tradition, a cordon sanitaire separating the narrator from the antics of the characters featured in the embedded tales (64).[5]

While many scholars have challenged what the cordon sanitaire separation implies or asserts, as a narrative device, the frame would become representative of the frontier humor genre as well as an important structural model for postbellum plantation authors, including Thomas Nelson Page, Joel Chandler Harris, and Charles Chesnutt. In his introduction to Chesnutt's *The Conjure Woman and Other Conjure Tales*, Richard Brodhead points out that

> with the official end of Reconstruction in 1877, Southern regionalism spawned a specialized subgenre, a form with the more or less overt function of excusing the North's withdrawal from the plight of the freed Southern slave. This subgenre, prefigured in Joel Chandler Harris's *Uncle Remus: His Songs and His Sayings* (1880) and perfected in Thomas Nelson Page's *In Ole Virginia* (1887), deployed a black rustic figure, an ex-slave but still-faithful retainer, to testify to his love of the old days and his lack of desire for equal social rights. Paradoxically, in order to deliver this reactionary message this form had to take a potentially progressive step. It handed the role of dialect speaker to the black character, and so made a literary place for an authentic-sounding black voice. (5)

Chesnutt distinguishes his work by the subversive quality of his tales, whereas Harris and Page are typically grouped together as authors whose fiction "served to perpetuate the carefully fabricated myth of genteel plantation owners and contented slaves with nothing but fond memories of bondage, which was created by southern writers after the Civil War" (Watkins, *On the Real Side* 72). Lucinda MacKethan, however, cautions: "Harris's Uncle Remus stories are in some measure complicated by the old storyteller's dual role; in one guise, he speaks to a postwar generation of whites about the good old days, but in a quite different voice he tells, and obviously identifies with, the folktales of that subversive animal anarchist, Brer Rabbit" ("Plantation Fiction" 651). Robert Cochran also identifies subversive elements in the Remus collections and contends that "Uncle Remus's control of the story-telling context and his persistent, if oblique, critique of plantation values" reveal Harris "quietly but insistently pursuing an anti-racist agenda" (23). Moreover, by examining Harris's extensive use of aspects of Southern folk art, black and white, his non-Remus fiction emerges as more subversive than it has traditionally been accorded.

In spite of many obvious differences between black and white folk cultures, these groups shared many values in common, such as community

unity, family loyalty, a distrust of outsiders (for the black community, this distrust included all whites), resistance toward authority, a keen sense of personal worth, and wit rather than formal education as a highly regarded social value. Furthermore, Harris's familiarity with black trickster tales not only enabled him to understand signifying strategies at work in the embedded stories but additionally allowed him to understand signifying as a creative device, which he then employs with a wide range of literary traditions to debunk nostalgic fantasies of the Old South, particularly stereotypes of African Americans and nonelite whites in order to promote greater sensitivity between the races and defuse white Americans' growing hostility toward its black citizenry.

Because Harris had to be careful to avoid offending his audience or failing to find publication outlets, he adopted the signifying tactics of the trickster.[6] Cochran notes that "George Terrell and Harbert, telling Brer Rabbit's wonderful tales to the listening boy, taught him not only the covert critique of their subject matter, but also the even more subversive lessons of their Signifying method," and Cochran adds, "Harris went to the world as the trickster Brer Rabbit" (29).[7] Harris's use of signifying as an aesthetic device gives him far more freedom to play on the sign systems of antebellum literary traditions and cultural discourses, black and white, written and oral, to ultimately undermine the myth of the Old South, a myth that was becoming regarded as history rather than fiction and perpetuating largely demeaning stereotypes of African Americans and nonelite whites that developed from antebellum proslavery discourses, most notably the plantation tradition.

The genre of frontier humor, however, stands in sharp contrast to traditional plantation fiction, particularly regarding the depiction of the plain folk. Thomas Inge and Edward Piacentino note that "some of the defining features of the humor of the Old South are the prominence of plain folk–lower-class rustics, backwoodsmen, and other marginal types—some of whom may be disreputable—as the principal players in the action. In addition, the situations depicted tend to be outlandish and sometimes bizarre, and the folk characters are given extensive voice, speaking in a colorful vernacular discourse. Moreover, the humorists favor the dialect of the vernacular speakers over the formal English of genteel characters, the latter usually relegated to the tale's or sketch's frame and consigned to the periphery" (2). The genre also shares many thematic and stylistic similarities with the tales that were "told night after night at the slaves' quarters," which also "favors colorful vernacular discourse" as well situations that "tend to be outlandish and sometimes bizarre" (2). Furthermore, the trickster figures celebrated in frontier humor and black folktale traditions share many interesting characteristics in common, most notably the emphasis on wit as a weapon in a contest of intellect and victory is measured by their ability to outsmart their opponents. These genres also often feature weak characters pitted against stronger, more powerful characters, but an important distinction between traditions is that for the frontier humorists, the playing field is more evenly matched due to race, but in the slave community, racial and legal distinctions cast the weaker character into much more vulnerable territory. As a result, as Lawrence Levine notes, these stories operated to "effect a rough sort of justice, and to protect themselves from some of the worst features of the slave system, slaves translated many of the tactics of their animal trickster tales into their own lives. Like Brer Rabbit, slaves learned to maneuver as well as they could from their position of weakness" (121). Harris is best known for his animal-tale collections featuring Uncle Remus, yet his negotiation with antebellum tricksters, black and white, suggests he was uniquely familiar with a variety of trickster figures.

In one of his most well-known short stories, "Free Joe and the Rest of the World," Harris features trickster figures drawn from both black folktales and frontier humor.[8] MacKethan notes that "the Southwestern humorists used the trickster figure to highlight class differences and satirize the rudeness of frontier life. The most important characters of this genre are Simon Suggs and Sut Lovingood" ("Trickster" 914). The frontier trickster figure, typically the con man, is further complicated by a more complex example of the con game, as Michael Oriard points out, in "tales of cheating the cheater, a local variation of the folklore tradition of tricking the trickster" (14). Oriard notes that "the best example of the former appears in Longstreet's *Georgia Scenes*, in the story 'The Horse-Swap'" (14). Similarly, in African American folklore, Watkins points out that "in the animal tales, the rabbit or hare, who could be mischievous, even arrogant and malicious, was occasionally tricked by weaker animals. This counter theme, which [Charles] Joyner designates as the 'trickster out-tricked,' accentuated another aspect of slave morality" (*On the Real Side* 73). In Harris's story, the character Major Compton closely resembles the frontier con man trickster. Compton is a "negro-specul[…] traveling through the "little village of Hillsborough on his way to […] sissippi region" (3). Compton believes himself much more "[…] than the inhabitants of this rural community and thus reg[…]g men" as "overgrown boys who needed to be introduced to so[…]e arts and sciences at his command. Thereupon the major pitched hi[s] tents, figuratively speaking, and became, for the time being, a part and parcel of the innocence that characterized Hillsborough. A wiser man would doubtless have made the same mistake" (4). Compton indulges in a number of the con man's typical activities, such as wagering on horse races, cockfights, as well as the dice and cards, "all with varying luck, until," Harris notes, "he began his famous game of poker with Judge Alfred Wellington, a stately gentleman with a flowing white beard and mild blue eyes that gave him the appearance of a benevolent patriarch" (4). Compton is, however, overconfident in his abilities and unwilling to accept defeat. Harris notes that "at various stages of the game Major Compton would destroy the cards with which they were playing, and send for a new pack, but the result was always the same" (5). After losing "his money, his horses, his wagons, and all his negroes but one, his body-servant," Compton becomes the trickster-tricked. He then "executed the papers that gave his body-servant his freedom" and "sauntered into a convenient pine thicket, and blew out his brains" (5).

Compton's newly manumitted body servant "came to be known as Free Joe," a label loaded with significance (5). Referring to the character as Free Joe rather than simply Joe marks his identity as distinct from the rest of the black population in the community by his legal status. Harris notes that in spite of his being "the humblest, the simplest, and the most serious of all God's living creatures . . . the sober-minded citizens of the little Georgian village of Hillsborough were not inclined to take a humorous view of Free Joe, and neither his name nor his presence provided a smile" (1). In spite of the white community's constant surveillance of Joe, they do not see an individual but rather the sign they impose on this man. To the white community,

> Free Joe represented not only a problem of large concern, but, in the watchful eyes of Hillsborough, he was the embodiment of that vague and mysterious danger that seemed to be forever lurking on the outskirts of slavery, ready to sound a shrill and ghostly signal in the impenetrable swamps, and steal forth under the midnight stars to murder, rapine, and pillage,—a danger always threatening, and yet never assuming shape; intangible, and yet real; impossible, and yet not improbable. Across the serene and smiling front of safety, the pale outlines of the awful shadow of insurrection sometimes fell. With this invisible panorama as a background, it was natural that the figure of Free Joe, simple and humble as it was, should assume undue proportions. Go where he would, do what he might, he could not escape the finger of observation and the kindling eye of suspicion. His lightest words were noted, his slighted actions marked. (2)

The white community regards Joe as a danger due to his legal status, race, and gender rather than his behavior, which deviates significantly from the myth of the Old South as an Arcadian ideal depicted in the postbellum plantation tradition.

When Joe first arrives in Hillsborough, he is an outsider, and his subsequent manumission becomes a dangerous threat to the slave community if they are suspected of any involvement with him. He is, therefore, excluded from their society as well. While Joe is at liberty to leave and find a more tolerant community, he remains in Hillsborough to be close to his wife, Lucinda. Harris's focus on a black couple in an obviously committed and loving relationship undermines antebellum and postbellum racial theories that blacks inherently lacked the ability to form deep, romantic bonds and also undermines another common feature of the postbellum plantation tradition. In Thomas Nelson Page's "Marse Chan. A Tale of Old Virginia," the embedded narrative is told by a former slave, Sam, who tells an unnamed traveler stories about life before and during the war.[9] Sam describes the antebellum era as "good ole times . . . de bes' Sam ever see! Dey wuz, in fac! Niggers didn' hed nothin' 't all to do—jes' hed to 'ten' do de feedin' an' cleanin' de hosses, an' doin' what de master tell 'em to do'" (10). Sam then recounts the story of the courtship between Marse Chan and Miss Anne as well as the feud between their families that destroys their relationship. Sam provides extensive details about his master's family but makes only a brief note regarding his own romantic relationship. Sam explains that his wife, Judy, was Miss Anne's maid but provides no further information regarding his courtship or details of his relationship with his wife, which suggests that the story of his master's family is more important than his own. The focus in Harris's story, however, features a character willing to endure a life of suspicion, isolation, and intolerance for the exclusive purpose of maintaining his relationship with his wife.[10]

In this hostile and dangerous environment, Joe has to maneuver carefully. He must present an image to the community that will defuse their suspicion and distrust, and, as Harris notes, "under all the circumstances it was natural that his peculiar condition should reflect itself in his habits and manners" (2). Joe presents an image of "something painfully plaintive and appealing in his attitude, something touching in his anxiety to please. He was of the friendliest nature" (2). And in spite of Joe's legal status, he cautiously addresses all white men as "master" (2). He is also required "under the law, to choose a guardian" and chooses "Judge Wellington, chiefly because his wife Lucinda was among the negroes won from Major Compton"

(5). Due to his carefully controlled behavior and Wellington's basic decency, Joe enjoys several years of being permitted to visit his wife, but when Wellington dies, his wife and the other slaves "went to his half-brother, a man named Calderwood, who was a hard master and rough customer generally,—a man of many eccentricities of mind and character. His neighbors had a habit of alluding to him as 'Old Spite;' and the name seemed to fit him so completely, that he was known far and near as 'Spite' Calderwood" (6). When Calderwood first meets Joe, he demands Joe's papers. Calderwood then tore "the pass in pieces and flung it away" and forbids Joe from visiting Lucinda (7). Joe, however, "soon found a way out of this difficulty" (9). He befriends an elderly brother and sister, Becky and Micajah Staley, "representatives of a class known as poor white trash" (9). The Staleys live "near the Calderwood place, but not on Calderwood's land," and Joe soon figures out that he can send his dog off to Lucinda's cabin and "for a long time after that he had no difficulty seeing his wife" (9-10). Calderwood, however, discovers this ruse and vindictively sells Lucinda, and as a result, Joe becomes the trickster-tricked.

In the presence of the Staleys, Joe appears unconcerned that his wife may have been sold, which baffles Micajah Staley. He tells his sister, "'I'd in-about give up my t'other hand ef I could stan' flat-footed, an' grin at trouble like that there nigger'" (19). Becky Staley, however, possesses much greater insight. She tells her brother, "'He grins,—an' that's nigger,—but I've ketched his under jaw a-trimblin' when Lucindy's name uz brung up'" (19). Becky's comment demonstrates that she understands that Joe's "grin" is simply a mask, but his performance is weakened by his intense emotional pain, which provides a glimpse into the reality concealed behind the mask. Becky is also highly critical of this particular master's abuse of authority and "bridling up a little, and speaking with almost fierce emphasis," she tells her brother, "'The Old Boy's done sharpened his claws for Spite Calderwood. You'll see it'" (20). In spite of their low status on the social hierarchy because of their poverty and lack of education, the Staleys' compassion suggests that they are much more worthy of the respect the upper class receive simply because of wealth, which again undermines the notion of genteel plantation owners and contented slaves featured in the postbellum plantation genre.

Harris's depiction of Joe's humanity, vulnerability, and commitment to his wife, moreover, also functions to undermine "the race hatred that grew during the 1880s and swept the white South in the 1890s" (Kinney, "Race in the New South" 236). The story is set in the 1850s but written and published in the 1880s, which "were years of turmoil in the South, especially for

African Americans" (243). James Kinney contends that the story "subverts the Radical racism that attempts to represent free blacks as savage beasts once they have been released from the constraints of slavery" (243). Kinney asserts that "Joe, the black man freed from slavery, becomes an emblem of all post-emancipation blacks in the 1880s. Just as the people who had feared slave revolt before the war were proven wrong . . . by the lack of revolt during the war, the text implies that those who in the 1880s fear the 'new Negro' as a dangerous beast are equally wrong" (249). Harris alludes to this position early in the story, noting that "the problems of one generation are the paradoxes of a succeeding one, particularly if war, or some such incident, intervenes" (2). The paradoxes for the post-Reconstruction generation reflect Joe's difficulties after he is freed, and Joe functions as a symbol of the dangers imposed on black men in the postbellum South. Harris writes, "Having no owner, every man was his master. He knew that he was the object of suspicion, and therefore all his slender resources (ah! How pitifully slender they were!) were devoted to winning, not kindness and appreciation, but toleration" (8). Charles S. Johnson points out that in the late nineteenth century, particularly in the rural South, African American men had to operate carefully because, as he notes, the main "reason for respecting them [is] . . . you know that they will get you killed for disrespecting them" (257). Joe's vulnerability functions as an appeal to white Southerners to practice the type of basic decency the Staleys, although poor and uneducated, show Joe.

Harris prominently features the social values of nonelite whites in several other short stories as well, specifically backcountry mountain culture and the animosity many mountain communities felt regarding outside interference, particularly what may be perceived as a threat to their intense sense of independence. Steven Hahn notes that throughout the backcountry, "'liberty' was more than a catchword. At heart, it meant a specific sort of independence—ownership of productive resources, control over farming operations, an emphasis on household self-sufficiency, and lack of subservience to outsiders or outside forces" (45). Indeed, the genre shares an important theme with the black trickster tradition by the community's emphasis on undermining and repudiating official forms of power and authority.

During the antebellum era, the backcountry regions of southwest Virginia and the Carolinas, as well as Georgia, Tennessee, Alabama, Arkansas, Mississippi, and Louisiana, were predominantly settled by Scots-Irish, "a quick-tempered but sensual and playful people [who] often dressed provocatively, acted with a volatile belligerence, drank to excess, engaged in constant and open competition in every form, and adamantly defied the attempts of outsiders to control them" (Webb 133). While there are no mountain men who reach the level of defiance demonstrated by George Washington Harris's Sut Lovingood of Frog Mountain, Tennessee, Joel Chandler Harris sets several stories in the Georgia mountains and depicts many characters who share much in common with Sut. Harris also offers a unique perspective of backcountry culture by developing narratives that often begin where the genre of frontier humor ends, with the Civil War. Other stories are set during the war and offer the perspective of the backcountry plain folk, "many of whom supported the Confederacy with great reluctance, if at all" (Hahn 45).

In several short stories published in various collections, Harris features mountain culture and demonstrates the animosity many mountain communities held regarding Southern secession, particularly the view that the Civil War was a rich man's war in defense of the property rights of slave owners, which is a theme evident in the tale "A Conscript's Christmas" (published in the collection *Balaam and His Master and Other Sketches and Stories* in 1891). The sketch also highlights a narrative element more commonly featured in the slaves' folktales as well as the slave narrative, which is the community engaged in subversively protecting a fugitive. In this story, however, the fugitive is not a slave but rather a deserter. The story is set in 1863 and depicts two Confederate representatives, Captain Dick Moseley and Private Bill Chadwick, who have been sent into the mountains to retrieve Israel Spurlock, an army conscript who had been "yerked" into the army but who had "yerked himself out" (49). Harris notes: "They were not in a friendly region. There were bushwhackers in the mountains. . . . They had that day ridden past the house of the only member of the Georgia State convention who had refused to affix his signature to the ordinance of secession, and the woods, to use the provincial phrase, were full of Union men" (46). As the men ride on, Chadwick complains: "'When I j'ined the army I thought I was goin' to fight the Yankees, but they slapped me in the camp of instruction over there at Adairsville, an' now here we are fightin' our own folks. If we ain't fightin' 'em, we are pursuin' after 'em, an' runnin' 'em into the woods an' up the mountains'" (48). When they encounter a mountain minister, Uncle Billy, they are given a chilly and critical reception. He lectures them, "'I've had Israel Spurlock in my min' off an' on' ev'ry since they run him down an' kotch him an' drug 'im off to war. He was weakly like from the time he was a boy. . . . He knowed that he was drug off right spang at the time he wanted to be getherin in his craps, an' savin' his ruffage, an' one thing an' another bekaze his ole mammy din't have a soul to help her but 'im'" (54–55). The humor throughout the story derives from the mountain community's repudiation of official authority, which is another common feature of the slaves' trickster tales, but due to race, the mountaineers are able to be more direct in expressing their contempt. Uncle Billy goads the men: "'You thought that while your Uncle Billy was a-moonin' aroun' down the hill yander you'd steal a march on your Aunt Crissy, an' maybe come a-*conscriptin' of her* into the army" (my emphasis 60). In another scene, a former colonel during the Mexican War, Dick Watson, lectures them "'that this hain't Mexico, an' that they hain't no war gwine on on this 'ere hill. You know that mighty well'" (67). As Watson's comment suggests, the mountaineers are not opposed to war, as evident by Watson's role in the Mexican War, but are opposed to a war they believe is dividing the Union in order to protect the wealth of, as one mountain character puts it, "'them dad-blasted Restercrats'" ("At Teague Poteet's," *Mingo, and Other Sketches in Black and White* 16).

Although the issues of war, conscription, and deserters are rather serious subjects, they are treated with playful humor, yet like numerous examples in the slave narrative tradition, the community's very serious commitment to protect one of their own is a persistent theme throughout the tale. Other themes evident in this story that are also commonly featured in the black trickster tradition are the depiction of the weak pitted against the strong and the use of wit to undermine more powerful forces. These officials are repeatedly thwarted in their mission by the community's unity, and the soldiers begin to sense the impotence of their authority. Chadwick confides his misgivings to Moseley: "'It's my belief that we are gwine on a fool's errand'" (83). His suspicion is confirmed when, after resting by a tree, he wakes to find himself "dragged backward from the log by strong hands . . . lying flat on his back, with his hands tied, and as helpless as an infant. He looked up and discovered that his captor was Israel Spurlock" (91). Moseley is also captured, and the men are held prisoner in the hope that the man who sent them on the mission, Adjutant Lovejoy, "would come in search of them" (101). Lovejoy takes the bait, and he and his men are also captured. Yet in spite of the prisoners' status as captives, they are treated to plain-folk hospitality and are invited by Danny Lemmons to "'stay over an' take Christmas wi' us, sech ez we'll have'" (100). During the Christmas festivities, they also attend Spurlock's wedding officiated by Uncle Billy. Harris notes that the sermon "was not the less meaty and sincere, not the less wise and powerful, because the English was ungrammatical and the rhetoric uncouth," which is a perspective reminiscent of North Carolina frontier humorist Hardin E. Taliaferro's mountain preachers (103). The scene also suggests that lack of education should not be taken as evidence of lack of intelligence, which is an important element for nonelite oral communities, black and white. One slave adage sums up the perspective: "De price of your hat ain't the measure of your brain" (Watkins, *African American Humor* 79). But in spite of the humor in the tale, the story takes a decidedly serious turn when one of the captives "seized a musket," but "before he could raise his gun, a streak of fire shot forth into his face, and he fell and rolled to the side of the road" (112). The story represents the cultural ethos of the mountaineers who treat outside interference with good-natured humor, which will, however, be tolerated only so far.

In one of his most interesting but largely overlooked stories, "Blue Dave" (published in the collection *Mingo, and Other Sketches in Black and White* in 1884), Harris deviates significantly from traditional elements of the plantation tradition. The story begins in 1850 during the funeral of one of the town's most prominent citizens, Felix Kendrick. As Harris provides Kendrick's personal history, he demonstrates the fluid nature of the Southern social hierarchy by depicting Kendrick's father as a man of humble origins who was a "hatter by trade, who had come to Georgia in search of a precarious livelihood" (52). The elder Kendrick was "shrewd, close-fisted, and industrious" and "became an overseer" (52). Due to his success, "he commanded a large salary, and saved money. This money he invested in negroes, buying one at a time and hiring them out. He finally came to be the owner of seven or eight stout field hands; whereupon he bought two hundred acres of choice land and set himself up as a patriarch" (52). This character portrait resembles Longstreet's narrator, Baldwin, who also rose from a plain farming community and moved into the upper ranks of Savannah society. Furthermore, while the elder Kendrick has no regard for the social distinction his hard-earned wealth makes possible, Kendrick's son Felix is more class conscious and in order to demonstrate the family's rise in social status, builds a house with a double veranda, tall chimneys, and a collection of gables "to show that 'some folks was as good as other folks'" (52).

The entire community turns out for Felix Kendrick's funeral, and Harris features two local farmers in attendance discussing the events of the day. Class distinctions are indicated by language, with plain-folk farmers using backcountry vernacular that is contrasted by characters such as George Denham using standard English and demonstrating formal education. In addition to evidencing the fluid nature of the social structure, this sketch also shows that while there were certainly instances of clashes between planter and plain folk, interaction between classes was customary.

Indeed, the narrative frame of the frontier humorists depended on sustained relationships and verbal exchanges between characters of different classes. These friendships, however, are dependent on and maintained by the mutual respect for the distinct cultural values of different sociopolitical groups, such as Alexander G. McNutt's Jim and Chunkey and their relationship with the governor, George Washington Harris's George and Sut, and Augustus Baldwin Longstreet's Baldwin and Hall and their interaction with a wide array of plain-folk characters.

Harris also introduces a unique narrative element in his characterization of Blue Dave, drawing this portrait from the hero featured in the slave narratives, the escaped slave. Susan Tracy notes that "the runaway represented the assertion of their humanity, and, if male, of black masculinity" (147). Furthermore, because of the often insurmountable obstacles deterring permanent escape attempts into the North or Canada, temporary flight was common. John Blassingame notes that "the ubiquitous runaway defied all the odds. Sometimes he stayed away until his anger or that of his master subsided. Cold and hungry, he frequently returned after a few days. . . . On other occasions, however, the runaway eluded his pursuers for weeks, months, or even years, safe in his bailiwick near the plantation" (110). Although the slave narratives focused on permanent escape and were a crucial component of the abolitionist press, temporary escape was much more common. Osofsky notes that "it was not only possible for slaves to escape and hide out for long periods of time, but the more skillful could also remain away almost as long as they chose. . . . They often arranged to contact friends and family on the plantation to supply them with food on secret visits" (15). Moreover, temporary flight demonstrated a psychological independence that the institution of slavery was structured to suppress, and by running, slaves were able to assert more control over their lives, often choosing when to return and on what terms.

The runaway also represented the appealing quality of simply defying authority and thus exasperating masters. Cowan notes that "it was that knowledge of runaways, defiant in the wilderness, that threatened the planter's conception of his slaves, and therefore his self-concept"—and, it is important to point out, his reputation in the community, which could be a source of keen embarrassment (23). Indeed, rumors about this slave are well known in the community, which is evident when, during the funeral, Brother Roach spots a "powerfully built negro" hiding behind "one of the gables on the roof" and immediately recognizes Dave (55). Roach tells Brannum, "'That nigger, roosting up there so slick and cool, is Bledser's

Blue Dave. Nuther more, nuther less'" (55). Blue Dave has been at large for seven years, and his "success in eluding pursuit caused the ignorant minded of both races to attribute to him the possession of some mysterious power. He grew into a legend; he became a part of the folk-lore of the section. According to popular belief, he possessed strange powers and great courage; he became a giant, a spirit of evil. . . . *The negroes had many stories to tell of him*" (my emphasis 56). Early in the narrative, the "stories" about Dave suggest that he is feared by "both black and white," but as the narrative develops, it becomes apparent that the slaves' "stories" operate covertly to protect him and thus generate fear in the white community, which suggests that the black community employs trickster wisdom to signify on the white community to enable Dave's unique form of freedom (56).

Dave is also a particularly bold and independent individual, thereby undermining nineteenth-century essentialist racial ideology as well as demeaning black literary and cultural figures. Osofsky notes that "even to conceive the possibility of escape required a special quality of mind: imagination, independence, cunning, daring, and a sense of self-pride. . . . It called for the use of subtle psychological weapons" (20-21). Harris endows Blue Dave with these qualities and notes that little was known of the history of Blue Dave before

> he was brought to the little village of Rockville in chains in a speculator's train,—the train consisting of two Conestoga wagons and thirty or forty forlorn-looking negroes. The speculator explained that he had manacled Blue Dave because he was unmanageable; and he put him on the block to sell him after making it perfectly clear to everybody that whoever bought the negro would get a bad bargain. Nevertheless Blue Dave was a magnificent specimen of manhood, straight as an arrow, as muscular as Hercules, and with a countenance as open and as pleasant as one would wish to see. He was bought by General Alfred Bledser, and put on his River Place. He worked well for a few weeks, but got into trouble with the overseer, and finally compromised matters by taking to the woods. He seemed born for this particular business; for the track dogs failed to find him, and all the arts and artifices employed for capturing and reclaiming runaways failed in his case. It was a desperate form of freedom he enjoyed; but he seemed suited to it, and he made the most of it. (57)

In this narrative, Harris deviates dramatically from characteristics of traditional plantation fiction, with which he is so commonly associated, by not only featuring a fugitive slave but further by noting that "it was a common thing to hear of fugitive negroes" (56). Tracy explains that in the antebellum plantation tradition, "recalcitrant or rebellious blacks are rarely portrayed, and those that are, are treated as exceptions. In fact, there are only three rebellious black men in all of the literature" (146). And this type of omission is not limited to fiction. Mark Reinhardt in his book *Who Speaks for Margaret Garner?* points out that although the Margaret Garner case was covered extensively throughout the course of the capture and the trial in northern presses, the South responded largely with silence or extreme "censorship" (207). Moreover, Harris endows this character with qualities of manhood that directly undermines antebellum and postbellum stereotypes of black masculinity. Blue Dave's flight challenges the submissive and loyal image of the antebellum era, and his intellect, sense of self, and compassion undermines the postbellum "degeneration" theorists who characterize free black men as reverting to bestial savagery and preying on vulnerable white women.[11]

Blue Dave is also a man of courage and risks his liberty by approaching Kitty Kendrick so she can warn George Denham that he should not attempt to cross the river due to the flood. When she asks him to identify himself, he replies, "'I mos' fear'd, Miss Kitty'" (58). Harris notes that "the tone of his voice was something more than humble. There was an appeal in it for mercy" (58). To alleviate her potential fear of him, Dave tells her to "'des ax yo' little br'er. Little Mars. Felix, he knows I ain't no bad nigger'" (58). Dave's statement indicates that the child has been aiding this runaway for an extensive amount of time, which is particularly evident because Dave has been at large for seven years and Felix is an eight-year-old. It is interesting to note that Harris also features a young boy, Joe Maxwell, in his semiautobiographical *On the Plantation*, depicting Joe assisting the fugitive slave Mink (40). Yet in spite of the risk Dave takes on Kitty's behalf, she lacks her brother's compassion and is more concerned with appearances. Kitty chastises her brother: "'You've disgraced us all. You knew Blue Dave was hiding on top of the house all the while. What would be done with us if people found out we had been harboring a runaway negro?'" (58). Young Felix, however, "had views of his own" and replies, "'I don't care if I did. If you tell anybody, I'll never run up the road to see if Mr. George is coming as long as I live; I won't ever do anything for you'" (59). Felix adds defensively, "'He's the best nigger man I ever saw, less'n it's old Uncle Manuel when he gets that old, 'cause Uncle Manuel said so'" (59). The information the boy inadvertently shares suggests that old Uncle Manuel is also in contact with Dave.

The implication of Manuel's involvement with Dave is verified when Kitty, relaxing her "principles" a bit *after* Dave has rescued George, visits Manuel's cabin. Harris describes Manuel as "old, wise, and cunning" as well as distrustful of this white woman. Thus, when Kitty asks him to deliver food to Dave, Manuel "hesitated a moment before replying; and even then his caution would not allow him to commit himself" (64). Manuel's caution reflects an important aspect of slave life. Lawrence Levine notes that throughout the trickster stories, an imperative message was repeated "over and over: 'It's bad to talk too much . . . don't tell all you see.' There is abundant evidence that the slaves thoroughly assimilated this lesson. Even their friends and defenders testified to the slaves' duplicity and secretiveness" (99-100). Winifred Morgan adds that "as important as speaking out and using language to out-fox the master is, the John and the Massa tales also emphasize the paramount importance of knowing when to be quiet" (*Trickster Figure* 22). Indeed, Harris commented on the cautious distrust of African Americans while collecting folktales in the 1880s. In the introduction to his first collection of Uncle Remus stories, he writes: "I have found few negroes who will acknowledge to a stranger that they know anything of these legends; and yet to relate one of the stories is the surest road to their confidence and esteem. In this way, and in this way only, I have been enabled to collect and verify the folklore in this volume" (xxv). The slaves' vigilant distrust of the white community is a common element in Harris's narratives of the Old South and undermines rather than reinforces "the myth of the contented slave" (Turner 29).

Manuel's prayer of gratitude for Kitty's offering, however, confirms his access to Dave. Moreover, when Dave approaches the Denham plantation to tell Mrs. Denham about her son's accident, Harris notes that "he was well acquainted with the surroundings at the Denham Plantation, having been fed many a time by the well-cared-for negroes" (65). The detail of the slave community's involvement with a runaway offers a unique glimpse behind the veil of carefully concealed information. Moreover, Dave functions as a slave trickster, exercising full control over his life with the added benefit of exasperating his master, "bidding defiance to the law of the State and Bill Brand's track dogs" as well as evading the patrollers for years (56). Lawrence Levine notes that the trickster "could outwit his master again and again, but his primary satisfaction would be in making his master look foolish and thus exposing the myth of white omniscience and omnipotence" (132). Indeed, the longevity of Dave's evasion suggests he is not only physically strong but also draws on sharp intellect to outwit and outmaneuver the white community, particularly with the covert assistance of the black community.

Dave is, however, supremely cautious and demonstrates an important lesson featured in the folktales. Levine notes that "while each tale may bring the satisfaction of the weak triumphing over the strong, the cycle itself has a more complicated message: Rabbits may win battles but they don't win wars. Rabbits don't replace foxes and wolves; they're rabbits! They have to use their wits all the time. They're always in danger. They never become secure. They're never on top. That was the lesson being taught to the young; not some simple fantasy of victory, but what you needed to *survive* in this world" (my emphasis xviii). Harris suggests that Dave's aid is motivated by sincerity and compassion but is also more subversively driven by a strategic survival strategy. Dave establishes his safety through his savvy understanding that the Denhams promise to be advantageous allies.

Dave's assessment proves accurate and introduces another example of the trickster-tricked motif. Harris concludes the tale by again featuring a discussion between Brother Roach and Brother Brannum. Roach recounts events from the previous Saturday when he had run into General Bledser, who boasted that he had made a trade that made him "'particular proud'" (69). Bledser bragged that he "'sold Blue Dave'" and believes he has duped Mrs. Denham by selling her a fugitive slave who has proven impossible to catch and made a profit (69). His delight is undermined, however, when the Denham carriage approached. Roach notes that he had asked Bledser to "'look clost at that nigger on the carriage,—look clost at him'" (69). Roach explains that when Bledser saw Dave driving the carriage, he exclaimed, "Why, what the thunderation!'" And as the carriage passed, Mrs. Denham called out, "'Good-morning, Giner'l, good-morning! David is a most excellent driver'" (69). Brother Roach tells Brother Brannum, "'The Giner'l managed for to take off his hat, but he was in-about the worst whipped-out white man I ever see. And arter the carriage got out of hearing, sir, he stood in that there door there and cussed plump tell he couldn't cuss. When a man's been to Congress and back, he's liable for to know how to take the name of the Lord in vain. But don't tell em about the wimmen, Brother Brannum. Don't'" (69). Bledser is embarrassed, infuriated, and loses his temper, and the conversation between the farmers suggests that they too enjoy the outwitting of this planter patriarch; indeed, Roach is described telling Brannum the story "laughing until he began to wheeze" (69).

While Darwin T. Turner asserts that Mrs. Denham's reward of buying Dave undermines the story's subversive potential, in the context of Georgia's slave codes, manumission was possible only by special legislative act and tended to be approved only "as long as local opinion supported manumission" (Ford 295). Given Dave's reputation as an elusive fugitive, legislative permission granting his manumission would have been highly unlikely. Moreover, Dave was at large for more than seven years, which indicates that he had a compelling reason to remain in the area, most likely because of ties to family and friends. Had Mrs. Denham successfully manumitted him, he would have lost access to his community connections because, as Lacy K. Ford notes, "in 1826, Georgia mandated that all newly manumitted slaves be removed from the state" (295). As Harris demonstrates in "Free Joe," this practice was not always enforced, but given Dave's history, it is unlikely he would have been permitted to remain in the community. The scene described by the farmers thus suggests that Dave and Mrs. Denham negotiated a deal that would satisfy both parties and simultaneously get the best of Bledser. Mrs. Denham's role also suggests characteristics of a trickster, yet like many of Stowe's characters, these traits have been overlooked likely due to gender. In this tale, Mrs. Denham and Dave are depicted as a trickster team, featuring a white woman as tricky and enigmatic as her black trickster partner.

Another trickster duo is depicted in "Balaam and His Master." In this story, Harris draws on the cultural ideal of the traditional Virginia gentleman in his portrait of William Cozart. Before the mid-eighteenth century, Virginia maintained a fairly tight-knit gentry class that wielded extensive power.[12] Webb notes that in the colonial era, the

> Virginia colony had evolved into a rigid, three-tiered society. At the top was a landed English-American aristocracy whose wealth and holdings owed much to the patronage of the ruling royalty in the mother country. Contrary to the prevailing mythology of a ruggedly competitive, rags-to-riches ethos among those who had braved the Atlantic to come to America, the majority of this privileged class was originally granted huge tracts of land by royal decree. Family names and quasi-royal prerogatives were taken seriously, and as the generations unfolded, this "Cavalier aristocracy" took great pains to protect and advance their own interests as well as those of others in their small circle of elites. (141)

But by the early 1760s, as Rhys Isaac demonstrates, the gentry's hegemony was weakened by the popular evangelical movement that conflicted with Anglican authority. Further deterioration of power occurred in the postrevolutionary era with the triumph of "republicanism" resulting in changes "to the traditional forms" that were replaced with "an ideology in which 'the individual' was the legitimating metaphor" (314). Isaac notes that "the old order had induced a sense of obligation to public service among those whose family and fortune had set them over their neighbors in parish and county. Within the new framework of contractual association the local units seemed to be less like patriarchal protectorates and more like outlets for the electoral ambitions of individuals. An acute sense of lost public spirit resulted" (314). By the late eighteenth century, the decline of the Virginia tobacco economy compelled many members of these formerly powerful families to seek new opportunities in the Southwest, particularly after the Louisiana Purchase and Eli Whitney's invention of the cotton gin, which combined to create a new market in cotton production as well as a revived market in the domestic slave trade. While these families transported rigid notions of class distinctions tied to lineage and bloodlines, the ideology of "the individual" replaced the planter aristocracy's sense of social responsibility with a more opportunistic sensibility. Furthermore, the upper class's hierarchical worldview often clashed with the backcountry ethos of independence and "lack of subservience to outsiders or outside forces" (Hahn 45).

William Cozart represents, as Harris notes, "the Old Virginia fashion," yet his portrait is depicted with greater emphasis on personal ambition than traditional protectorate ideology, and with his "wagons and his negroes," he settles in middle Georgia, "bought hundreds of acres of land," and became "the leading citizen of the place" (8-9). This "thrifty village" grew into "a flourishing town" and the "Cozarts remained the leading family, socially, politically, and financially" (9). The family's peace is disturbed, however, by the birth of Berrien Cozart in the 1830s, and the child grew to become "a thorn in the side of those who loved him best" (10). Harris undermines first families of Virginia (FFV) ideology through the character of Berrien Cozart, who had "a temper of extreme violence and an obstinacy that had no bounds," which suggests that the Cozarts' class status is simply a matter of wealth rather than notions of inherently superior bloodlines (12).

Harris introduces another interesting feature in this character portrait through his relationship with his body servant Balaam. Whereas Berrien's father lacks the ability to exert control over his rebellious son, "only one person in the world had any real influence over him—a negro named Balaam" (10). Balaam is introduced as a "negro with an independence and a fearlessness extremely rare among slaves," and he is the only character in the text able to exercise any influence on Berrien (12). Furthermore, due to Balaam's limitations as a slave, with no legal or social rights, his power derives from the only resource available to him, his intelligence, which Harris emphasizes throughout the narrative. For example, Berrien's father hires a tutor to educate him, but he "was not very much to Berrien's taste," and he insults and assaults the young teacher (13). Balaam then enters the room, "closing the door carefully behind him, and almost immediately the tumult ceased. Then the negro appeared leading his young master by the arm. . . . The negro, with his hand on the boy's shoulder, was saying something unpleasant, for the tutor observed one or two fierce gestures of protest. But these soon ceased" (14). Harris does not recount what Balaam says to subdue Berrien, but he is depicted as the only person able to control this "sensual, cruel, impetuous, and implacable" young man; indeed, he is repeatedly described giving the appearance of "leading his young master" through his influence and intelligence (15).

Balaam's sway over Berrien also functions to undermine William Cozart's role as a patriarch. Fischer notes that in the Virginia tradition, child rearing was geared toward preparing "the child to take its proper place in the social hierarchy. The child's will was not broken, but in a phrase that Virginians like to use, it was 'severely bent against itself.' This end was accomplished primarily by requiring children to observe elaborate rituals of self-restraint" (*Albion's Seed* 313). In spite of William Cozart's social, economic, and political power, he is unable to bend the will of his rebellious son, yet his slave Balaam possesses an influence and authority the elder Cozart lacks.

As the narrative progresses, Harris draws on frontier and slave trickster traits in developing the character portraits of this unique duo. After Berrien is expelled from college and disinherited by his father, he tells Balaam: "'You belong to me, but I'll give you your choice; you can go with me, or you can stay. If you go, I'll probably get into a tight place and sell you; if you stay, Pap will make a pet of you for my sake" (19). Balaam chooses to go with Berrien because the alternative is to "'go to the overseer and tell him to put you to work,'" which means picking "five hundred pounds of cotton every day" (18). Berrien sets out to make his way in the world as a con man and seems to live by Simon Suggs's credo: "It's good to be shifty in a new country."[13] Balaam, however, lives by African American folk wisdom. Morgan points out that "southwestern tricksters struggle to win; African-American tricksters struggle to *survive*," which is a perspective especially relevant to this unique story as well ("Signifying" 212).

Berrien Cozart is particularly well suited to the frontier trickster lifestyle and embraces the con game as a livelihood. Harris notes that "there were few games of chance in which he was not an adept. No conjurer was so adroit with the cards or the dice" (25). But like other frontier tricksters, Berrien eventually becomes a trickster-tricked when "one fine day luck turned her back on him, and he paraded on fine afternoons in front of Lloyd's Hotel a penniless man" (25). Furthermore, when Balaam discovers that Berrien "had made up his mind to sell him," he draws on black trickster wisdom for his own protection. He tells Berrien, "'Well, suh,' said Balaam, brushing his master's coat carefully, 'you kin sell me, but de man dat buys Balaam will git a mighty bad bargain'" (25). Berrien asks what he means, and he replies, "'You kin sell me, suh, but I ain't gwine stay wid um.' . . . 'I got legs, Marse Berry. You know dat yo'se'f'" (26). The two decide to embark on a scheme to sell Balaam, who will then run "armed with a 'pass' which formally set forth to all to whom it might concern that the boy David had express permission to join his master in Nashville, and this 'pass' bore the signature of Elmore Avery, a gentleman who existed only in the imagination of Mr. Berrien Cozart" (30). During Balaam's journey, he uses trickster wit on a number of occasions to evade trouble. For example, he is asked by a white man who his master is and having forgotten the name on his pass, Balaam explains, "'I runned my han' und' de lindin' er my hat an' pulled out de pass, an' say, 'Boss, dis piece er paper kin talk lots better dan I kin.' De man look at me right hard, an' den he tuck de pass an' read it out loud. Well, suh, w'en he come ter de name I des grabbed holt un it wid my min', an' I ain't never turned it loose tell yit'" (31). Berrien Cozart is eventually arrested and jailed, and Balaam is captured in a rather perplexing escape attempt. Harris notes that the jailer discovers Berrien dead, "and crouching beside him was Balaam. How the negro had managed to make his way through the masonry of the dungeon without discovery is still one of the mysteries of Billville" (43). While Balaam superficially appears to conform to, as Turner contends, the literary and cultural stereotype of the devoted servant, Balaam's trickster traits suggest loyalty to a lifestyle rather than to a master, which is far more preferable to the alternative and common condition of most slaves working from sun to sun in a cotton field. Ultimately, the narrative highlights the frontier humor trickster-tricked motif, but the black trickster featured in this story demonstrates the trickster's most important message, survival, and Balaam does just that.

In the story "Where's Duncan?" (published in the collection *Balaam and His Master and Other Sketches and Stories* in 1891), Harris introduces a character representing a unique amalgam of frontier humor and black folktale trickster traits. The tale is particularly compelling in the subversive content implied throughout, which addresses the taboo topic of "the forbidden theme of black/white miscegenation" as well as the implied sexual exploitation of a female slave (Kinney, *Amalgamation!* 45). James Kinney notes that in the antebellum era, "the nearly two-century struggle to contain miscegenation amounted to this—they prohibited legal intermarriage, punished illicit unions between black men and white women, but tolerated those between white men and black women as long as the mulatto children followed the condition of their slave mothers" (6). While Harris does not provide the personal story of the mulatto woman introduced later in the narrative, the detail that she is racially mixed and, as we later learn, has a child by her master implies white male sexual exploitation of a black woman.

Harris establishes the narrative structure by using the common frontier humor frame technique, opening the sketch with "old man Isaiah Winchell a-gabbling about old times" (149). And like the frontier humorists, Harris also utilizes a narratee, a character who functions as the listener of the tale, which is evident when Winchell uses second-person "you" in telling what Winchell calls not a story but "a happening" (149). Winchell notes that in 1826, he was a young man of eighteen and put in charge of "ginning and packing cotton" when their overseer quit. After preparing the cotton for market, Winchell and Crooked-leg Jake load the wagon and start for Augusta, but when Winchell learns that Jake is drunk, he is compelled "to drive six mules, and there was only one rein to drive them with" (151). During the trip, "there came out of the woods a thick-set, dark-featured, black-bearded man with a bag slung across his shoulder" (152). The man helps with the team and joins Winchell in his journey. Harris introduces a particularly intriguing element when Jake wakes up and asks who is driving. After Winchell recounts the stranger's arrival, Jake asks: "'Is he a sho' 'nuff w'ite man?'" (153). Winchell replies: "'Well, he looks like he is,' said I; 'but I'm not certain about that'" (154). The element of confusion regarding clarifying the stranger's racial identity complicates the racial binary of black and white, which is a particularly important distinction in an era defending racial slavery and later racial segregation; in other words, the era in which the story is set and the era in which it was published.

Jake's question also implies that a black character is privy to information about this "stranger" that his master lacks. His master is thus not equipped to understand the full implications of the stranger's behavior or figurative speech. Toward the end of their journey, the character identifies himself as "Willis Featherstone" and claims: "'I am simply a vagabond'" but adds, "'I have a rich daddy hereabouts, and I'm on my way to see how he is getting along'" (157). Featherstone then poses a "riddle" but advises: "'If you can't unriddle it, it will unriddle itself'" (157). He tells Winchell, "'A father had a son. He sent him to school in Augusta, until he was fifteen. By that time, the father grew to hate the son, and one day, in a fit of anger, sold him to a nigger speculator'" (157). Unable to "unriddle" the riddle, Winchell simply shrugs off the odd exchange.

Another strange encounter occurs later that evening when "a tall mulatto woman" approaches the camp and relays an invitation from her master, Giles Featherstone, to join him for dinner. While Winchell does not appear to notice that the stranger and the woman's master share the same surname, the stranger's question to the woman shows it is not simply coincidence. He asks her, "'Where's Duncan?'" (163). Her reaction indicates that the question is a source of intense pain. The woman "stood like one paralyzed. She gasped for breath, her arms jerked convulsively, and there was a twitching of the muscles of her face pitiful to behold" (163). When Featherstone repeats the question, she rose and "ran off into the darkness, screaming;—'He sold 'im!—he sold Duncan! He sold my onliest boy!'" (164). As the narrative events unfold, so too does the riddle. During the night, Jake wakes Winchell to tell him about a "'mighty rippit up dar at dat house on de hill'" (164). Jake urges Winchell to take action, stating, "'Dey gwine ter be trouble up dar, sho ez you er born'" (165). His insistence suggests that he possesses disturbing insight regarding the potential for further "trouble," but Winchell ignores Jake's appeal and returns to sleep. Winchell is again awakened by Jake as the trouble escalates and the house becomes engulfed in flames. Winchell rushes to the house and through a window, he witnesses the mulatto woman "engaged in an encounter with a gray-haired white man . . . like two bull-dogs fighting. The woman had a carving-knife in her right hand, and she was endeavoring to push the white man against the wall. He, on his side, was trying to catch and hold the hand in which the woman held the knife, and was also making a frantic effort to keep away from the wall. But the woman had the advantage; she was younger and stronger, and desperate as he was, she was more desperate still" (166–67). During the fight, Winchell explains that "once, and only once, did I catch the sound of a voice; it was the voice of the nigger woman; she had her carving-knife raised in the air in one hand, and with the other she had the white man by the throat. 'Where's Duncan?' she shrieked" (168). After the woman "plunged the carving-knife into his body, not only once, but twice," the house collapses in flames (168). Winchell concludes the story by noting that "Crooked-leg Jake insisted to the day of his death that the man who had driven our team sat in a chair in the corner of the dining-room, while the woman and the man were fighting, and seemed to be enjoying the spectacle" (169). While Harris presents Winchell as the narrator of the story, Crooked-leg Jake provides key elements necessary to "unriddle" the riddle, and it becomes clear that the woman is the stranger's mother and that he is the son referenced in the riddle, which implies the sexual exploitation of a female slave resulting in the son whose father (and master) sold him to a slave speculator and, therefore, profited from the sale of his own child.

The stranger's amalgam of black and white trickster traits are evident by his "vagabond" freedom, which would have involved some form of escape from the slavery his father sold him into as well as the use of wit to survive; whereas, his frontier trickster traits are suggested by his mission to see "how his father is getting along," which indicates that he is carrying out a plan (157). MacKethan identifies Simon Suggs and Sut Lovingood as representative examples of frontier humor trickster figures, but these characters are driven by distinctly different motives. Suggs is notorious for being "shifty" in a new country as an opportunist, but Sut Lovingood is more often driven by an important backcountry attitude toward justice ("Trickster"). Fischer notes that "backsettlers shared an idea of order as a system of retributive justice. The prevailing principle was *lex talionis,* the rule of retaliation. It held that a good man must seek to do right in the world, but when wrong was done to him he must punish the wrongdoer himself by an act of retribution that restored order and justice in the world" (*Albion's Seed* 765). Many of Sut's antics are motivated by this principle; indeed, the sketch "Parson Bullin's Lizards" is subtitled "retribution."[14] As the story of the stranger concludes, it becomes evident that retaliation is also the motivating force of the son's "visit" to his father. Harris's narrative also strategically integrates controversial elements rarely featured in nineteenth-century fiction, such as the issue of miscegenation, particularly as a result of the sexual exploitation of a slave woman, as well as a chronicle of the long-lasting devastation resulting from the separation of a mother from her child.

Turner justifiably chastises Harris for his metaphorical reference to slavery as "a university," but in the context of an era reneging on the social and civil rights of black Americans at an alarming rate, this figurative device suggests that Harris was again signifying. Harris writes, "Here is a university of slavery that shall lead the savage to citizenship" (7). Although use of the word *savage* has understandably outraged a number of readers, the word was also commonly employed by radical racists in the post-Reconstruction era perpetuating the theory that free of the "civilizing" influence of slavery, black Americans were reverting to bestial "savagery." Harris's use of the word *savage* undermines the connotation of his contemporaries by relegating it into an era that has passed and thus indicating a transitional phase that has resulted in citizenship, which Harris suggests African Americans have earned and are therefore entitled to. Harris expresses similar sentiments in his nonfiction, as Jeremy Wells points out, and "was insistent in several essays published during his lifetime that African Americans had not yet been given the chance to show whether they could contribute to U.S. civil society and that they deserved the opportunity" (54). Furthermore, by drawing on aesthetic traditions of the antebellum era, Harris celebrates the rich artistry of written and oral folktales featuring the cultural, social, and community values of nonelite Southerners, highlighted by frontier humor and African American folktale traditions.

Chapter 5

Twain's Tricksters

Slip the Yoke and Poach the Joke[1]

Like his close personal friend Joel Chandler Harris, Mark Twain was also uniquely familiar with many facets of African American culture. Twain frequently expressed his esteem for black art forms as well as his highly controversial appreciation for the minstrel tradition, which many scholars contend was a prominent influence in his work.[2] Other creative influences derive from "Southwest humor, Northeastern humorists, and the picaresque novel" as well as the "fugitive slave narratives" (Mensh and Mensh 34). Scholars have also addressed various aspects of African and African American oral traditions in his work as well. Jennifer Hildebrand examines "the African philosophy behind some beliefs in witches and ghosts" in *Adventures of Huckleberry Finn* and contends that "the witchlore and other folk beliefs" held by both black and white characters undermines the perspective of associating "Jim's 'superstitious' behavior with the racist caricatures presented by the nineteenth-century minstrel show" (152). Shelley Fisher Fishkin, in her provocative study *Was Huck Black?*, examines "the ways in which African-American voices shaped Twain's creative imagination" (4). Fishkin notes that the most significant influences came from the young waiter depicted in "Sociable Jimmy," the captivating tale of Mary Ann Cord's personal history recounted in "A True Story," and a slave named Jerry, "a master of the African-American art of 'signifying' who helped introduce Clemens, at age fifteen, to the power of satire as a tool of social critique" (54).[3] Fishkin also notes Twain's regard for the minstrel tradition and contends that "Twain's sympathy for Jim may have been genuine, but Jim's voice retains enough of minstrelsy in it to be demeaning and depressing" (107). Fishkin asserts that the African American voices that influence Twain indicate that "the model for Huck Finn's voice was a black child instead of a white one" (4). Twain, however, claimed that he based the character Jim on a particularly gifted and memorable storyteller, a slave known as Uncle Dan'l.

Twain commented frequently on his regard for storytelling as a largely underappreciated art form in numerous letters, lectures, and his autobiography. Twain considered the humorous story a "high and delicate art" and claimed that "only an artist can tell it" (156).[4] His love of a great story began early in his life. During summer visits to his uncle's farm, he was introduced to Uncle Dan'l. In his autobiography, Twain recalls

> the look of Uncle Dan'l's kitchen as it was on privileged nights when I was a child, and I can see the white and black children grouped on the hearth, with the firelight playing on their faces and the shadows flickering upon the walls, clear back toward the cavernous gloom of the rear, and I can hear Uncle Dan'l telling the immortal tales which Uncle Remus['s] Harris was to gather into his book and charm the world with, by and by; and I can feel again the creepy joy which quivered through me when the time for the ghost story of the "Golden Arm" was reached—and the sense of regret, too, which came over me, for it was always the last story of the evening, and there was nothing between it and the unwelcome bed. (217)

During these formative years, Twain was not only exposed to a gifted storyteller but also to an oral tradition that was typically restricted to black listeners, giving this young auditor rare access to a cultural tradition that would profoundly influence his work as an adult. Indeed, Uncle Dan'l provided Twain a unique and privileged education in his kitchen, which included access to ghost stories and trickster tales as well as the aesthetic complexities of signifying. In this chapter, I contend that Twain's most complex (and controversial) black characters, Jim and Roxy, operate as subversive trickster figures developed by Twain's use of black aesthetic traditions.

In Twain's masterpiece, *Adventures of Huckleberry Finn*, the character Jim has become one of the most controversial figures in American literature. The most negative criticism derives from numerous scholars who view him as an offensive example of the minstrel tradition. Fredrick Woodard and Donnarae MacCann contend that the novel is "thoroughly embedded in the convention of blackface minstrelsy" and that Jim remains "forever frozen within the convention of the minstrel darky" (145). Although Ralph Ellison identifies a complex duality in the character, he felt that Twain, "standing closer to the Reconstruction [than Faulkner] and to the oral tradition, was not so free of the white dictum that Negro males must be treated as either boys or 'uncles'—never as men," and, as a result, "Nigger Jim" is "a white man's inadequate portrait of a slave" ("Change the Joke" 51,

64). The terms *boy* and *uncle* were common throughout the nineteenth and twentieth centuries, as Ellison indicates, as a means to deny the manhood of black men, yet Twain does not use these terms to refer to Jim anywhere in the novel. Furthermore, Twain's proximity to the oral tradition was also an important influence in Ellison's work as well, and he explains, "I use folklore in my work not because I am Negro, but because writers like Eliot and Joyce made me conscious of the literary value of my folk inheritance. My cultural background, like that of most Americans, is dual (my middle name, sadly enough, is Waldo). I knew the trickster Ulysses just as early as I knew the wily rabbit of Negro American lore" (58). Twain was also clearly conscious of the literary value of folk art and demonstrates a similar cultural duality as well, drawing on, as many have noted, trickster elements of frontier humor, particularly regarding the con men the king and the duke, yet few studies have addressed the extensive influence of black folklore, particularly Jim's resemblance to the wily Rabbit.

The novel's characters have generated a wide range of debate over the years and, as Kevin Michael Scott notes, "as the critical view of Tom has grown increasingly negative, interestingly, the critical view of Jim has become steadily more complex and positive, elevating him from stage prop to active participant, even during the evasion. Jim has evolved from the stereotypical minstrel 'darky' to [Leo] Marx's tragic hero to the current critical view, promoted most persuasively by Forrest G. Robinson, of a fully realized but concealed character" (188).

Jim's "concealed" characteristics are, I contend, accessible by examining him in the context of the novel's perspective on slave culture and black folklife, which reveals a bold, cunning, highly intelligent individual and suggests characteristics representative of the trickster figure featured in black folklore. Furthermore, the trickster's most important agenda is survival, which is Jim's driving force throughout the novel, yet Jim's commitment to survival is not exclusively self-serving but motivated by his goal to eventually safeguard his family. In many of the Brer Rabbit tales, the Rabbit is often operating to protect his little brood from the dangers of Brer Fox as well.

Jim is first introduced in the novel in chapter 2 "setting in the kitchen door," a location Twain utilizes to provide several features of the slave community in St. Petersburg, Missouri (18). After Tom plays his prank on Jim, Huck explains Jim's interpretation of waking to find his hat on a tree above him and the "five center" he discovers on the kitchen table. According to Huck, "Jim said the witches bewitched him and put him in a trance, and rode him all over the State. . . . And the next time Jim told it he said they rode him down to New Orleans, and after that, every time he told it he spread it more and more" (19). While numerous critics regard Jim's account as evidence of minstrel characteristics, including gullibility, superstition, and low intellect, this perspective depends on an assumption that Jim believes he has been ridden by witches, but as Lott points out, "this moment of apparent blackface foolishness is in fact an occasion in which Jim seizes rhetorical and perhaps actual power. . . . One notes that Jim's actual words are not rendered here, which in the orthographic hierarchy of white dialect writing might have had the effect of reducing their impact. This is a moment when Jim, as he does in other ways throughout Huck Finn, uses tricks and deceits to his advantage" ("Mr. Clemens and Jim Crow" 136). Indeed, tricks and deceits are representative characteristics of the trickster figure, which are traits that Jim demonstrates throughout the novel, but the scene also highlights the slaves' storytelling traditions and the esteem the community accorded gifted raconteurs. Storytellers do not simply repeat an event or pass along a tale but engage in figurative craftsmanship regarding the material they are working with.[5] Twain implies that Jim is a particularly talented storyteller by the rapid circulation and popularity of his tale, which suggests that Jim should be regarded as an artist because it is clear he is in narrative control, choosing what elements to add, emphasize, and elaborate upon.

An additional indication that Jim is not simply demonstrating his superstitious belief in witches or his literal belief in the night ride is evidenced by similar manipulation of figurative elements in the tale he crafts for his hair ball. Huck goes to Jim for information regarding Pap's return because Jim has a hair ball, which he claims has "a spirit inside of it, and it knowed everything" (29). In this scene, it is clear that Jim does not actually believe he has an all-knowing hair ball but is manufacturing a story for material gain. According to Jim, the hair ball often "wouldn't talk without money" (29). Jim's tale of the hair ball's avaricious eccentricities and Huck's claim that the only money he has is a "slick counterfeit quarter" pit the pair in a contest of wit. Robinson contends that Jim's tactic is "in fact shrewdly resourceful" (145), whereas Mensh and Mensh claim that "the essential point is that Jim does not best the boy by demonstrating adult wit or mature consciousness, but by knowing a little trick. That Jim knows the trick and Huck does not is of no significance" (32). Jim's "little trick" is, however, embedded in an extensive cultural signifying system that depends on black insight in order to dupe, deceive, and survive. While Jim only receives a counterfeit quarter,

Huck walks away believing he has gained important information but has accomplished nothing more than to rid himself of his questionable quarter. In this contest, Jim is clearly the victor.

It is certainly reasonable to assume that Jim's witch tale is also figurative rather than evidence of minstrel-like gullibility. Moreover, Jim's witch tale serves him in many ways. The popularity of the story contributes to his reputation and, as David L. Smith points out, he becomes "a local celebrity" in the black community (109). Twain notes that "niggers would come miles to hear Jim tell about it, and he was more looked up to than any nigger in that country. Strange niggers would stand with their mouths open and look him all over, same as if he was a wonder" (19). Jim not only gains the regard of his community but his story strategically benefits him materially as well. Jim carries the five-center around his neck, and "niggers would come from all around there and give Jim anything they had, just for a sight of that five-center piece" (19). Twain's note that strange slaves traveled for miles to hear the story and look at the five-center additionally suggests a mobility that was not likely authorized by their masters. These strange slaves either slipped away and evaded the patrollers or secured passes by duping their masters with deceptive explanations for their requests. An additional feature of slave culture provided in this section is an element of the black community's activities free from white involvement or interference. After they are relieved of their duties for the day and the widow's routine of gathering them in the parlor for prayers, they then congregate in the kitchen "talking about witches in the dark," an activity Twain also loved (19). This brief reference, moreover, demonstrates the ways in which the black community took advantage of opportunities for privacy, the types of entertainment they engaged in together, and the pleasure they took in each other's company. While Huck is aware of this routine, he is not a participant but simply an observer, privy to these activities during his night excursions with Tom.

During the early chapters of the novel, the relationship between Huck and Jim is familiar rather than personal. As Tom points out at the end of the novel, Huck and Tom have "knowed" Jim "all his life" (291). The boys are approximately "thirteen or fourteen," as Huck notes in gauging the age of Buck Grangerford, so while Jim has known them all their lives, he is a grown man with a wife and two children, and there is little information provided regarding his life prior to these thirteen or fourteen years. Huck's relationship with Jim at this point is limited to his basic familiarity with one of the slaves owned by Miss Watson. Twain reiterates the social and personal distance between Jim and Huck by Huck identifying Jim as "Miss Watson's nigger, Jim" on two occasions early in the novel, and on Jackson's Island, Jim addresses Huck as "sah."

The relationship between Jim and Huck changes dramatically and quickly on Jackson's Island, and Jim's trickster traits become much more evident. Several scholars contend that Jim's reaction to Huck's appearance again suggests minstrel-like superstition, believing Huck is a ghost, but as Hildebrand points out, "Jim is not the only one to conclude that the figure of Huck appearing before him was a ghost: when Tom Sawyer saw Huck alive at the Phelps', he said, 'I hain't ever done you no harm. You know that. So then, what you want to come back and ha'n *me* for?'" (170).[6] For both it is simply a surprising and disorienting moment, but after determining that Huck is indeed alive, Jim is depicted quietly and attentively listening to Huck's account of his escape from Pap. Jim also takes stock of Huck's extensive inventory and after a particularly satisfying breakfast after living on berries for five days, Jim begins to more carefully analyze Huck. Jim considers Huck's strategy of staging his "murder" as "smart," which shows his ability to discern sharp intelligence regarding Huck's plan in spite of Huck's minimal education, which demonstrates another aspect of black insight (54). Walter Johnson points out that the "slaves' life-long vulnerability to white brutality often provided them with the experience of what [former slave] John Brown called 'a long habit of studying the expression of countenance' born of being 'forced to watch the changes of my master's physiognomy, as well as those of the parties he associated with, so as to frame my conduct in accordance with what I had reason to believe was their prevailing mood at any time'" (165). Thus, black insight not only helped slaves conceal and protect their real emotions, intentions, opinions, and sense of self but also functioned as an analytical tool to gauge the veracity, integrity, and intelligence of whites they had to deal with daily in order to determine how to operate in a given situation.

Jim is highly reluctant to trust Huck when Huck asks him why he is on Jackson's Island, but he is in an enormously dangerous and vulnerable situation. After eliciting Huck's promise to keep his secret, Jim confides that he "has run off" (55). As Jim provides details of his flight, his story signifies repeatedly on the slave narrative tradition. Jocelyn Chadwick-Joshua notes the influence of the slave narratives in the novel and contends that "by allowing us to hear Jim's voice, Twain enhances the whole notion of the Southern slave's integrity and self-reliance in the face of the grotesque predicament that the 'milder' forms of slave plantation life created" (xvi).

While Jim certainly demonstrates integrity and self-reliance, it is important to note that he is not a plantation slave, mild or otherwise. Indeed, it is the prospect of plantation slavery and all its horrors that sends Jim into flight. Jim explains that he overheard his mistress telling the widow of her plan to sell him to New Orleans, which would mean the permanent separation from his family, the indignities of the slave market, and the likelihood of *plantation* slavery. Kolchin observes that "life on a large cotton plantation in Mississippi, where slaves worked in gangs under the watchful eyes of an overseer and drivers, was very different from that on a small hemp-producing farm in Kentucky [or other border states], where the master personally directed and toiled alongside his hands" (100). While Jim regards his mistress as "pooty rough," he is a farm laborer living in close proximity to his wife and children in the border state of Missouri. His responsibilities regarding the care of the livestock is mild work compared to life-draining plantation field labor. Jim is also a respected member of a specific black community and engages in activities such as stories in the kitchen after dark as well as visits to his wife and children, but, as Walter Johnson points out, slaves were keenly aware that at any time, "any slave's identity might be disrupted as easily as a price could be set and a piece of paper passed from one hand to another" (19). Jim, after hearing that his mistress stands to gain eight hundred dollars for his sale, tells Huck: "'I never waited to hear de res'. I lit out mighty quick'" (55).

In spite of the urgency of Jim's escape, his flight requires another quality regularly featured throughout the slave narrative tradition, as well as the folktales, which is the ingenuity necessary to form a strategic plan. Woodard and MacCann claim that while "Jim may reasonably be viewed as a model of goodness, generosity, and humility, he is characterized without an equally essential intelligence" (141). Yet in this scene, and many others, Jim demonstrates his intelligence by forming a well thought out plan, which also functions to emphasize the danger he is in. He tells Huck, "'I tuck out up de river road, en went 'bout two mile er more to whah dey warn't no houses. I'd made up my mine 'bout what I's agwyne to do. You see ef I kep' on tryin' to git away afoot, de dogs 'ud track me; ef I stole a skift to cross over, dey'd miss dat skift, you see, en dey'd know 'bout whah I'd lan' on de yuther side en whah to pick up my track. So I says, a raff is what I's arter; it doan' *make* no track'" (55). The scene not only demonstrates Jim's cunning and quick wit, like Brer Rabbit, but functions intertextually to signify on the harrowing accounts of numerous fugitive slaves who were pursued by men armed with guns, dogs, and the law, which are threats to Jim that are reiterated throughout the course of the novel. Like Brer Rabbit, Jim is *always* in danger and is keenly aware of his vulnerability.

The weeks they spend on the island are described by Huck as a sort of vacation from "sivilization" as well as Pap, but several scholars regard Jim's time on the island as a retreat from an independent to a dependent role. Mensh and Mensh contend that "it is hopeless for Jim to stay on the island. . . . That Jim suddenly veers from a quick-thinking fugitive bent on his freedom to a fugitive unconcerned with his perilous situation and content with ephemeral comforts would be inexplicable were it not for his roots in blackface minstrelsy as well as the fugitive slave narratives" (41). But given Jim's clear comprehension of the danger he is in, this duration suggests a strategic opportunity to bide his time during the most intense period of the search for him, which will eventually lose its momentum. The slave hunters are also much more likely to search for a fugitive in a nearby free state rather than an island in plain sight of the slaveholding community from which he fled, which is a particularly bold tactic and similar to Harriet Jacobs's strategy of hiding in her grandmother's attic while her pursuers relentlessly search everywhere *but* the attic for years.[7]

Huck, however, begins to become bored with their routine and wants to slip over to the Illinois shore "to find out what was going on," yet the risk to Huck is minimal (66). Woodard and MacCann observe that "Jim is often scared stiff in contrast to Huck's calm, confident demeanor" and contend that this fear indicates "Jim's childishness" (146). However, if Huck's identity is revealed, the worst-case scenario is that he could be returned to either Pap or the widow, but Jim runs the risk of being killed or seriously injured in an attempt to catch him, and if he is captured, he would most likely be sold because, as Huck notes later in the novel, his mistress "would be mad and disgusted at his rascality and ungratefulness for leaving her, and so she'd sell him straight down the river again; and if she didn't everybody naturally despises an ungrateful nigger" (221). Twain suggests, however, that "everybody" refers to the white community because the fugitive is a hero in the quarters and is often aided, abetted, and protected by other slaves. Jim thus forms a strategic plan to minimize the risk by sending Huck off dressed as a girl. When Huck returns from his reconnaissance mission, Twain reiterates the danger Jim is in by his intense fear. Huck shouts, "'Git up and hump yourself, Jim! There ain't a minute to lose. They're after us!' Jim never asked no questions, he never said a word; but the way he worked for the next half an hour showed about how he was scared" (72). Jim's actions demonstrate his acute appreciation of the danger he is in, and the information also indicates that the search for him is still active, which means that at this point, Miss Watson has not yet undergone the change of heart revealed later in the novel. The scene also highlights Jim's insight after Huck has the chance to explain why they had to leave the island so quickly. Jim regards the woman who saw through Huck's disguise as "a smart one" and contends that "'if she was to start after us herself she wouldn't set down and watch a camp fire—no, sir, she'd fetch a dog'" (74). Jim surmises that she had likely advised her husband to fetch a dog, which Jim believes accounts for the delay, or as he tells Huck, "'we wouldn't be here'" (74).

Jim's decision to run with Huck is a highly strategic move that yields many benefits. Huck functions as a cover (a tactic similar to the one used by William and Ellen Craft), can read and write, has demonstrated his intelligence, and, while a gamble early on, seems worthy of Jim's trust. In light of the circumstances, particularly the lure of the three-hundred-dollar reward, it is a smart move toward securing his freedom and the eventual freedom of his family. Indeed, Jim's familial role also operates to develop his character portrait, condemn inhumane slave-market practices, and debunk essentialist racial ideology, particularly race theorists who claim that blacks were incapable of forming deep family bonds. Jim's commitment to his survival is motivated by his devotion to his family and his goal to eventually secure their freedom. Jim tells Huck that he is worth eight hundred dollars and notes, "'I wisht I had de money, I wouldn' want no mo'" (58). Lawrence Howe claims that "by identifying his value in dollars, he points to the influence of slavery on his identity," and as a result, he is unable to extricate his sense of self from his status as a commodity (10). However, Jim's family is the commodity he is interested in, and his goal is to shift his wife and children's status from commodity to family and eight hundred dollars would come close to if not cover the cost of a woman and two young children. Throughout the novel, Jim never loses sight of his main goal to work and save "up money and never spend a single cent, and when he got enough he would buy his wife, which was owned on a farm close to where Miss Watson lived; and then they would both work to buy the two children, and if their master wouldn't sell them, they'd get an Ab'litionist to go and steal them" (110). Jim's comment that after purchasing his wife (if granted permission by her master), he and his wife will "both work to buy the two children" suggests that Jim and his wife have considered and discussed this issue before and that his wife is as devoted to her husband and children as Jim is, which demonstrates a loving family unit.

Twain reiterates Jim's commitment to his family in Huck's depiction of private moments as well and notes that on one occasion, Huck woke to find Jim "with his head down betwixt his knees, moaning and mourning to himself" (170). Huck notes, "I didn't take notice, nor let on. I knowed what it was about. He was thinking about his wife and his children, away up yonder, and he was low and homesick" (170). This passage is often noted as a marker of Huck's growing understanding regarding Jim's humanity, particularly when Huck muses: "I do believe he cared just as much for his people as white folks does for theirn. It don't seem natural, but I reckon it's so" (170). Yet the scene also reiterates Jim's role as a husband and father as well as the pain that separation from his family produces. Furthermore, Twain demonstrates an important aspect of slave culture regarding the physical arrangement of many slave families, which were often made up of members owned by different masters, and they were, therefore, unable to live together. Because of these arrangements, slaves were dependent on their masters' permission to maintain family ties. A master's refusal to permit visits or the sale of loved ones destroyed countless numbers of black families for centuries, an issue Twain addresses in "A True Story, Repeated Word for Word as I Heard It."[8]

Twain recounts a conversation he had with Mary Ann Cord following his observation that her cheerful disposition must mean she has had little trouble in her life. She corrects this flawed assessment, telling him: "'My olc man—dat's my husban'—he was lovin' an' kind to me, jist as kind as you is to yo' own wife. An' we had chil'en—seven chil'en—an' we loved dem chil'en jist de same as you loves yo' chil'en. Dey was black, but de Lord can't make no chil'en so black but what dey mother love 'em an' wouldn't give 'em up, no, not for anything dat's in dis whole world. . . . Well, bymeby my olc mistis say she's broke, an' she got to sell all de niggers on de place. An' when I heah dat dey gwyne to sell us all off at oction in Richmon', oh de good gracious!'" (591-92). In spite of her pleas and eventual physical resistance, her husband and all seven children are sold. With the exception of one of her sons, Cord never sees her family again. Walter Johnson notes that "of the two thirds of a million interstate sales made by the traders in the decades before the Civil War, twenty-five percent involved the destruction of a first marriage and fifty percent destroyed a nuclear family—many of these separating children under the age of thirteen from their parents. Nearly all of them involved the dissolution of a previously existing community" (19). Because Miss Watson has the authority to sell Jim but not his family, like other fugitive slaves,

Jim must run from his family to maintain hope of ever seeing them again, which clearly fuels his flight and commitment.

Twain makes a similar point regarding the devastation suffered by the breakup of a family when the Wilkses' slaves are sold to a slave trader, "the two sons up the river to Memphis, and their mother down the river to Orleans" (195). The scene functions to reiterate the constant vulnerability of slave families, and because there is no father mentioned, Twain introduces a rather interesting narrative omission, insinuating that he is either dead, was sold, is owned by a different master, or that his identity is not public knowledge. The heartbreak suffered by this family also functions in sharp contrast to the family dynamic between Huck and his abusive father. After Pap's return to town, Judge Thatcher's refusal to give him Huck's money prompts the widow and the judge to, as Huck explains, "get the court to take me away from him and let one of them be my guardian; but it was a new judge that had just come, and he didn't know the old man; so he said the courts mustn't interfere and separate families if they could help it; said he'd druther not take a child away from its father" (33). Jim, however, has no legal recourse available to him to protect his family from harm or keep them together. These father figures also function as a scathing critique of the judicial system authorized to award an abusive, selfish, alcoholic father legal custody of his child yet not only deny the same legal considerations to a caring and loving father but also deny him any legal rights regarding his family at all. While the legal identity of children followed the mother, the masters of slave children had total legal authority over them, many of whom (as numerous slave narratives demonstrate) were their own children.

Jim's role as a father has been commented on by a number of critics and several contend that Jim transfers his parental instincts onto Huck; indeed, Myra Jehlen describes the character as "Twain's motherly Jim" (112).[9] This perspective is typically supported by Jim's advice to Huck to avoid looking at the dead man's face while they are exploring the house floating down the river. When Jim discovers the dead man, he tells Huck, "'It's a dead man. Yes, indeedy; naked, too. He's ben shot in de back. I reck'n he's ben dead two er three days. Come in, Huck, but doan' look at his face—it's too gashly'" (61-62). Tuire Valkeakari claims that when Jim "discovers that the dead man inside the house floating down the river is Pap Finn, he decides to temporarily withhold this information from Huck. . . . Huck obeys Jim without as much as a word of protest when Jim tells him not to look at the dead man's face. In this scene, it is clear who is a boy (Huck) and who is an adult (Jim), or who is the 'son' and who is his new surrogate 'father,' although this is not sustained in later chapters" (35). Like Jehlen, Woodard and MacCann regard this act as a maternal rather than paternal characteristic and contend that several scenes suggest that "Jim resembles a 'mammy' stereotype clucking over her surrogate child" (146). Other critics have, however, questioned Jim's motives in this particular event. Mensh and Mensh sum up the various perspectives: "Jim is noble if he tells Huck the news of Pap's death to comfort him or withholds the news to protect him, but Jim is selfish if he withholds it to protect himself" (43). Mensh and Mensh claim that "Jim deceives Huck to protect his own escape and his chances of rescuing his family" and contend that his reason for doing so falls under one of two options: it is either a reflection of "the minstrel tradition, he is dependent upon whites; or, conversely, that he has reason to believe Huck will help or at least can be manipulated into providing help" (44). The perspectives of Jim as either dependent on whites or manipulating Huck into helping him reiterate the common assumption of Huck leading Jim throughout their journey. However, the only risk in this situation is that Huck's reason for leaving is to get away from Pap, which implies that the omission is neither selfless nor selfish but rather self-serving, suggesting the trickster's survivalist agenda. Furthermore, because it is not until Jim learns of his freedom at the end of the novel that he chooses to disclose this information also indicates that he is strategically protecting his protection and thus utilizing his wits to lead Huck.

Jim's relationship with Huck is, moreover, simply too complex for easy categorization. While he certainly benefits from this friendship, it is neither purely mercenary nor parental but in many respects resembles the relationship in Toni Morrison's *Beloved* between Amy Denver and Sethe. Morrison writes: "A pateroller passing would have sniggered to see two throw-away people, two lawless outlaws—a slave and a barefoot whitewoman" (85). When Paul D asks Sethe if she delivered her baby alone, Sethe replies, "'A whitegirl helped me'" (8). Paul D responds, "'Then she helped herself too, God bless her'" (8). The complicated dynamic between Amy and Sethe is similar to Huck and Jim, who are also two throwaway people, two lawless outlaws—one a slave, the other a barefoot white boy—one on the run, the other helping yet thoughtlessly insulting and demeaning with words like *nigger* throughout their journey, yet well intended and sincere nonetheless.

The most significant insight regarding the relationship between Huck and Jim is depicted when they are free from the interference of outsiders, particularly on the raft, "floating along, talking, and singing, and laughing" (222). During their nights alone on the river, Twain repeatedly references

Jim and Huck "talking" but does not include the content of the dialogue in these general scenes; based on Jim's earlier history, it is likely this talking included storytelling. For example, the scene in which Huck decides, in a battle of moral uncertainty, to head out in the canoe to "tell on Jim" suggests that Huck has been tutored in the slaves' folktale tradition. William J. Scheick contends that Twain drew from either Joel Chandler Harris's Uncle Remus tales or from the tales he heard from Uncle Dan'l yet does not address how Huck would have become familiar with the trickster tactics featured in the black folktales, which would have come from Jim as a storyteller. When Huck encounters two men in a skiff searching for five runaway slaves from "up yonder above the head of the bend," they ask him if the man on Huck's raft is "'white or black'" (111). Huck replies, "'He's white'" and notes, "'I tried, for a second or two, to brace up and out with it, but I warn't man enough—hadn't the spunk of *a rabbit*'" (my emphasis 111). He does, however, demonstrate the clever wit of the wily Rabbit, and as Scheick points out, employs a tactic identical to the escape method of the most well-known tale in the Brer Rabbit cycle, "How Mr. Rabbit Was Too Sharp for Mr. Fox." When Brer Fox catches Brer Rabbit, Brer Rabbit tells him, "'Hang me des ez high as you please. . . . Drown me des ez deep ez you please. . . Skin me . . .'snatch out my eyeballs, t'ar out my years by de roots, en cut off my legs,' seesee, 'but do please, Brer Fox, don't fling me in dat brier-patch'" (Harris, *Complete Tales of Uncle Remus* 12). Similarly, when the men become suspicious and state, "'I reckon we'll go and see for ourselves,'" Huck has to think quickly. He replies, "'I wish you would, says I, 'because it's pap that's there, and maybe you'd help me tow the raft ashore where the light is. He's sick—and so is mam and Mary Ann'" (111). Huck claims that no one will help, and the men become concerned and ask: "'What *is* the matter with your pap? Answer up square, now, and it'll be the better for you'" (112). Huck states, "'I will, sir, I will, honest—but don't leave us please. It's the—the—gentlemen, if you'll only pull ahead, and let me heave you the head-line, you won't have to come a-nearer the raft—please do'" (112). The men quickly "backed water" but send forty dollars out of pity for Huck's dilemma, and as they make their hasty departure, advise: "'If you see any runaway niggers, you get help and nab them, and you can make some money by it'" (113). Huck responds, "'Good-by, sir,' says I, 'I won't let no runaway niggers get by me if I can help it'" (133). The scene is strongly reminiscent of Brer Rabbit's clever ploy and also sends a dual message. Huck's claim that he "'won't let no runaway niggers get by'" him shares much in common with William Craft's comment when a white man in the North advises that he leave his master and enjoy his freedom. Craft replies: "'I shall never run away from such a good master as I have at present'" (267). Similarly, Huck won't let a runaway "get by" him because he is aiding and abetting him. This scene and several others also demonstrate that runaway slaves were common and that there was money to be had in assisting in their capture, reinforcing the dangers of escape. Those who chose to oppose slavery by, according to the cultural adage, "voting with their feet" took enormous risks, requiring courage, intelligence, and a commitment to freedom, qualities that undermine the myth of the contented slave as well as the minstrel buffoon stereotype.

Huck also demonstrates that he has learned the art of signifying with the arrival of the duke and the king. The men ask Huck if Jim is a runaway, likely hoping to cash in on a reward, but Huck responds, "'Goodness sakes, would a runaway nigger run south?'" (143). Because a runaway is indeed running south, the tone of incredulity of Huck's question leads them to conclude, "No, they allowed he wouldn't" (143). Huck then manufactures a tale the men not only accept but, indeed, are unwittingly duped into assisting. The tactics Huck employs in several situations are notably different from the method he had used to escape from Pap, which indicates a shift in his strategic methodology. Huck does not escape from Pap by verbally duping him but rather waits until he departs and plants physical signs that suggest he has been murdered, which as Jim points out, is certainly "smart." His tactics during his journey with Jim, however, shift from utilizing physical signs to a more sophisticated manipulation of appearances and linguistic devices and suggest that these are tools Huck learns from Jim. Early in their journey, Huck engages in the Solomon debate with Jim, which several critics cite as an example of minstrel foolishness or as evidence of Jim's lack of intelligence. David L. Smith, however, contends that "Jim clearly possesses a subtlety and intelligence which 'the Negro' allegedly lacks" (111). Smith asserts that the debate "demonstrates [Jim's] impressive reasoning abilities, despite his factual ignorance. . . . The humor in Huck's conclusion, 'you can't learn a nigger to argue,' arises precisely from our recognition that Jim's argument is better than Huck's" (111). This scene also indicates Jim's intellectual independence as well as his repudiation of theories of white intellectual superiority and authority when he tells Huck, "'I doan k'yer what de widder say'" (87). Jim's flight similarly indicates that he "doan k'yer" what the authorities "say" who make and impose the law that defines him as property. Unlike Huck's periodic twangs of conscience for breaking the law and defying cultural morality, Jim *never* shows signs of an internal conflict nor does he demonstrate regret for his actions.

Throughout the early chapters, Jim's intelligence is demonstrated by multiple plans. Linda Morris points out that it is Jim's "idea to dress Huck in girl's clothing, he shortens the dress for him, he fastens it, he observes Huck practicing to be a girl, and he critiques Huck's performance" (37). Their main plan to use the river to get to Cairo where they can then board a steamboat up the Ohio is also Jim's idea because it is the location, as Jim tells Huck, where "'the two big rivers joined together there, that would show'" (96). Jim also demonstrates his knowledge of the area when Huck wonders if they are near Cairo, but Jim explains that there is "no high ground about Cairo" (114). However, the morning after their confusing night in the fog when they see "the clear Ohio water in shore, sure enough, and outside was the old regular Muddy," Jim notes that it was "'all up with Cairo'" (114). They are forced to form an alternative plan, but this is also derailed when the steamboat barrels down on the raft.

The various communities Jim and Huck spend time in introduce important features that distinguish significant elements between the white community and the slave community. Indeed, the black community is often depicted engaging in autonomous activities intentionally independent of the white community's knowledge. For instance, Jim tells Huck about "'a nigger name' Bob, dat had ketched a wood-flat, en his marster didn' know it; en I bought it off'n him'" (57). The reference implies that Bob's knowledge of his master's character suggests that if he hopes to benefit from the wood-flat, rather than his master, he must conceal this information from him. The secretive nature of the slave community is also evident in the Grangerford section, particularly the black community's carefully concealed assistance and thus regard for the fugitive. The section also highlights the trickster wisdom of the quarters when Jack, one of the Grangerfords' slaves, asks Huck to "'come down into de swamp,'" claiming that he will show him "'a whole stack o' water-moccasins'" (131). Huck thinks: "That's mighty curious; he said that yesterday. . . . What is he up to anyway?" (131). When Huck meets up with Jim, Jim tells him, "'Dey's mighty good to me, des niggers is, en whatever I wants 'm to do fur me, I doan' have to ast 'm twice, honey. Dat Jack's a good nigger, en pooty smart'" (132). Huck agrees with Jim's assessment, adding "'Yes, he is. He ain't ever told me you was here; told me to come, and he'd show me a lot of water-moccasins. If anything happens, he ain't mixed up in it. He can say he never seen us together, and it'll be the truth'" (132). The scene features Jack employing the trickster's characteristic double voice to entice Huck to get to Jim without implicating himself or the other slaves who are involved in concealing a runaway slave from their master, which, had they given Jim up, may have garnered a reward. Had their clandestine activities been discovered, however, they would have been disciplined, and, Twain implies, likely severely given Jack's supreme caution as well as the Grangerfords' penchant for violence in carrying on their feud with the Shepardsons for decades.

The Grangerfords' slaves demonstrate loyalty to a fellow bondsman, indeed a stranger, rather than their master, which undermines theories of mutual love and devotion between masters and slaves, particularly the alleged loyalty of slaves toward their masters. Jim explains that "'early in de mawnin' some er de niggers come along, gwyne to de fields, en dey tuck me en showed me dis place, whah de dogs can't track me on accounts o' de water, en dey brings me truck to eat every night, en tells me how you's a gitt'n along'" (131). The scene highlights the trickster wisdom of the quarters and also functions in rather glaring contrast to the family who owns these slaves. While the black community is featured protecting and caring for a fellow bondsman in great danger, the "elite" white community is depicted basically hunting one another—and hunting to kill at that. Indeed, the section concludes with the Colonel and his sons Tom, Bob, Buck and cousin Joe as well as "two or three" Shepardsons dead as a result of their feud (133).

Twain also satirizes theories of white superiority in the Boggs section as well, yet this event is not limited to a critique of the antebellum era but more subversively allegorizes racial tensions in the post-Reconstruction era as well. The scene begins similarly to many stories of the frontier humor tradition, featuring a "one-horse town" on the banks of the Mississippi in Arkansas. As the whiskey passes between men loafing at a country store around noon, old Boggs rides in on his "little old monthly drunk" threatening to kill old Colonel Sherburn for, as he claims, swindling him. The men good-naturedly dismiss his antics and state: "'He don't mean nothing; he's always a carryin' on like that, when he's drunk. He's the best-naturedest old fool in Arkansaw—never hurt nobody, drunk nor sober'" (157). Another man jokes, "'I wisht old Boggs'd threaten me, 'cuz then I'd know I warn't gwyne to die for a thousan' year'" (156). But when Colonel Sherburn tells Boggs that he will permit his foolishness until one o'clock and not a minute after, the scene quickly becomes serious. Just after one, in spite of Boggs's plea, "'O Lord, don't shoot,'" Sherburn takes aim and shoots twice, killing Boggs. The community gathers and determines to lynch Sherburn, but he stands his ground and mocks them: "'The idea of you lynching anybody! It's amusing'" (161). Sherburn chastises the crowd, "'I was born and raised in the south. . . . Your newspapers call you a brave people so much that you think you are braver than any other people. . . . If any real lynching's going to be done, it will be done in the dark, southern fashion; and when they come, they'll bring their masks, and fetch a man along" (162). While the account is set in the antebellum era and the mob's target is a white man, in the post-Reconstruction era, the lynching of black men had become, as Twain put it, an "epidemic of bloody insanities." In his essay "The United States of Lyncherdom," Twain writes: "When there is to be a lynching the people hitch up and come miles to see it, bringing their wives and children. Really to see it? No—they come only because they are afraid to stay at home, lest it be noticed and offensively commented upon. . . . When I was a boy I saw a brave gentleman deride and insult a mob and drive it away" (676). While Twain clearly esteems this gentleman's bravery and his disgust with lynching is clear in this essay, he too lacked the courage to have his opinions "offensively commented upon." He wrote the essay in 1901 after reading a newspaper report of a lynching in Missouri and indeed intended to write a book on lynching in America but decided not to pursue the project. Fishkin explains that "Twain wrote his publisher that he would not have a friend left in the South if he went through with that book" (*Lighting Out* 114). His perspective regarding lynching, however, becomes an important critical aspect at the end of the novel.

While several scholars contend that Jim remains "forever frozen within the convention of the minstrel darky," minstrel characteristics are much more evident in the characters of the king and the duke.[10] Many critics have demonstrated the pair's similarities to the trickster con men featured in the frontier humor tradition, particularly Johnson Jones Hooper's character Simon Suggs. Indeed, these two take Suggs's motto "it's good to be shifty in a new country" to a higher level and are often shifty with each other as well as various unsuspecting communities.[11] But as their antics continue, Twain begins to subtly shift their frontier trickster traits for characteristics much more representative of the minstrel fool, which suggests a blurring of the line between these genres. The men are at their ludicrous best in their Shakespeare performances, which was a common routine on the minstrel stage and featured inept "black" characters butchering Shakespearean roles, dialogues, and soliloquies.[12] Some of the most ridiculous scenes in the novel are the "rehearsals" on the raft of the balcony scene in *Romeo and Juliet*, featuring the king as Juliet, as well as Hamlet's soliloquy to "answer for encores with" (151). During rehearsals, the duke advises the king: "'You mustn't bellow out *Romeo*! That way, like a bull—you must say it soft, and sick, and languishy, so—R-o-o-meo! That is the idea; for Juliet's a dear sweet mere child of a girl, you know, and she don't bray like a jackass'" (151). The king practices so often that Huck has also memorized "Hamlet's soliloquy" and its absurdity is evident by the first line alone: "'To be, or not to be; that is the bare bodkin'" (152). After their first performance, however, the king is not given the opportunity to perform his encore material because the audience "laughed all the time, and that made the duke mad; and everybody left, anyway, before the show was over, but one boy which was asleep" (165). While Twain depicts the men as unscrupulous buffoons, he reserves his harshest critique for the way they (particularly the king) betray Jim by selling him out for, as Huck puts it, "forty dirty dollars."

While the king and the duke serve Jim badly, he does not submit to their treachery passively and, indeed, avails himself of an opportunity to pay them back, which is another characteristic feature of Brer Rabbit. Bernard Wolfe points out that in spite of the Rabbit's physical weakness and vulnerability, he could be vindictive, malevolent, and aggressive, which are characteristics that are suggested of Jim when the Phelpses' children ask to go to the show that evening.[13] Silas Phelps tells them: "'No,' says the old man, 'I reckon there ain't going to be any; and you couldn't go if there was; because the runaway nigger told Burton and me all about that scandalous show, and Burton said he would tell the people; so I reckon they've drove the owdacious loafers out of town before this time'" (239). Jim's disclosure suggests that his intentions are motivated more toward settling the score with these "rapscallions" rather than to protect an unfamiliar white community from being hoodwinked. Jim's information is also likely a strategy to gain the good graces of this strange white community holding him against his will. Jim's tactic is ultimately highly successful, and the men are tarred, feathered, and run out of town on a rail, whereas Jim's detention is relatively mild.

The location of the Phelpses' farm provides additional insight into antebellum slave culture. In spite of many critics regarding this section as a structural failure and Hemingway's infamous advice to stop reading at the evasion, many crucial aspects of the novel are presented in the final chapters.[14] While 75 percent of the white population in the antebellum South owned no slaves, Kolchin notes that farms with fewer than thirty slaves "constituted more than nine-tenths of rural slaveholdings and contained the majority of the slaves. . . . On farms with fewer than ten slaves, which contained a quarter of the slaves but a majority of the owners, masters could typically be found in the field, toiling alongside their slaves while bossing them and casually interacting with them" (102).[15] The plantation was a common setting in the proslavery romance novels, the slave narratives, and the post-Reconstruction plantation tradition, yet large planters owning more than one hundred slaves made up only 1 to 2 percent of the slaveholding population, and smaller planters owning fifty or more slaves constituted approximately 25 percent (Kolchin 101).

Silas Phelps is depicted as a typical hardworking farmer, like Twain's Uncle, and represents the majority of the slaveholding population. When Huck first arrives in search of Jim, he describes a modest farm with a "big double log house for the white folks" and "three little log nigger-cabins in a row" for the slaves (228). The three slave cabins suggest a modest number of slaves, likely no more than ten to fifteen, if that. Because it is early morning, "the hands was all gone to the fields" with the exception of Lize, who comes "tearing out of the kitchen" with a rolling pin in her hand trailed by her three young children (229). Because the family is able to utilize one of their slaves as a domestic worker rather than field hand suggests that they are economically stable and firmly in the middle ranks of the yeoman slaveholding class. Sally Phelps is depicted throughout the section performing the common duties of a farm wife: spinning, sewing, cooking, cleaning, and supervising her children. Silas and Sally Phelps are described throughout the section as hardworking, moral, and kind people; indeed, Silas Phelps is, as Huck explains, not "only just a farmer, he was a preacher, too, and had a little one-horse log church down back of the plantation, which he built it himself at his own expense" (235). The extensive and highly flattering portrait Twain crafts for this family is, however, sharply undermined by a significant flaw—their racism. One of the most controversial sentences in the novel is when Huck fabricates the tale of an explosion on the steamboat to account for his delay, and Aunt Sally asks if anyone was hurt. Huck has learned to become much more analytical regarding his audience and frequently changes his linguistic tactics to suit the situation. David L. Smith points out that "Huck is playing on her glib and conventional bigotry" when Huck replies, "No'm. Killed a nigger" (106; 230). She responds, "Well, it's lucky; because sometimes people do get hurt," which demonstrates that she considers white lives as more valuable than black lives (230).

Furthermore, in spite of the Phelpses' admirable personal qualities, they are detaining a man they believe to be a fugitive in a shed shackled by a chain for monetary compensation. While Jim could easily slip the chain from the bed, it is secured to his ankle, which would make his flight far more dangerous and difficult, if not impossible. The first chance he has to talk to Huck and Tom privately, he asks them to "'hunt up a cold chisel to cut the chain off of his leg with, right away'" (255). Tom Sawyer, however, thinks this plan, as well as all of Huck's ideas, lacks "style." While several critics claim that Jim acquiesces to Tom's foolish antics, which undermines the novel's subversive potential, Jim is in an enormously dangerous and vulnerable situation and has only one person he can trust, Huck. He thus puts his faith in Huck rather than Tom, which is suggested throughout the final chapters by his continuous reference to Tom as "mars Tom" and "sah." Jim's use of these terms indicate that his relationship with Tom never progresses beyond the familiar to the personal and demonstrates his clear lack of confidence in Tom. Furthermore, Jim endures many indignities as a result of Tom's schemes but does so out of his commitment to survival rather than diminished sense of self. Life as a slave—more important, the New Orleans slave market that typically resulted in plantation slavery—is a much greater threat to dignity and sense of self, as well as physical safety.

The failed escape at the end of the novel also reinforces Jim's vulnerability. While Jim has shown himself to be a compassionate human being, he is also keenly cognizant of his perilous situation. After their disastrous evasion, Jim is fully aware that there is a search for him under way with men, dogs, and guns, as well as an injured white boy who has been involved in his escape attempt, which significantly amplifies the risk factor, particularly if this boy dies. He thus comes out of hiding to help the doctor not only out of compassion but also as a survival strategy. Twain emphasizes the danger he is in when he is brought back to town with his hands tied behind his back, and the men "wanted to hang Jim, for an example to all the other niggers around there, so they wouldn't be trying to run away like Jim done," but "the others said, 'don't do it, it wouldn't answer at all, he ain't our nigger, and his owner would turn up and make us pay for him'" (287–88). The men are deterred only by reason of the potential expense. The commercial value of slaves protected many from outright murder in the antebellum era, but in the post-Reconstruction period, monetary value no longer protected black Americans and the number of "southern fashion" lynching soars.

The issue of money has been noted by several critics as another failure of the novel, particularly Jim's "joy" regarding the forty dollars Tom gives him, suggesting that he has sold his dignity for this paltry sum. However, Jim's identity, escape attempt, and participation in the recent chaos has been exposed, which puts him in an enormously vulnerable position relative to the power (as well as the caprices) of this white community, a community that had recently wanted to lynch him as a warning but was deterred only by his value as property, which, as a manumitted slave, no longer protects him. Jim, therefore, must maneuver carefully, yet there is nothing to suggest that his plans to buy or steal his wife and children have changed; indeed, it is certainly reasonable to assume that his expressed joy regarding the money signifies the satisfaction of the strategist, or trickster, in moving his plan forty dollars closer toward this goal. Moreover, Jim needs to stay in the good graces of not only this white community but also the white community Tom will return to, which is where his wife and children are as well. Because he is now free, it is more than likely that Jim will return to St. Petersburg to reunite with his family. It is also important to note that it is when Huck expresses interest in Tom's suggestion that they "go for howling adventures amongst the Injuns, over in the Territory" that Jim decides to enlighten Huck with information regarding Pap (295). Huck has proven a loyal friend throughout the novel and, furthermore, is in possession of six thousand dollars, which could be beneficial to Jim. Moreover, because he is now free, he is susceptible to Missouri state code requiring free blacks to leave the state within six months, as we learn during Pap's rant about the black college professor.[16] Huck has been a crucial ally to Jim, and Jim's timely disclosure suggests he hopes to maintain this allegiance. Although the novel ends with Huck's intention to "light out for the Territory" because Aunt Sally wants to adopt him, the information he provides that "Tom's most well, now, and got his bullet around his neck on a watch-guard, and is always seeing what time it is" suggests that Tom and Huck have either returned home or soon will.

Ultimately, Jim does get his freedom and does so because he ran. Woodard and MacCann contend that Miss Watson's freeing Jim is "an extraordinary sign of benevolence on Miss Watson's part since she has no way of knowing before she dies that Jim has not slain Huck, as many townsfolk believe and as evidence about Huck's disappearance indicates" (150). However, it is highly unlikely that any slave owner would express regret for offering a reward for the capture of a fugitive the community believes is a murderer, particularly of a white boy, or publicly announce that she has manumitted him in her will. Tom's knowledge that "she was ashamed she ever was going to sell him down the river, and *said* so; and she set him free in her will" suggests that her motive was in response to public disapproval (291). The duration of their time on Jackson's Island indicates that Miss Watson does not experience a change of heart for several weeks, and because Jim ran at the same time the community discovers that Huck has been "murdered," his flight generates more attention than usual when suspicion turns from Pap to Jim, which likely exposed her intention to sell a slave south and break up a family. Given the public criticism when the Wilkses' slaves are sold, Miss

Watson may have also been subjected to public disapproval, particularly when suspicion shifts back to Pap, which implies that she manumitted Jim as a way to save face in the community rather than as a sincere gesture of remorse. Furthermore, by manumitting him in her will, Miss Watson indicates she is not willing to inconvenience herself while she is still alive. Had Jim not run after overhearing her discussion with the widow, it is highly likely she would have followed through with her plan to sell Jim and could have regretted her actions while counting her cash. Ultimately, Jim has the last laugh at the expense of the white community, particularly his mistress who has treated him "pooty rough" and intended to break her promise that she would never sell him "down to Orleans" (55). At the end of the novel, he is a free man with the liberty to work to buy or steal his family because he ran. Miss Watson did not free Jim; Jim's flight and the subsequent public opinion that resulted in shame did. Moreover, the months that Huck and Jim elude capture demonstrate that numerous whites were duped by an illiterate slave and a barely literate representative of the poor white class, frequently as a result of the covert assistance of the black community, which presents "the quality," more often than not, as rather foolish.

Twain again draws from a range of cultural and literary sources in his novel *Pudd'nhead Wilson* to create, I contend, his most crafty trickster, Roxy. The character Roxy is highly complex and functions as mammy and anti-mammy, tragic mulatto figure and subversive operator, but more important, she is also the speaking subject of sexual exploitation.

Dean McWilliams points out that the issue of the sexual exploitation of black women in Charles Chesnutt's story "'The Dumb Witness' allegorizes the problem of black speechlessness and its consequences during these years. . . . The silence imposed on blacks by violent intimidation is an important chapter in white America's denial of black personhood. Before Ellison's invisible man, there was Chesnutt's inaudible woman" (79). However, because of his editor's rejection of this particular tale, Chesnutt's inaudible woman would remain silent until the tale was finally published in 1974.[17] Twain also takes on these highly charged issues but turns to more covert tactics to challenge America's "denial of black personhood," particularly the denial of black womanhood that functioned to rationalize the sexual exploitation of black women.

Twain presents an account of sexual exploitation by completely omitting the story and then generating all of the narrative events out of this omission. Twain provides a brief history of the town and introduces each leading figure in a lengthy paragraph—with one exception. Twain writes,

"Then there was Colonel Cecil Burleigh Essex, another F.F.V. of formidable caliber—however, with him we have no concern" (4). Essex is briefly mentioned on two other occasions; the first reference notes his death, which is quickly overshadowed by the death of another important community figure, Roxy's master, Percy Driscoll. Essex is again mentioned in a much more compelling context when Roxy tells Tom the identity of his father: "'You ain't got no 'casion to be shame' o' yo' father, I kin tell you. He was de highest quality in dis whole town—Ole Virginny stock, Fust Famblies, he was. Jes' as good stock as de Driscolls en de Howards, de be's day dey ever seed'" (43). Twain's description of FFV ideology infuses this and other passages with rather biting satire, exposing, as Hilton Obenzinger points out, "the men of the First Families of Virginia [who] maintain their airs of moral superiority unaffected by the crude reality of their sexual exploitation. They regularly force themselves sexually on their slaves" (95). This section also more strategically satirizes theories of race by a character who looks white but is by birth—and thus legally—black and a slave who is passing as white but doesn't know it for most of his life. Because the details of the relationship between Roxy and Essex are left unrecorded, we do not know how or why the union occurred. Roxy may have been maneuvering to avoid more unwelcomed advances, like Harriet Jacobs, or may have been sexually victimized by Essex. There is also the possibility that there was genuine affection but laws and social mores kept them apart; nevertheless, the fact of the union, evidenced by the child, indicates that the story could not be told even in fiction, an enormously important omission. What we are given is the story of a woman with the sole responsibility of the care of her child and her master's child but with no legal rights to defend herself or protect her child.

Furthermore, because Roxy is "only one-sixteenth" black, she literally embodies four generations of the sexual exploitation of black women by white men; in other words, her mother, grandmother, great-grandmother, and great-great-grandmother were also subjected to the sexual advances of white men and bore their children. If these women were of similar age to Roxy when she gave birth, at twenty years old, the sexual victimization of Roxy's maternal ancestors dates back to the 1750s, close to—if not beyond—a one-hundred-year chronicle of this particular family's history of sexual exploitation. Moreover, because Roxy is a slave, inherited by the mother, none of these men freed their children. The constant references throughout the novel regarding the community's elite as descendants of the first families of Virginia suggest that, in addition to carrying into the Southwest rigid class distinctions and maintaining "the nicest requirements of the Virginia rule," these men of privilege and power also transported the practice of sexually violating black women (4). Indeed, the list of colonial and early American men of the Southern "aristocracy" alleged to have been engaged in sexual relationships with their slave women is a long one.[18]

Because Roxy bore only one child suggests that the relationship with Essex ended with her pregnancy. Further indication that the relationship was limited to a purely sexual rather than affectionate or romantic union is implied when Roxy is forced to confront the possibility of losing her baby. When the threat is made by Percy Driscoll to not only sell his slaves but to sell them "DOWN THE RIVER," Twain writes, "a profound terror had taken possession of her. Her child could grow up and be sold down the river! The thought crazed her with horror" (12-13). Roxy vows to kill her child and herself rather than allow her son to be sold, feeling she has no other options. Walter Johnson notes that "the disquieting stories of slaves who mutilated themselves to avoid the trade or women who killed their children to spare them from slavery" were common aspects of the slave trade (11). Twain notes that Roxy "gathered her baby to her bosom, now, and began to smother it with caresses," telling him "'Mammy's got to kill you,—how *kin* I do it! But yo' mammy ain't gwyne to desert you,—no, no; *dah*, don't cry—she gwyne *wid* you, she gwyne to kill herself, too'" (13). The scene highlights a mother's deep devotion to her child, the slaves' constant vulnerability of sale, and also indicates Roxy's isolation. Unlike Harriet Jacobs, who appealed to the father of her children to help her protect them, Roxy does not so much as consider going to her baby's father for help in spite of her desperate predicament. This omission suggests that she was simply sexually used by Essex and callously discarded once she became pregnant. Roxy has nowhere to turn and no one to turn to and considers infanticide and suicide her only option, a rather chilling reminder of the desperation of this powerless young mother. However, while preparing herself and her child for death, Roxy strikes upon an ingenious idea. Roxy turns to trickster tactics to orchestrate a brilliant plan to safeguard her child by switching the identities of the babies in her care.[19]

Roxy's plan is enormously risky and requires courage, cunning, and keen insight into members of the community, most notably its wealthy, powerful, and highly educated elite. Her master is not only a privileged white man, but his brother is "the chief citizen" of Dawson's Landing and is "Judge of the county court" (4). Roxy's bold scheme involves not only her master's son but this man's nephew, which is particularly risky because the Judge and his wife had for years longed "for the treasure of a child" but "the blessing never came—and was never to come" (4). The Judge's attachment to his nephew is strengthened by his own personal disappointment in having no children of his own. Furthermore, his "dearest friend" is the lawyer Pembroke Howard, "a fine, brave, majestic creature, a gentleman according to the nicest requirements of the Virginian rule, a devoted Presbyterian, and authority on the 'code,' and a man always courteously ready to stand up before you in the field if any act or word of his had seemed doubtful or suspicious to you, and explain it with any weapon you might prefer, from brad-awls to artillery" (4). Howard's readiness to stand against another man on the "field of honor" and risk death to defend his reputation, as well as his education and status in the community, indicates that to underestimate the power these men wield is highly dangerous.[20] Roxy is, however, up to the challenge and makes her move by strategically "calculating her chances," demonstrating keen insight regarding the members of this community (16).

Percy Driscoll's preoccupation with his problematic land deals are a constant distraction from his family and Roxy is, therefore, not overly concerned with him, and because the house servants have been sold and will be replaced by "'some mo' dat don't' know de chillen,'" Roxy surmises, "'—so *dat's* all right'" (16). Because it will be necessary to take the children in public, Roxy devises a plan to "'gaum dey mouths all aroun' wid jam, den dey can't *nobody* notice dey's changed. Yes,'" Roxy tells herself, "'I gwinter do dat till I's safe, if it takes a year'" (16). Roxy is confident in her ability to successfully carry out her plan but maintains one reservation. She notes, "'Dey ain't but one man dat I's afeard of, en dat's dat Pudd'nhead Wilson. Dey calls him a pudd'nhead, en says he's a fool. My lan', dat man ain't no mo' fool den I is! He's de smartes' man in dis town, less'n it's Jedge Driscoll, or maybe Pem. Howard'" (16). In spite of the community's assessment of Wilson, Roxy is a much shrewder judge of character and intelligence, which not only highlights her own superior intelligence but also shows her confidence in her intellect by noting that he is no more a fool than she is. Her only regret is compassion for her master's baby. She tells the child, "'I's sorry for you, honey; I's sorry, God knows I is,—but what *kin* I do, what *could* I do? Yo' pappy would sell him to somebody some time, en den he'd go down de river, sho', en I couldn't, couldn't, *couldn't* stan' it'" (15). Her pity is reserved only for the child because, as she states regarding his father, "'He ain't got no heart—for niggers he haint, anyways. I hates him, en I could kill him!'" (13). Roxy's opinion would likely be quite a revelation to Percy Driscoll, who considers the act of selling his slaves locally rather than down the river as "a noble and gracious thing, and he was privately well pleased with his magnanimity; and that night he set the incident down in his diary, so that his son might read it in after years and be thereby moved to deeds of gentleness and humanity himself" (12). Had Driscoll possessed Roxy's keen insight regarding his slaves, particularly Roxy's opinion (and likely the others as well) of his "magnanimity," there is little doubt she would have quickly found herself on a boat to New Orleans.

Roxy's switch has the added benefit of allowing her to fully indulge her love for her child and privately relish the privileges his new identity bestows upon "her darling." Twain notes that "with all her splendid common sense and practical every-day ability, Roxy was a doting fool of a mother" (19). Furthermore, because he is now "her master," Roxy must alter her behavior toward her son, but she has been trained by a lifetime and lifestyle that demands various performative masks and thus makes a rather smooth transition. Roxy is, however, no martyr and when her son's character flaws threaten her own security, she demonstrates the most crucial element of the trickster figure, survival. After losing her hard-earned savings, she appeals to "Marse Tom" for assistance but is rebuffed and insulted and "the fires of her old wrongs flamed up in her breast and began to burn fiercely. She raised her head slowly, till it was well up, and at the same time her great frame unconsciously assumed an erect and masterful attitude, with all the majesty and grace of her vanished youth in it" (38). Roxy boldly threatens to go to his uncle and "'tell him every las' thing I knows about you,'" and Tom quickly realizes that "even a former slave can remember for ten minutes insults and injuries returned for compliments and flatteries received, and can also enjoy taking revenge for them when the opportunity offers" (38). Tom drops to his knees and pleads to know what Roxy has on him, and Twain notes that "the heir of two centuries of unatoned insult and outrage looked down on him and seemed to drink in deep draughts of satisfaction" (39). Roxy's satisfaction is not simply personal but speaks for centuries of similar inheritors of "unatoned insult and outrage." It is a particularly satisfying moment in Roxy's life, and she tells Tom: "'Fine nice young white gen'lman kneelin' down to a nigger wench! I's wanted to see dat jes' once befor' I's called. Now, Gabrel blow de hawn, I's ready'" (39). Roxy's statement demonstrates Twain's insight into the private animosity and concealed hatred many slaves harbored regarding their masters, which again undermines the myth of mutual devotion and affection.

Roxy's most satisfying moment is the opportunity to abandon her performative mask and inform Tom of his racial and legal identity. The revelation is dangerous, particularly due to her keen insight into his character, but she has equipped herself with a stratagem to secure her safety. When Tom not only denies the information but comes at her with "a billet of wood," Roxy laughs at him and tells him, "'Does you think you kin sk'yer me? It ain't in you, nor de likes of you. I reckon you'd shoot me in de back, maybe, if you got a chance, for dat's jist yo' style, I knows you, thoo en thoo—but I don't mind gitt'n killed, becaze all dis is down in writin', en it's in safe hands, too, en de man dat's got it knows wharh to look for de right man whin I gits killed'" (41). Roxy is, however, signifying and "could have proven nothing to anybody, and her threat about the writings was a lie; but she knew the person she was dealing with, and had made both statements without any doubts as to the effect they would produce" (42). Roxy's strategy is not only effective but, because she is unable to read or write, it also insinuates that whomever Roxy solicited to document her account is also in possession of this dangerous information. Her intelligence is simply no match for this Yale dropout and is superior to the most educated and powerful members of this community as well.

Roxy comes up with several strategies to help Tom get out of debt to avoid further risk to his inheritance and her material security. However, when Tom learns that Wilson has devised a "scheme" to retrieve the twin's expensive dagger but does not reveal how "the thing was done," Tom tries for days to figure out Wilson's plan but fails. He then decides to "give Roxana's smarter head a chance at it"; she "thought it over, and delivered her verdict upon it. Tom said to himself, 'She's hit it, sure'" (76). Tom then exposes Wilson's secret scheme, noting that the reward for the knife was advertised but the reward for the thief was offered by "'private letter'" (76). Wilson "said to himself, 'Anybody with a reasonably good head would have thought of it. I am not surprised that Blake didn't detect it, I am only surprised that Tom did'" (76). Wilson would likely have been more surprised to learn that an illiterate former slave woman figured out his scheme in minutes while Tom, Justice Robinson, John Buckstone, and Constable Blake puzzled over it for days.

Roxy's "smarter head" is again necessary when Tom is robbed by "a brother-thief," and his inheritance is once more at risk. Roxy works out another especially bold plan, agreeing to allow Tom to sell her as a slave for a year and then buy her "free agin" (80). In this event, however, Roxy becomes the trickster-tricked. As she sits on the boat, "her practiced eye fell upon the tell-tale rush of water," and she quickly realizes, "'Oh, de good Lord God have mercy on po' sinful me—I's sole down de river!'" (82). The Arkansas cotton planter who buys her, however, makes a particularly bad bargain by purchasing an intellectually gifted woman who is also physically beautiful. As a result, he is able to benefit from her services for only just over two months rather than the lifetime servitude he believes that, because he paid for, he is entitled to.

For slave women, beauty could be a particularly sharp double-edged sword, drawing the unwanted sexual attention of white masters, male family members, friends, and overseers as well as the wrath of white women who often blamed the victims rather than the victimizers. Elizabeth Fox-Genovese notes that "ladies often displaced their anger at the husbands who 'protected' them onto the slave women whom their husbands' power entitled them to bully" (326). Indeed, many white women of the slaveholding class viewed slave women as Jezebels, "the dark, sensual temptress who seduced" white men into sinful allegiances (McLaurin 28). In her personal journal *A Diary from Dixie*, Mary Boykin Chesnut writes, "Under slavery, we live surrounded by prostitutes, yet an abandoned woman is sent out of any decent house. Who thinks any worse of a Negro or mulatto woman for being a thing we can't name" (21). While there is no textual evidence to suggest that the planter has any improper intentions toward Roxy, his wife is "not right down good lookin'" and becomes consumed with jealously over Roxy's superior beauty. She demands that her husband send Roxy out of the house to work with the "common fiel' han's" (85). Twain not only undermines many demeaning stereotypes of African Americans throughout the novel but also debunks many of the cultural binaries on which black stereotypes were established. The conflict between Roxy and her mistress functions in stark contrast to highly flattering stereotypes of white women, particularly of the planter class. Deborah Gray White explains that white women, "according to the prevailing Victorian image, were supremely virtuous, pious, tender, and understanding" and were "regarded as nurturing, empathetic, and morally directive," which are characteristics that this particular woman lacks entirely (56). The contrast between these women not only undermines antebellum racial and gender stereotypes but signifies on late nineteenth-century stereotypes as well, which is particularly important in light of the dangerous racial environment in the post-Reconstruction South. Susan Gillman contends that *Pudd'nhead Wilson*

> implicitly reminds readers that racial codes regulating miscegenation and classifying its mixed offspring did not disappear after Emancipation but rather were reenacted or reaffirmed, with even more rigorous definitions

> of whiteness, during the nineties, when anti-black representation took multiple forms, legal and extralegal. *Pudd'nhead Wilson* was serialized in *Century Magazine* in the middle of a decade that saw not only an epidemic of lynchings but also the beginnings of newly enacted Jim Crow laws defining the "Negro's place" in a segregated society, laws paralleled in the political sphere by a variety of voting restrictions to disenfranchise most blacks. (*Dark Twins* 55)

Furthermore, the practice of lynching black men was defended by the claim of protecting white women, and in this era, class became much less important than race. Ultimately, a white woman's word, any white woman, was incredibly dangerous to black men.[21]

Twain provides his most glaring condemnation of slavery in this section as well. Twain depicts this master as not "a bad man, he's good enough, as planters goes," but his "benevolent" authority is undermined by his difficult wife and her influence with the plantation's overseer (85). Not satisfied to simply send Roxy to the field, Roxy tells Tom that her mistress "'worked up de overseer agin me, she 'uz dat jealous en hateful; so de overseer he had me out befor' day in de mawnins en worked me de whole long day as long as dey 'uz any light to see by; en many's de lashin' I got becaze I couldn't come up to de work o' de stronges'. Dat overseer 'uz a Yank, too, outen New Englan', en anybody down South kin tell you what dat mean. *Dey* knows how to work a nigger to death, en dey knows how to whale 'em, too—whale 'em till dey backs is welted like a washboard'" (85–86). Twain not only undermines the nostalgic depictions of plantation life that were enormously popular in the post-Reconstruction era but also demonstrates the ambivalence of many Northerners regarding the institution in the antebellum era as well. The scene also sheds a rather glaring light on the brutalities of common slave-management practices.

Roxy's only comfort during this time is a "'little sickly nigger wench 'bout ten year ole dat 'uz good to me, and hadn't no mammy, po' thing, en I loved her en she loved me'" (86). When the girl attempts to slip Roxy a "roasted tater" because she knew the overseer did not give her enough to eat, he "'ketched her at it, en give her a lick acrost de back wid his stick which 'uz as thick as a broom-han'le, en she drop' screamin' on de ground', en squirmin' en wallerin' aroun' in de dust like a spider dat's got crippled'" (86). This act of cruelty inflames Roxy's bold nature, and she "'snatch de stick outen his han' en laid him flat'" (86). She then jumps on his horse and heads to the river. The slave community's commitment to protect one of their own is demonstrated when Roxy tells Tom, "'I had a pow'ful good start, caze de big house 'uz three mile back fum de river en on'y de work mules to ride dah on, en on'y niggers to ride 'em, en *dey* warn't gwyne to hurry—dey'd gimme all de chance dey could. Befo' a body could go to de house en back it would be long pas' dark, en dey couldn't track de hoss en fine out which way I went tell mawnin', en de niggers would tell 'em all de lies dey could 'bout it'" (87). In this scene, Twain highlights the trickster wisdom of the quarters by featuring the slaves signifying on the master to buy Roxy time, which also indicates their regard and support for the courageous fugitive.

Roxy's return to St. Louis and her confrontation with Tom has been interpreted as evidence of internalized racism and that she regards her and her son's "black blood" as inferior to their "white blood." Arthur G. Pettit contends that "although Mark Twain implies that the mulatto may have been warped by six generations of decadent FFV blood rather than by his drop of Negro blood, Driscoll's mother Roxana is convinced that her son's wickedness flows from his invisible mark of blackness . . . his whiteness thoroughly conceals both his wickedness and his blackness, until his bad behavior exposes them both" (350). The dialogue most noted to support this perspective is when Roxy chastises Tom for avoiding a duel with Luigi, which she regards as cowardly, and claims, "'It's de nigger in you, dat's what it is. Thirty-one parts o' you is white, en on'y one part nigger, en dat po' little one part is yo' *soul*'" (70). The comment, however, features Roxy engaging in another type of signifying known as playing the dozens, a verbal exchange of clever insults. This linguistic "game" is featured earlier in the novel between Roxy and Jasper. When Jasper "threatens" to "'come a-court'n'" Roxy, she responds, "'*You* is, you black mud-cat! Yah-yah-yah! I got sump'n better to do den 'sociat'n wid niggers as black as you is. Is ole Miss Cooper's Nancy done give you de mitten?'" (8). Jasper accuses Roxy of jealousy and calls her a "'huzzy,'" and she replies, "'Oh, yes, *you* got me, hain't you. 'Clah to goodness if dat conceit o' yo'n strikes in, Jasper, it gwyne kill you, sho'. If you b'longed to me I'd sell you down de river 'fo' you git too fur gone. Furst time I runs acrost yo' marster, I's gwyne to tell him so'" (8). Twain notes that "this idle and aimless jabber went on and on, both parties enjoying the friendly duel and each well satisfied with his own share of the wit exchanged" (8). Similarly, in her confrontation with Tom, Roxy is well aware that his "nigger blood" is a sore subject as well as a dangerous secret, and her comment functions as a painful jab. His inability to return an insult demonstrates his fear of Roxy. He avoids Roxy's verbal duel because of the same cowardice that led him to decline the physical duel. Furthermore, Roxy's ancestral list includes John Smith, Pocahontas, and "a nigger king outen Africa" (70). The amalgam of various types of "superior" blood functions to reinforce Roxy's insult by indicating that he is unworthy of any of his elite blood and also operates to satirize pseudoscientific theories regarding bloodlines and pedigrees. Gillman notes that the issue of "how biological differences determine the natural capacities of racial groups" functions as a "satire of racial classification by fractions of blood [and] mirrors problems in American race relations during both the antebellum period in which the novel is set and the 1890s when it was written" ("'Sure Identifiers'" 87).

Roxy engages in a similar dialogue with Tom after she makes her way back to St. Louis. When she confronts Tom in his hotel room, he attempts to outwit her by claiming to need get out of the room "to clear his brain in the fresh air," but Roxy, by far his intellectual superior, is not fooled by his feeble attempt to dupe her and tells him: "'Gwyne out to cle'r yo' brain! In de fust place you ain't got none to cle'r, en in de second place yo' ornery eye tole on you. You'd de low-downest hound dat ever—but I don tole you dat, befo'" (91). Roxy then explains her plan to reestablish her freedom and gives Tom several instructions emphasized by a knife in his back. Tom, however, rejects Roxy's plan and attempts to work out a scheme of his own; lacking his mother's sophisticated intelligence, he ultimately murders his "uncle."

The revelation at the end of the novel is made by the one man Roxy deduces, quite astutely, is her intellectual equal and thus a constant source of concern. When Wilson exposes Tom, Roxy does not register shock but rather "flung herself upon her knees, covered her face with her hands, and out through her sobs the words struggled—'De Lord have mercy on me, po' misable sinner dat I is!'" (113). Roxy's plea is, however, more likely an appeal for the mercy of the white community packed into this courtroom rather than "de Lord" because her "trick" has been exposed, which puts her in an enormously vulnerable position. "Tom" is ultimately sentenced to "imprisonment for life" (114). However, his "father's" creditors complain of irregularities regarding his status as inventory, and he is then sold "down the river" (114–15). In this scene, Twain also implies a critique of the community by Tom's sale south, which indicates that they put money ahead of their alleged "principles" and ultimately allow a "slave" to get away with the murder of his "master." Furthermore, several scholars regard the end of the novel as concluding with the defeat of both Roxy and her son. Jehlen contends that in the end, "Roxy's punishment is quite moderate," and "Roxy and her baby exit as the villains of a story they entered as the innocently wronged" (107). Obenzinger claims that "the 'tragedy' of the novel is partly Roxana's vain effort to outwit the system and its consequences in ruined lives and murder" (97). But Roxy did outwit "the system" for years, and moreover, was not punished at all. While she is heartbroken by her son's villainy and guilt-ridden by the real Tom continuing to pay her thirty-five dollars a month, she does find solace "in her church and its affairs" (114). The white community's lack of action regarding her deception suggests resistance to acknowledge that for twenty-three years, the entire white community has been duped by this illiterate former slave woman.

Throughout *Adventures of Huckleberry Finn* and *Pudd'nhead Wilson*, both Roxy and Jim operate by drawing on the trickster wisdom of the slaves' folktales to maneuver within an oppressive social and political environment. They are legally powerless to protect themselves or their families but use cunning to outwit much more powerful and, according to cultural wisdom, allegedly more intelligent characters. Yet in spite of the legal, educational, and financial advantages of many of the white characters featured in the novels, they are routinely undermined, outwitted, and often depicted as highly gullible victims of Jim's and Roxy's signifying skills. The tales of the storytellers Twain heard as a child not only exposed him to a form of entertainment but also introduced him to a rich cultural heritage that features prominently in two of his most compelling literary works, one of which became one of the most celebrated as well as controversial novels in American literary history.

Conclusion

The Tellers

"Not without Laughter"[1]

From the earliest years of the nation's history, the processes used to deny the full humanity of black Americans in order to justify slavery or impede the civil, political, or social rights of free blacks frequently shifted according to religious, political, legal, and scientific factors, but at the most fundamental level, the subject of race in America has consistently operated on the simple binary of white superiority and black inferiority. Religious leaders, social theorists, politicians, scientists, and authors (with several notable exceptions) incessantly revised a script asserting the natural superiority of whites and the inherent moral, cultural, and intellectual deficiencies of blacks. Because the majority of black Americans in the antebellum era were slaves, the theory of paternalistic protection of an inferior race informed the rhetoric of both proslavery advocates as well as most white abolitionists. Staunch advocates of emancipation and racial equality were typically regarded as extremists, and indeed, this point of view often led to violent if not deadly reactions. Writing in the 1830s, John Pendleton Kennedy was freer to critique slavery than later Southern authors would be, yet Kennedy cautiously approaches the issues of race and slavery satirically and subversively. His depiction of two distinct cultures, the white master class and the black slave community, demonstrates the unique cultural features of the slave community and highlights a black male character who functions as an antithesis to negative cultural stereotypes of black masculinity. Abe is independent, courageous, devoted to his mother, and highly intelligent. As a member of Swallow Barn's slave community, Abe is also guided by the community's elders rather than his master. These more experienced slaves pass along their cultural wisdom in the form of stories, providing Abe with a nontraditional education in the black community's trickster wisdom. Abe draws from his own superior intelligence as well as trickster tactics to form an ingenious plan of escape and does so with the unwitting assistance of the white community, ultimately exposing the "master class" as gullible dupes of Abe's master plan.

As the country grew progressively more divided over the controversies regarding slavery, Southern authors were pressured to either avoid the issue or vehemently defend the institution in their fiction. Kennedy revised and republished *Swallow Barn* in 1851, but because his readers were resistant to acknowledge the more critical and subversive elements of the text, the novel was simply considered an idyllic depiction of plantation life and did not generate the harsh criticism that authors more overtly criti[illegible] ery received. An essay published in the South's most pres[illegible] al, the *Southern Literary Messenger*, demonstr[illegible] ited political and artistic atmosphere for So[illegible] Duty of Southern Authors," the anonymous writer c[illegible]

> it is because of the world's ignorance of African slavery, as it exists at the South, that the world is arrayed against it. Let there be light upon this subject—let it be understood—and we need not fear to stand alone; for then, against the fanatical tide that threatens to overwhelm us, there will be raised a great moral break-water in our defense. As literature has been the most powerful weapon which the enemies of African slavery have used in their attacks, so, also, to literature we must look for the maintenance of our position, and our justification before the world. Let southern authors, men who see and know slavery as it is, make it their duty to deluge all the realms of literature with a flood of light upon this subject. . . . Southern literati, read here your duty to the South, your duty to yourselves and to posterity! With great moral force of literature overturn the unholy citadel erected by the slander, fanaticism, and malignity of your enemies. (242)

The author identifies Harriet Beecher Stowe as one of the South's greatest enemies and claims that "the success of 'Uncle Tom's Cabin,' is an evidence of the manner in which our enemies are employing literature for our overthrow. [It] is that effusion, in which a woman, instigated by the devil, sows the seeds of future strife" (243).

In a book review of *Uncle Tom's Cabin* in the same journal, another anonymous writer publishes not only a scathing review of the novel but a personal attack of Stowe as well. The reviewer addresses what he considers the controversial issue of women writers and adds, "But we beg to make a distinction between *lady* writers and *female* writers. . . . Where a writer of the softer sex manifests, in her production, a shameless disregard of truth and of those amenities which so peculiarly belong to her sphere of life, we hold that she has forfeited the claim to be considered a lady, and with that claim all exemption from the utmost stringency of critical punishment" (630). The novel was banned throughout the South, and Stowe received death threats from angry Southerners; indeed, one package contained the severed ear of a slave. Southern readers were infuriated over Stowe's depiction of slavery, but the novel has also been a constant source of controversy regarding her black character portraits. Yet, like Kennedy, Stowe also features two distinct cultures, the white community and a black community that is often pitted against the white community. Stowe demonstrates keen insight into the distinct cultural mores and social values of the black community and creates several characters who undermine oppressive circumstances by drawing on the cultural wisdom of their folktales. Moreover, several of Stowe's most crafty and intelligent characters are females, notably Chloe, Topsy, and Cassy.

In spite of the South's angry reaction to *Uncle Tom's Cabin*, Stowe refused to be intimidated and continued to critique slavery in her writing. In 1856, Stowe published her second antislavery novel, *Dred: A Tale of the Great Dismal Swamp*. The novel was largely written in response to Southern criticism as well as to black intellectual leaders like Martin Delany who felt that Stowe drew on negative cultural stereotypes in *Uncle Tom's Cabin*, particularly Tom's passivity. The revolutionary protagonist of *Dred* is an escaped slave living in the swamp, and in this novel, Stowe is much more direct in presenting her views on slavery and race. In his introduction to the novel, Robert S. Levine contends that Stowe "attempts new strategies of point of view that would allow for a fuller development of black revolutionary perspectives and implicitly rejects African colonizationism—endorsed in *Uncle Tom's Cabin*—as a solution to the nation's racial problems. . . . In many respects, *Dred* is Stowe's most honest and vulnerable fiction, revealing an antebellum novelist who is willing to take risks" (x). Because Stowe shifts her aesthetic tactics, *Dred* is simply not as rich as *Uncle Tom's Cabin* and the characters lack the complexities of her most well-known novel, particularly the subversive trickster tactics featured throughout *Uncle Tom's Cabin*. In *Dred*, Stowe overtly demonstrates highly intelligent black characters who aggressively react to their oppression by running and creating a community of fugitives living in the swamp. And like Stowe's George Harris and Jim Selden, these fugitives are also prepared to defend their liberty with deadly force if necessary. Stowe remained a leading figure in the abolitionist movement and, as she put it in a letter to a friend, committed "to inspire universally through the country a kindlier feeling toward the negro race" (qtd. in Reynolds 130).

In his last novel, *The Confidence-Man: His Masquerade,* Herman Melville again features trickster tactics but his ambiguous narrator much more closely resembles the con-men tricksters featured in the Southwest humor tradition than the trickster heroes celebrated in black folktales. Reviews of the novel were negative and dismissive and, in addition to a number of personal issues, led Melville to abandon writing and take up professional lecturing. In his later years, he worked as an inspector at New York's Custom House. *Benito Cereno* is Melville's most aggressive attack on the institution of slavery as well as racism, and it is in this work that Melville drew most heavily on black aesthetic techniques in creating one of the craftiest trickster figures in American literary history. The novella is unique because, although Melville drew from a number of sources, the similarities between Babo and the Signifying Monkey—as well as the similar dynamics between the Signifying Monkey, the Lion, and the Elephant and Babo, Captain Delano, and Benito Cereno—suggest that this unique cycle was an important influence in Melville's creative process. Moreover, Babo does not simply expose the flawed logic of racist ideology but mocks the tenets of racial theorists as well.

After emancipation, advocates of equal civil rights and political protection for African Americans were met with "massive resistance" by the white South. Leon Litwack notes that "whites employed terror, intimidation, and violence to doom Reconstruction, not because blacks had demonstrated incompetence but because they were rapidly learning the uses of political power, not because of evidence of black failure but the far more alarming evidence of black success. This was clearly unacceptable to a people who deemed themselves racially superior and who resisted any evidence to the contrary" (xiii). In the post-Reconstruction era, black Americans were systematically disenfranchised, deterred from educational opportunities, economically trapped in the practice of sharecropping or the convict-lease system, denied due process in the courts, socially and physically controlled by Jim Crow laws and ordinances, and routinely terrorized by violence.

From the end of Reconstruction to the civil rights movement, an estimated thirty-five hundred black Americans were lynched by white mobs. The victims were typically men accused of anything from petty theft, impudence, attempting to vote, or, the most dangerous allegation, raping a white woman. Most were, as Litwack points out, "simply at the wrong place at the wrong time" (307). Moreover, white lynch mobs were not content to merely hang the accused but often engaged in vicious torture, including dousing the victim with gasoline and burning him alive, castration, dismemberment of body parts (which participants kept as souvenirs), and then terminating the victim's life by gunshot or at the end of a rope. As DuBois notes in *Black Reconstruction in America*, "The slave went free; stood for a brief moment in the sun; then moved back toward slavery. The whole weight of America was thrown to color caste. . . . A new slavery arose. The upward moving of white labor was betrayed into wars for profit based on color caste. Democracy died save in the hearts of black folk" (30). To cope in this oppressive white world of injustice and intimidation, African Americans responded in much the same way they had during slavery: by utilizing trickster wit as a means of survival. John W. Roberts explains that

> the continued performance of the trickster tales in freedom suggests that, despite the insertion of the "law" between African Americans and the types of rewards often associated with the trickster during slavery, they still discovered situations and ways in which the subversive and manipulative behaviors associated with the trickster could be advantageous in dealing with white power. For example, the ease with which black storytellers substituted Old Boss for Old Master without altering the plots of tales in which John served as the central character strongly suggests a black perception of the work situation as one little changed from slavery. Certainly individual whites still maintained and exercised enough control over the economic lives of African Americans to make aggressive behavior in dealing with them extremely costly. In addition, the work situation remained one in which the kinds of face-to-face interaction between African Americans and whites which made the trickster an effective model of behavior were little altered. (187)

While trickster tactics allowed African Americans to "create a world of their own 'behind the veil,'" as W. E. B. DuBois described it, the white authors studied in this project were not only given rare access to this world but astute enough to understand the artistic merits and the complexities of a culture and lifestyle dramatically different from their own (Litwack xvi). Indeed, black aesthetics would feature prominently in many of their most celebrated narratives. Moreover, as Wayne Mixon points out, "it required great courage for a white southerner to take the black man's part in the highly charged atmosphere around the turn of the century. . . . The opponents of racist thinking were perceived as 'sickly humanitarians who refused to face facts'" (465). Mixon credits Joel Chandler Harris as an author who "fought the almost hopeless battle against racism in the only way he could—subversively, through fiction" (465). Harris's Uncle Remus collections continue to dominate scholarly attention of Harris's writing, but a number of less well known short stories also feature Harris subversively battling racism. In his fiction, Harris depicts the slaveholding master class, the slave community, and the plain-folk white community. Harris suggests that nonslaveholding rural farmers share more cultural features in common with the black community than with wealthy whites, most notably rich oral storytelling traditions featuring distinct trickster figures. Yet while the trickster figures highlighted in the frontier humor tradition tend use wit in the con game or as a form of retaliation, black tricksters use wit as a means of survival. Free Joe, for example, must perform the role of a humble and nonthreatening black man, whereas Blue Dave uses trickster tactics to evade his pursuers for years. Balaam manipulates his master to avoid fieldwork, and Duncan strategically draws on his mixed racial identity to escape the slavery his father sold him into as well as retaliate for his father's betrayal. Harris's short fiction also provides very different perspectives regarding life in the South during the antebellum and post-Reconstruction eras than many of his contemporaries, such as Thomas Dixon and Thomas Nelson Page. Page engages in the nostalgic perspective of the Old South of the plantation tradition, which was enormously popular, particularly with Northern readers, whereas in *The Clansman*, Thomas Dixon draws on and energizes the myth of the black as beast, sexually preying on vulnerable white women. Harris's works strategically undermine both of these narrative points of view.

Harris was, moreover, much more direct regarding his view of race relations in his editorial pieces. Harris frequently cited the work and perspectives of the era's leading black intellectuals, Booker T. Washington and W. E. B. DuBois. Harris biographer Walter M. Brasch notes that "in one of his most forceful editorials, published in the *Constitution* of 11 May 1883, Harris struck out against racism, arguing, 'There is no reason why any southern man, woman or child should have any prejudice against the negro race. There is no ground for it, no excuse for it. . . . The southern editor who makes the discussion of this problem an excuse for attacking and abusing the negroes grossly misrepresents his reader and the people of his section'" (121-22). Against intense Southern opposition, Harris "called for a repeal of numerous Jim Crow laws" and "in his folklore, in articles, and in editorials, Harris deplored the belief, advanced by the science of the day and advocated by Grady (his co-editor), that Blacks were genetically inferior to Whites" (122). Numerous biographers have noted Harris's shyness, but as his fiction and editorial writing demonstrates, this particular character trait did not deter him from writing against the political grain in an increasingly dangerous social and political environment.

Like Harris, Twain was also deeply concerned with racial issues and chose to allegorize these problems by setting his novels *Adventures of Huckleberry Finn* and *Pudd'nhead Wilson* in the antebellum era. This distance allowed Twain to comment on racial issues in an era that was growing increasingly more hostile toward black Americans. Twain's regard for the minstrel tradition has had a tendency to overshadow his admiration for black folk art, particularly storytelling traditions, but Twain, I contend, drew much more heavily on the black trickster tradition in his character portraits of Jim and Roxy than from minstrelsy. Throughout both novels, Twain depicts an oppressive world governed by white laws and social mores, requiring black characters to maneuver subversively and strategically. After overhearing the widow's plans to sell him, Jim is forced to take immediate action, particularly in order to maintain any hope of seeing his family again. Throughout the course of the novel, Twain emphasizes the constant danger Jim is in, and as a fugitive, he is no longer pitted against a single owner but now against all whites. He has to maneuver carefully and strategically, and his smartest move is aligning himself with Huck, who functions as a cover for his flight. Jim's freedom at the end of the novel demonstrates that he survives by trickster wit rather than minstrel dependence.

In *Pudd'nhead Wilson*, Twain creates his most savvy and complex trickster through the character Roxy. Twain also satirically critiques the white community's violence, injustice, and the sexual abuse of black women. Moreover, this is the world Roxy must maneuver within, but she is a bold and intelligent woman who draws on her cultural inheritance to battle the injustices of her powerlessness. With no social or legal protection, Roxy's only weapon is her intelligence, which she draws on to form an ingenious plan to protect her baby. Roxy switches the identities of the children in her care, which requires cunning insight into the powerful members of the white community. But for her son's character flaws, he would likely have enjoyed his position as an upper-class white man for the rest of his life. His insulting treatment of the woman who raised him, particularly in a time of great need, is his most egregious mistake. When Roxy asks him for help, Tom saw simply a humble former slave groveling for his assistance rather than the bold and intelligent woman Roxy soon reveals herself to be. He also quickly learns that after years of abuse from the son for whom she sacrificed so much, like Brer Rabbit, this woman could also be vindictive when provoked. Twain's depictions of Jim and Roxy feature black characters drawing on the wit and wisdom of the black oral tradition to accomplish the trickster's most important agenda, survival.

A significant amount of the material I use in this book originated from artists who are anonymous and remain nameless because they were slaves. I am regretfully unable to credit their gifts by including their names in the bibliography. The best I can do is to dedicate to them this book. It is not enough. The tellers were not only artisans in their own right but cultural preservers, teachers, and leaders. But more important, they were real people who lived real lives. They were men, women, and children who loved, lost, hated, fought, worked, suffered, played, prayed, danced, and—what seems so difficult to comprehend in light of the historical fact of their enslavement—laughed. Most lived their entire lives as slaves, but they defied and repudiated the injustices of the masters' authority by demonstrating that while their blood, sweat, and tears could be compelled to flow by the force of the lash, the spirit, the song, the story, their sense of self-worth, their compassion, and their language could not be enslaved. They not only provided their fellow bondsmen and bondswomen with entertainment; they passed along their culture's wisdom and its art as well. Glenda Carpio notes that "black American humor began as a wrested freedom, the freedom to laugh at that which was unjust and cruel in order to create distance from what would otherwise obliterate a sense of self and community. Until well into the twentieth century, it had to be cloaked in secrecy lest it be read as transgressive and punished by violence" (4). The secretive nature of black folk culture in general and black humor traditions in particular lead to assumptions about the black community that persisted well into the twentieth century. Lawrence Levine points out that slaves were regarded as "the community-less, culture-less, atomized slaves pictured in so many history books and history classes—the tabula rasa upon whom the whites could write anything they wished" (xvii).

Throughout the nineteenth century, the perspective of the cultureless black community was widely held by whites because of the oral nature of slave culture, which was largely a result of systematic oppression as well as laws prohibiting teaching slaves to read and write. As Ralph Ellison's Invisible Man asks: "We who write no novels, histories or other books. What about us?" (432). As many scholars have observed, the answer to this question has often been the erroneous assumption that those who did not write did not create and thus had no culture. In spite of many studies that challenge this notion, Stephen F. Soitos observes that this perspective has proven particularly tenacious. He notes that

> the issue of African American cultural identity has long been debated, and the debate is far from over. Current African American vernacular criticism attempts to establish a coherent system of principles derived from the rural and urban culture of everyday African Americans. Therefore, an important question lies at the root of any discussion of African American accomplishments: Is there an African-American culture? If so, how does one define it? Berndt Ostendorf pinpoints the problem in his book *Black Literature in White America* (1982): "The history of blacks in America has too often been treated as a progress report on acculturation." . . . Perspectives such as these demean African Americans by suggesting that their historical reliance on white culture was their only motivation. In essence this line of argument denies a distinct heritage of black culture, rejects the possibility that the African past had any psychological or cultural influence on American blacks, and implies that African Americans were completely fragmented and destroyed as social entities in America. (5–7)

However, as Lawrence Levine points out, were these assumptions accurate, slaves

> would have been incapable of creating a music so deeply dependent upon a shared culture and a sense of community. Slaves had a reservoir of musical lines, phrases, and structures into which they dipped as they sang and told tales. It gave onlookers the sense of improvisation, but they weren't totally improvising. They were utilizing elements of their cultural reservoir even as they engaged in acts of pure creation and shaped new lines to the songs and new incidents in the stories, some of which would find a place in the reservoir. Their acts of creation were both individual and communal, looking both back to the African cultures from which they had come and around to the American cultures they lived amidst. (xvii)

Folklorists such as Zora Neale Hurston, Melville Herskovits, J. Mason Brewer, Richard M. Dorson, and others worked to not simply validate black folk culture but further to preserve an important American artistic tradition.

Later twentieth-century scholars such as Henry Louis Gates Jr., Toni Morrison, Houston Baker, Trudier Harris, and many others provide the theoretical tools necessary to approach the various complexities of black vernacular expressive art. Soitos notes that

> vernacular criticism is an exciting and enlightening tool that can be used for support and defense of the heritage of African Americans and their humanitarian and community values. This type of criticism helps to connect the varied and powerful creations of African Americans by developing a critical vocabulary based not on Euro-Americentric models but on African American and Afrocentric worldviews. Vernacular criticism challenges negative attacks on black Americans which suggested or suggest that African Americans have no real culture of their own. Furthermore, rather than divorce itself from the social value of African American texts, it enhances these values by demonstrating ways in which average rural and urban African American people transformed the dominant folk and formal cultural formulas, indicating their own cultural survival and triumph over oppression. (xii)

Cultural survival was often maintained by the cathartic humor of the trickster tales, which served many purposes in the slave community, yet these oral traditions also provide important information regarding their daily lives as well. A few examples demonstrate a wide range of cultural and historical insights. For example, a common theme in many tales features the trickster subversively acquiring food, which suggests that slaves routinely suffered from insufficient diets. A brief tale often cited (indeed, a version is featured in Toni Morrison's novel *Beloved*) develops by the dialogue between a master accusing his slave of stealing. The master states: "'You scoundrel, you ate my turkey,' the master said to the slave. 'Yes, suh, Massa,' the slave replied, 'You got less turkey but you sho nuff got mo' Nigger'" (qtd. in Watkins *African American Humor* 25). Another tale also features a subversive strategy to procure food and highlights the slaves functioning as a trickster community as well. In *Black Culture and Black Consciousness*, Lawrence Levine includes the "Malitis" story:

> Josie Jordan, born a slave in Tennessee, recalled a story her mother told her about a stingy master who fed his slaves so poorly that "they ribs would kinda rustle against each other like corn stalks a-drying in the hot winds. But they gets even one hog-killing time, and it was funny, too, Mammy said." The day before seven fat hogs were to be killed, one of the field hands ran to the master and told him, "The hogs is all died, now they

won't be any meats for the winter." When the master arrived on the scene he found a group of sorrowful-looking slaves who informed him that the hogs had died of "malitis" and acted as if they were afraid to touch the dead animals. The master ordered them to dress the meat anyway and to keep it for the slave families. "Don't you all know what is malitis?" Mrs. Jordan's mother would ask while she rocked with laughter. "One of the strongest Negroes got up early in the morning, long 'fore the rising horn called the slaves from their cabins. He skitted to the hog pen with a heavy mallet in his hand. When he tapped Mister Hog 'tween the eyes with that mallet, 'malitis' set in mighty quick." (127)

Other tales violate highly serious taboo subjects, such as physical violence against white women. Mel Watkins includes a tale titled "The Fight":

One plantation owner said to the other, "My colored guy can whip your guy." The other boss said, "I'll be damned if he can." So they signed up for a fight, them two farm owners. And so each man went and told the tough colored guy on his place that he got a fight coming up. Each tough guy went off to himself thinking, "I can't whip that bastard." Jim said, "I can't whip John," and John said, "I can't whip Jim." But back in slavery times you can't back out. So they set a date for the fight. So the boss said to each colored guy, "What do you want for the fight? What are you going to wear?" Jim he thought he'd make a display to frighten John. He asks his boss to make a link chain, about four feet long, with an iron stake at the end of it, to drive into the ground, and to put an iron ring in his nose. And he'll be scratching and kicking up dirt when John comes, like a bull, and running back and forward on the chain. And his boss would be trying to keep him quiet. "Steady, steady there, Jim, whoa, just a few minutes." When John's boss asked him what he wanted, he said, "Just give me Old Puss to ride down to the battling ground." He was quiet-like, tough but quiet. He was slow riding down—he almost like to be late, and forfeit the bet. That was a great big day, a holiday, people from twenty miles around was there in their horses and buggy and ox teams. So when he was late, his Missus got worried, and as soon as he came riding down she went over to him. John saw Jim on the chain and he was studying how to scare him, he was already scared himself. He's thinking fast, working his brain. When his Missus come over, he knew she would say something pretty flip. So he thinks: the minute she opens her mouth, I'll slap her. Missus said, "What kept you? Why you so late?" (*Very rough*) John he slapped her face. Jim pulled up the stake and ran, sold out, forfeited the fight. So the loser, Jim's master, had to pay off John's boss the three or four thousand dollars they'd put in a bag. Still, John's boss got mad about his wife being slapped. He asked John, "What was the idea slapping my wife?" "Well, Jim knowed if I slapped a white woman I'd a killed him, so he ran." (*African American Humor* 49–50)

In another story, a slave outwits his master to gain his freedom with the added benefit of insulting his master in the story "The Laugh That Meant Freedom":

Nehemiah, a clever slave who had a reputation for avoiding work with his wit and humor, had been transferred from one master to another because of his ability to outwit his owners. Then David Wharton, known as the most cruel slave master in Southwest Texas, heard about Nehemiah. He bought him and vowed to "make that rascal work." The morning after Nehemiah was purchased, David Wharton approached him and said, "Now you are going to work, you understand. You are going to pick four hundred pounds of cotton today." "Wal, Massa, dat's aw right," answered Nehemiah, "but ef Ah meks you laff, won' yuh lemme off fo' terday?" "Well," said David Wharton, who had never been known to laugh, "if you make me laugh, I won't only let you off for today, but I'll give you your freedom." "Ah decla', Boss," said Nehemiah, "yuh sho' is uh good lookin' man." "I am sorry I can't say the same thing about you," retorted David Wharton. "Oh, yes, Boss, yuh could," Nehemiah laughed out, "yuh could if yuh tole ez big uh lie ez Ah did." David Wharton could not help laughing at this; he laughed before he thought. Nehemiah got his freedom. (*African American Humor* 24)

In her essay, "Unspeakable Things Unspoken: The Afro-American Presence in American Literature," Toni Morrison suggests that a "re-examination of founding literature in the United States for the unspeakable unspoken may reveal those texts to have deeper and other meanings, deeper and other power, deeper and other significances" (14). The names of the white authors studied in this project are widely familiar, and they made important contributions to America's literary history, but the names of the slaves who shared their art with these authors remain largely "unspoken," yet the traces of their voices in these literary works reveal deeper, other, and powerful significances, and, I contend, we would not have these masterpieces of American literature without these nameless artisans.

NOTES

INTRODUCTION

1. Ellison, *Invisible Man*, 130.

2. Thomas, *From Folklore to Fiction*, 81.

3. For more information regarding call and response, see Floyd, "Ring Shout!"

4. Emory Holms II interview, *Los Angeles Times*, "Heavyweight with the Gift of Gab," Dec. 21, 1997.

5. Ellison, "Change the Joke."

6. Peter Kolchin notes that "the basis of the seventeenth-century work force in the southern two-thirds of the English mainland colonies—were European laborers. Most came as indentured servants. . . . During their indenture, servants were essentially slaves, under the complete authority of their masters; masters could (and readily did) apply corporal punishments to servants, forbid them to marry, and sell them (for the duration of their terms) to others" (9).

7. For information regarding slave laws and codes in the South by state, see Clayton E. Jewett and John O. Allen, *Slavery in the South: A State-by-State History* (Westport, CT: Greenwood Press, 2004).

8. In the original draft, Jefferson writes: "He has waged cruel war against human nature itself, violating its most sacred rights of life and liberty in the persons of a distant people who never offended him, captivating & carrying them into slavery in another hemisphere, or to incur miserable death in their transportation thither. This piratical warfare, the opprobrium of INFIDEL powers, is the warfare of the CHRISTIAN king of Great Britain. Determined to keep open a market where MEN should be bought & sold, he has prostituted his negative for suppressing every legislative attempt to prohibit or to restrain the execrable commerce" (242). See "Sources and Revision" in William Wells Brown's *Clotel; or The President's Daughter: A Narrative of Slave Life in the United States*, ed. Robert S. Levine (Boston: Bedford/St. Martin's, 2000).

9. In *Defending Slavery: Proslavery Thought in the Old South: A Brief History with Documents* (Boston: Bedford/St.Martin's, 2003), Paul Finkelman provides a number of examples of proslavery speeches and essays.

10. Owen Lovejoy was an Illinois congressman and brother of abolitionist leader Elijah P. Lovejoy, who was shot and killed in the warehouse of his abolitionist paper in 1837. See Reynolds, *Mightier Than the Sword*, 95.

11. See Fox-Genovese, *Within the Plantation Household*; Gray White, *Ar'n't I a Woman*; and Victoria E. Bynum, *Unruly Women: The Politics of Social and Sexual Control in the Old South* (Chapel Hill: University of North Carolina Press, 1992).

12. See Melville Herskovits, *The Myth of the Negro Past* (repr. Boston: Beacon Press, 1990); Babacar M'Baye, *The Trickster Comes West: Pan-African Influence in Early Black Diasporan Narratives* (Jackson: University Press of Mississippi, 2009); Gates, *Signifying Monkey*, 4.

13. For collections of folktales, see Abraham, *Deep Down in the Jungle*; Hughes and Bontemps, *Book of Negro Folklore*; Zora Neale Hurston, *Mules and Men* (Philadelphia: Lippincott, 1935); Harold Courlander, *A Treasury of Afro-American Folklore: The Oral Literature, Traditions, Recollections, Legends, Tales, Songs, Religious Beliefs, Customs, Sayings and Humor of Peoples of African Descent in the Americas* (New York: Marlowe, 1996); Henry D. Spalding, ed., *Encyclopedia of Black Folklore and Humor*, 3rd ed. (Middle Village, NY: Jonathan David, 2010); and Mel Watkins, ed., *African American Humor: The Best Black Comedy from Slavery to Today* (Chicago: Lawrence Hill Books, 2002).

14. Fishkin, *Was Huck Black?*

15. William L. Andrews in *To Tell a Free Story: The First Century of Afro-American Autobiography, 1760–1865* (Urbana: University of Illinois Press, 1988) also notes that fugitives utilized trickster wisdom in their escapes but associates trickster tactics with negative qualities, such as duplicity, and contends that trickster traits are then abandoned when fugitives have attained freedom.

16. In her introduction to *Swallow Barn*, Lucinda MacKethan notes that when Kennedy revised the 1832 edition, "Kennedy satirizes the setting less and the characters more," specifically the white characters. MacKethan also points out that "in the 1851 edition, Meriwether's monologue takes on more pointed political overtones. Yet the 1851 edition also reveals Kennedy's increased sensitivity to some of the degrading remarks about blacks in the first edition" (xxv).

17. See also Trudier Harris's book, *The Scary Mason-Dixon Line: African American Writers and the South* (Baton Rouge: Louisiana State University Press, 2009); and Gunning, *Race, Rape, and Lynching*.

Chapter 1

1. For examples of the antebellum plantation school, see George Tucker's *The Valley of Shenandoah; or, Memoirs of the Graysons* (1825); G. P. R. James's *The Old Dominion* (1831); and James Hungerford's *The Old Plantation and What I Gathered There in an Autumn Month* (1859). For literary treatment of cavalier ideology, see William Alexander Caruthers's *The Cavaliers of Virginia*, 2 vols. (1834–35).

2. Nat Turner led a rebellion in Virginia in 1831 that resulted in the deaths of sixty whites and an estimated one hundred blacks. Turner eluded capture for over a month but was eventually convicted, sentenced to death, and hanged on November 5, 1831. The rebellion resulted in new laws and codes throughout the South that imposed much greater restrictions on blacks and increased white fear of slave rebellion. For more information, see Scot French, *The Rebellious Slave: Nat Turner in American Memory* (New York: Houghton Mifflin, 2004); for an examination of the relationship between Kennedy's novel and Thomas Gray's *The Confessions of Nat Turner* (1831), see the essay by Andrews, "Inter(racial)textuality in Nineteenth-Century Southern Narrative."

3. It is possible that without the chapters "The Quarter," and "A Negro Mother, Abe," Kennedy's novel would have fallen into the obscurity from literary history of other antebellum plantation novels.

4. For an extensive literary and historical treatment of Meriwether's flaws, see Mayfield, *Counterfeit Gentlemen*.

5. For a perspective on this national holiday from the slave community's point of view, see Frederick Douglass's 1852 speech, "What to the Slave Is the Fourth of July," in *Great Speeches by African Americans: Frederick Douglass, Sojourner Truth, Dr. Martin Luther King, Jr., Barack Obama, and Others*, ed. Janet Baine Kipito (Mineola, NY: Dover, 2006), 13–34.

6. For more information on the theory of noblesse oblige, see Paul Finkelman, *Defending Slavery: Proslavery Thought in the Old South: A Brief History with Documents* (Boston: Bedford/St.Martin's, 2003), notably, the Reverend A. T. Holmes's 1851 essay, "The Duties of Christian Masters," and for proslavery defense of the institution, see South Carolina governor and senator James Henry Hammond's 1858 "Mudsill Speech." In this speech, Hammond claims that "the greatest strength of the South arises from the harmony of her political and social institutions. This harmony gives her a frame of society, the best in the world. . . . In all social systems there must be a class to do the menial duties, to perform the drudgery of life. That is, a class requiring but a low order of intellect and but little skill. Its requisites are vigor, docility, fidelity. Such a class you must have, or you would not have that other class which leads progress, civilization, and refinement. It constitutes the very mud-sill of society. . . . Fortunately for the South, she found a race adapted to that purpose to her hand. A race inferior to her own, but eminently qualified in temper, in vigor, in docility, in capacity to stand the climate, to answer all her purposes. . . . Our slaves are black, of another and inferior race. The *status* in which we have placed them is an elevation. They are elevated from the condition in which God first created them, by being made our slaves. None of that race on the whole face of the globe can be compared with the slaves of the South. They are happy, content, unaspiring, and utterly incapable, from intellectual weakness, ever to give us any trouble by their aspirations" (86–87).

7. For more information regarding slave laws in Virginia, see Sally E. Hadden's *Slave Patrols: Law and Violence in Virginia and the Carolinas* (Cambridge, MA: Harvard University Press, 2001).

8. Hiring an overseer was also a way to signify class status, but as Peter Kolchin, Bertram Wyatt-Brown, Eugene Genovese, and other scholars point out, white overseers were a constant problem for masters due to issues such as sexual misconduct with female slaves, excessive abuse of slaves that restricted their ability to work, stealing, and a host of other matters.

9. For more information on clothing for adult slaves, see Genovese, *Roll, Jordan, Roll,* 550.

10. For more information regarding housing conditions for slaves, see Genovese, *Roll, Jordan, Roll,* 524–35.

11. See ibid., 535-40.

12. For an extensive perspective regarding the changing aspects of the image of African Americans and the swamp, see Cowan, *Slave in the Swamp.*

13. Wilma King in *Stolen Childhood: Slave Youth in Nineteenth-Century America*, 2nd ed. (Bloomington: Indiana University Press, 2011), also notes the importance and influence of parents and older slaves on younger slaves rather than the master or other whites.

14. For information on the Denmark Vesey plot and others, see Davis, "Some Nineteenth-Century Slave Conspiracies and Revolts" (205–30) in his book *Inhuman Bondage,* and Stuckey, "Remembering Denmark Vesey" (19–31) in *Going through the Storm.*

15. For a complete list of Virginia's slave laws, see Guild, *Black Laws of Virginia.*

16. Douglass, *My Bondage and My Freedom.*

17. Twain addresses this dilemma in *Adventures of Huckleberry Finn* when Jim overhears Miss Watson telling the widow that she stands to gain eight hundred dollars for selling Jim. Jim tells Huck, "I never waited to hear the rest, I lit out mighty quick."

18. Jean Fagan Yellin contends that Abe is the novel's "closest approximation of a true hero" (59). Lucinda MacKethan also regards Abe as a "a real hero" and adds that his "noble enactment of a code" is "suicidal" ("Introduction" xxvi). Scott Romine sees this character as operating according to the cavalier code and contends that the story of Abe functions as the narrator Mark Littleton's "fantasy text" (90). By allowing this character to go beyond the limits of plantation life, Romine asserts that Abe's "truculence begins to appear nothing more than a thirst for adventure" and that the cavalier code "is not simply a code that allows Abe's actions to be domesticated after the fact; it is a code that he has lived by, after his fashion, all along" (90). William L. Andrews also sees Abe as a type of "chivalric hero" but reads the character in the context of the Nat Turner rebellion and contends that Kennedy transforms "negro subversion into negro heroism" and that Abe's heroism is "noble self-sacrifice" (310).

19. See Hamilton, *People Could Fly.*

20. Reed parodies the fugitive slave narrative and the flying African folktale in his novel *Flight to Canada* by featuring his fugitive escaping on board a jumbo jet to Canada.

Chapter 2

1. This chapter title signifies on Leslie Fiedler's essay, "Come Back to the Raft Ag'in, Huck Honey!"; *Partisan Review* (June 1948). Another essay that signifies on this title is Mark Royden Winchell's essay "Come Back to the Locker Room Ag'in, Brick Honey!"; *Mississippi Quarterly* 48 (Fall 1995).

2. Stowe lived in Cincinnati from 1832 to 1850.

3. Frederick Douglass published the exchange of the letters between Martin Delany and himself in *Frederick Douglass' Paper* between 1852 and 1854. See Robert S. Levine's "*Uncle Tom's Cabin* in *Frederick Douglass' Paper*" for an extensive examination of the letters.

4. Baldwin's essay was first published in the *Partisan Review* in 1949 and later collected in *Notes of a Native Son* (1955).

5. For more information on controversies regarding the sentimental tradition, see Gillian Brown, *Domestic Individualism: Imagining Self in Nineteenth-Century America* (Berkeley: University of California Press, 1990); Jane Tompkins, *Sensational Design: The Cultural Work of American Fiction, 1790-1860* (New York: Oxford University Press, 1985); Jean Fagan Yellin, *Women and Sisters: The Antislavery Feminists in American Culture* (New Haven, CT: Yale University Press, 1992); Elizabeth Ammons, ed., "Introduction" and her essay "Freeing the Slaves and Banishing the Blacks: Racism, Empire, and Africa in *Uncle Tom's Cabin*" in *Harriet Beecher Stowe's "Uncle Tom's Cabin": A Casebook* (New York: Oxford University Press, 2007), 3–14; 227-46.

6. Although the *National Era* was known as an abolitionist paper, the periodical also published stories, essays, and poetry on women's issues, labor reform, and temperance, as well as fashion, social events, and a number of other topics as well.

7. Stowe's father and husband became embroiled in controversy when a group of students wanted to organize a protest against slavery but were prohibited from doing so by the school's trustees. Stowe's father was then president and her husband was a professor. The opposition led many outraged students to withdraw from Lane Theological Seminary.

8. For more information regarding Ohio's "Black Codes ," see Melvin I. Urofsdy and Paul Finkelman's *A March of Liberty: A Constitutional History of the United States*, vol. 1, *From the Founding to*

1890 (New York: Oxford University, 2001). For information regarding race riots in Cincinnati, see Gloria J. Browne-Marshall's *Race, Law, and American Society: 1607–Present* (New York: Routledge, 2007).

9. In spite of Southern readers' angry reaction to the novel, several scholars contend that Stowe attempted to "appease the South" by creating highly positive character portraits of white Southerners (Piacentino 135). See Edmund Wilson, *Patriotic Gore: Studies in the Literature of the American Civil War* (New York: Oxford University Press, 1962); Forrest Wilson, *Crusader in Crinoline: The Life of Harriet Beecher Stowe* (Philadelphia: Lippincott, 1941); Yarborough, "Strategies of Black Characterization"; Piacentino, "Stowe's *Uncle Tom's Cabin.*"

10. See Lott, *Love and Theft*; and Meer, *Uncle Tom Mania.*

11. For more information regarding the social requisites for Southern gentlemen, see Bertram Wyatt-Brown's seminal study, *Southern Honor: Ethics and Behavior in the Old South* (New York: Oxford University Press, 1982).

12. In *Honor and Slavery*, Kenneth Greenberg explains that "the words of the master had to be accorded respect and accepted as true simply because they were the words of a man of honor. The words of the slave could never become objects of honor. Whites assumed that slaves lied all the time—and that their lies were intimately connected to their position as slaves" (11). Stowe's depiction of Shelby in contrast to Tom debunks this common assumption.

13. Another excellent study of slave life focusing on children is Wilma King, *Stolen Childhood: Slave Youth in Nineteenth-Century America*, 2nd ed. (Bloomington: Indiana University Press, 2011).

14. Barbara Welter in her essay "The Cult of True Womanhood: 1820–1860," *American Quarterly* 18.2 (1966): 151–74, defines the four cardinal virtues of the ideal woman: piety, purity, submissiveness, and domesticity. Other scholars who view Mrs. Shelby as the novel's matriarchal ideal include Jean Fagan Yellin, "Doing It Herself: *Uncle Tom's Cabin* and Woman's Role in the Slavery Crisis," in *New Essays on Uncle Tom's Cabin*, ed. Eric J. Sundquist (Cambridge: Cambridge University Press, 1986), 85–105; and Autumn Lauzon, who, in "Just Another 'Poke in the Ribs,' contends that the "real 'Mas'r' is in the home, Mrs. Shelby" (23).

15. Wallace-Sanders notes that the Aunt Chloe figure is featured in Isabel Drysdale's 1827 novel *Scenes in Georgia.*

16. For information regarding black stereotypes in film, see Donald Bogle, *Toms, Coons, Mulattoes, Mammies, and Bucks: An Interpretive History of Blacks in American Films* (New York: Continuum, 1989).

17. In addition to aspects of the minstrel tradition, scholars have explored other aspects of Stowe's humor. Autumn Lauzon contends that Stowe employs "Calvinist humor" to "reflect the irony of human characteristics, or to mock certain types of people in general, and oftentimes as a cover for her own personal commentary on human nature" (15). Mimosa Stephenson, in "Humor in *Uncle Tom's Cabin,*" contends that "the humor of the novel adheres closely to the tragedy as it draws attention to the absurdity of human behavior. Humor is rooted in the ridiculous, the ludicrous, the incongruous, the foibles of humankind" (5).

18. For information regarding typical food rations, see Kolchin, *American Slavery*, 113.

19. In addition to Baldwin, see Joel Dinerstein, "'Uncle Tom Is Dead!': Wright, Himes, and Ellison Lay a Mask to Rest," *African American Review* 43.1 (Spring 2009): 83–98.

20. In *A Key to Uncle Tom's Cabin*, Stowe notes that this is based on a published account (22–23).

21. Ellison, "Change the Joke."

22. See George M. Fredrickson, "Uncle Tom and the Anglo-Saxons: Romantic Racialism in the North," in his book *Black Image in the White Mind*, 97–129.

23. See John Blassingame, *Black New Orleans: 1860–1880* (Chicago: University of Chicago Press, 1973).

24. See Lawrence Buell, *New England Literary Culture: From Revolution through Renaissance* (Cambridge: Cambridge University Press, 1986).

25. See also Edward J. Blum and Paul Harvey, *The Color of Christ: The Son of God and the Saga of Race in America* (Chapel Hill: University of North Carolina Press, 2012).

26. For more information regarding slaves' folk music, several essays are included in the "Folk Music" section in Dundes, *Mother Wit from the Laughing Barrel*. Numerous essays are also included in part 1, "Music and Dance," in Caponi, *Signifyin(g), Sanctifyin', and Slam Dunking*.

27. Sarah Meer provides an extensive history of the dramatic renditions of the play and minstrel characters in *Uncle Tom Mania*.

28. It was also more difficult for women to escape with men, particularly in the guise of passing and traveling with a male servant. And, as Mark Reinhardt explains, "about 80 percent of runaways were young men seeking freedom alone. Often these men had no wives, or at least no children. Most male runaways who were married or had children left their families behind. Women, more strongly tied to children, were less likely to run (and typically slave girls had begun having children by their late teens)" (15).

29. Debra Rosenthal also contends that Cassy's power derives from voodun.

30. In *Going to the Territory*, Ralph Ellison writes, "Negroes were seen as ignorant, cowardly, thieving, lying, hypocritical and superstitious in their religious beliefs and practices" (174).

31. Richard Wright insinuates a very different perspective regarding the prospects for *Uncle Tom's Children* in his 1938 collection of short stories.

Chapter 3

1. This stanza is included in Gates, *Signifying Monkey*, 55.

2. For further biographical information, see Delbanco, *Melville*.

3. See Horth, *Correspondence*, 191.

4. Wyn Kelley explains that *Putnam's Monthly* also published "many works on Abolition and social reform in its pages" and notes that "in one of the issues of *Putnam's* in which *Benito Cereno* appeared also contained an extremely positive review of Douglass's second autobiography, *My Bondage and My Freedom*" (21–22).

5. In her essay "Interrogating 'Whiteness,' Complicating 'Blackness,'" Shelley Fisher Fishkin notes that "Eric Sundquist in *To Wake the Nations* (1993) and Viola Sachs in *L'Imaginaire Melville* (1992) have demonstrated Herman Melville's deep interest in African customs, myth, languages, and traditions and have pointed out the African influences on works such as *Moby-Dick* and 'Benito Cereno.' (Sachs, for example, has uncovered numerous references to the Yoruba god Legba in *Moby-Dick*. Stuckey and Sundquist have examined the use of Ashanti drumming and treatment of the dead in 'Benito Cereno,' suggesting that the treatment of the corpse of the rich slaveholder Aranda in 'Benito Cereno' was not a racist allusion to African savagery, as critics have argued, but rather, evidence of Melville's insight into Ashanti rituals and the shrewd political use his characters made of those traditions)" (432).

6. The perception of the character Babo, as Stuckey explains, "breaks down into two large, overlapping schools which perceive Babo as (1) the diabolical, and/or (2) savage leader of a culturally inferior people" (*Going through the Storm*, 58).

7. Ezra Tawil claims that although most scholars regard the plot as a story of slave insurrection, he contends that "it is in fact the story of a captain who, having boarded a slave ship on which a slave rebellion has already taken place, completely misapprehends the reality aboard" (197).

8. Stuckey, *Going through the Storm*, 167.

9. Tawil contends that Babo's performance "suggests, in effect, that Babo is putting on a 'Tom-Show' for Delano" (206), and Lott, in *Love and Theft*, regards "the story as Melville's version of the minstrel show, in which he ingeniously brings together the narrative paradigm of the slave insurrection with the ironies and conundrums of minstrel acts. The slaves-turned-mutineers disguised as slaves aboard the San Dominick are in virtual blackface, performing for the liberal northern visitor too blindered to know better" (234).

10. For connections to the *Amistad* revolt, see Karcher, "Riddle of the Sphinx"; and Maggie Montesinos Sale, *The Slumbering Volcano: American Slave Ship Revolts and the Production of Rebellious Masculinity* (Durham, NC: Duke University Press, 1997). Sundquist addresses the *Amistad* and the *Creole* revolts in his chapter "Melville, Delany, and New World Slavery" in *To Wake the Nations*.

11. In *The Method of Melville's Short Fiction*, Bickley contends that Babo's "mask" conceals his malevolence and adds that he functions throughout the novella as a "symbol of depravity and hatred" (107).

12. See Goldberg, "Benito Cereno's Mute Testimony"; and Jason Richards, "Melville's (Inter)national Burlesque: Whiteface, Blackface, and 'Benito Cereno,'" *American Transcendental Quarterly* 21.2 (2007): 73–94. Stuckey, in *Going through the Storm*, claims that Delano shows no "hesitation in using all his means to re-enslave" the rebels and describes Babo's capture as "defeat" (169, 170).

13. Versions of the poem appear in Gates's *Signifying Monkey*, Watkins's *African American Humor*, and Hughes and Bontemps's *Book of Negro Folklore*.

CHAPTER 4

1. In *The Book of American Negro Poetry* (New York: Harcourt, Brace, 1922), James Weldon Johnson writes: "These creations by the American Negro may be summed up under four heads. The first two are the Uncle Remus stories, which were collected by Joel Chandler Harris, and the 'spirituals' or slave songs, to which the Fisk Jubilee Singers made the public and the musicians of both the United States and Europe listen. The Uncle Remus stories constituted the greatest body of folklore that America has produced, and the 'spirituals' the greatest body of folk song" (14). In *Going to the Territory*, Ralph Ellison writes, "Aesop and Uncle Remus had taught us that comedy is a disguised form of philosophical instruction; and especially when it allows us to glimpse the animal instincts lying beneath the surface of our civilized affectations" (146).

2. Longstreet's *Georgia Scenes: Characters, Incidents, &c. in the First Half-Century of the Republic* was published in 1835, and many scholars consider the book as the foundational text in the frontier humor tradition. Thompson's *Major Jones's Sketches of Travel* was published in 1848.

3. For more biographical information, see Brasch, *Brer Rabbit, Uncle Remus, and the "Cornfield Journalist."*

4. In *Vengeance and Justice: Crime and Punishment in the 19th-Century South* (New York: Oxford University Press, 1984), Edward L. Ayers notes that race relations "had deteriorated dramatically in the short span between Reconstruction and the early 1890s" and notes that a "phobia seemed to emerge rather suddenly in those decades," which was white fear of "the rape of white women by black men," and this fear led to an "epidemic" of black men lynched by white mobs (237). Ayers notes that lynching "reached epidemic proportions in the early 1890s. Nearly 700 people died at the hands of lynchers between 1889 and 1893" (238). In *Crucible of Race*, Williamson notes that "the number of lynchings decreased after 1892, [which] might be attributed primarily to a rising caution among black men that led them to avoid occasions that could possibly be twisted into a semblance of rape or an attempt at rape. Almost certainly, black men came generally to avoid being alone with white women, were careful not to meet feminine eyes with a level gaze, and guarded the tone of their voices in the presence of white females" (117).

5. See Lynn, *Mark Twain and Southwestern Humor*, 50.

6. Harris's collections were published by companies in New York and Boston.

7. George Terrell and Old Harbert were slaves owned by Joseph Addison Turner. Cochran notes that Harris was "an illegitimate child who never knew his father" and "went to work as a boy of fifteen in the printshop of Joseph Addison Turner's Turnwold plantation, near his home town of Eaton in Putnam County, Georgia. While there he heard from slave storytellers the Brer Rabbit tales that would make him famous" (22).

8. "Free Joe and the Rest of the World" was originally published in the New York literary journal the *Century* in 1886 and later in the collection *Free Joe, and Other Georgian Sketches* in 1901.

9. "Marse Chan. A Tale of Old Virginia" was originally published in the *Century* in 1884 and later published in the collection *In Ole Virginia; or, Marse Chan and Other Stories* in 1887.

10. Page further distances himself from Harris regarding race relations in the South by his book *The Negro: The Southerner's Problem* (New York: C. Scribner's Sons, 1904). In this book, Page contends that "the charge that is often made, that the innocent are sometimes lynched, has little foundation. . . . The crime of lynching is not likely to cease until the crime of ravishing and murdering women and children is less frequent than it has been of late. . . . As the crime of rape of late years had its baleful renascence [*sic*] in the teaching of equality and the placing of power in the ignorant Negroes' hands, so its perpetuation and increase have undoubtedly been due in large part to the same teaching. The intelligent Negro may understand what social equality truly means, but to the ignorant and brutal young Negro, it signifies but one thing: the opportunity to enjoy, equally with white men, the privilege of cohabitating with white women" (113).

11. Williamson notes that some of these theorists "were academicians in leading universities," including natural scientist and Harvard professor Nathaniel Southgate Shaler; Walter Francis Willcox, a social science professor at Cornell University; and Edward Drinker Cope, professor of zoology and comparative anatomy at the University of Pennsylvania (121–23).

12. For more information on Virginia's colonial cultural history, see "The South of England to Virginia: Distressed Cavaliers and Indentured Servants, 1642–1675," in Fischer, *Albion's Seed*, 202–418.

13. See Johnson Jones Hooper's "Simon Plays the 'Snatch' Game," reprinted in *Humor of the Old Southwest*, 2nd ed., ed. Hennig Cohen and William B. Dillingham (Athens: University of Georgia Press, 1994), 257.

14. I provide a more extensive discussion of Sut Lovingood's motives in "Sut Lovingood and the Principle of Lex Talionis" in Gretchen Martin, *The Frontier Roots of American Realism* (New York: Peter Lang, 2007), 101–24.

Chapter 5

1. My title signifies on Ralph Ellison's essay, "Change the Joke and Slip the Yoke."

2. See Lott, *Love and Theft*; Bell, "Twain's 'Nigger' Jim"; and Mensh and Mensh, *Black, White, and Huckleberry Finn*. Twain was also an admirer of black musical traditions. In *Highbrow/Lowbrow: The Emergence of Cultural Hierarchy in America* (Cambridge, MA: Harvard University Press, 1988), Lawrence W. Levine notes that "after hearing the Jubilee Singers in 1897, Mark Twain wrote a friend, 'I think that in the Jubilees and their songs America has produced the perfectest flower of the ages; and I wish it were a foreign product, so that she would worship it and lavish money on it and go properly crazy over it'" (143).

3. Jennifer Hildebrand identifies other potential storyteller influences. She notes that "it is possible that at least one other storyteller shared the stage with Daniel. When narrating his life to biographer Albert Paine, Twain recalled 'Uncle Ned' 'a man of all work' who, with Jennie, was 'in real charge of the children and supplied them with entertainment.' In this remembering, Ned supplied 'Golden Arm,' the ghost story that Twain would later make famous (in most other places Twain attributed the story to Daniel). Cousin Tabitha Quarles Greening wrote of Daniel and Ned as two separate storytellers, however, and suggested a third person whose information about black cultural beliefs may have influenced *Huckleberry Finn*: 'The folk lore and strange African legends of 'Daddy Ned' and Uncle Dan'll [*sic*] with the weird and distorted superstitions of the slave girl, Mary, Little Sam's playmate, developed the romantic nature that he inherited from his visionary father.' Atlantic African understandings of the world might also have been imparted to Twain by 'Aunt' Hannah and 'Aunty' Cord" (155).

4. See Twain, "How to Tell a Story." In this essay, Twain also notes: "I do not claim that I can tell a story as it ought to be told. I only claim to know how a story ought to be told, for I have been almost daily in the company of the most expert story-tellers for many years" (155).

5. In West African culture, an important role in the community was known as the griot, a storyteller, historian, and authority of the oral tradition. In "Sounds of a Tradition: The Souls of Black Folk" in *The Cambridge History of African American Literature*, ed. Maryemma Graham and Jerry W. Ward Jr. (Cambridge: Cambridge University Press, 2011), 21–38, F. Abiola Irele notes that "the function, status, and role of the oral bards in the indigenous cultures of Africa were central and remain today indispensable. The singularity of oral artists emerges in this perspective. . . . It is important to stress, however, that although an exceptional development of the powers of memory, as a physical endowment, constitutes a basic requirement for their role, they combine this prowess with individual creative and performance skills which form an essential part of their artistic vocation. As Albert Lord has pointed out, the role of the oral bard goes beyond passive reproduction and recital of texts, but also implies an active process of composition, even in the course of performance" (26).

6. See Mensh and Mensh, *Black, White, and Huckleberry Finn*, 38.

7. Jacobs lived hidden in a crawl space in her grandmother's attic for close to seven years.

8. "A True Story, Repeated Word for Word as I Heard It" was originally published in 1874 in the *Atlantic Monthly*, one of the most prestigious literary journals of the nineteenth century.

9. One of the most controversial essays regarding the relationship between Huck and Jim is Leslie Fielder's claim of a homoerotic relationship between the two in his essay "Come Back to the Raft Ag'in, Huck Honey!"; *Partisan Review* (June 1948).

10. Mensh and Mensh, *Black, White, and Huckleberry Finn*, 145.

11. See Johnson Jones Hooper's "Simon Plays the 'Snatch' Game," reprinted in *Humor of the Old Southwest*, 2nd ed., ed. Hennig Cohen and William B. Dillingham (Athens: University of Georgia Press, 1994), 257.

12. For information regarding Shakespeare in the minstrel tradition, see the essay by Lisa M. Anderson, "From Blackface to 'Genuine Negroes': Nineteenth-Century Minstrelsy and the Icon of the 'Negro,'" *Theatre Research International* 21.1 (Spring 1996): 17–23; Lawrence W. Levine, *Highbrow/Lowbrow: The Emergence of Cultural Hierarchy in America* (Cambridge, MA: Harvard University Press, 1988); and W. T. Lhamon Jr., *Jump Jim Crow: Lost Plays, Lyrics, and Street Prose of the First Atlantic Popular Culture* (Cambridge, MA: Harvard University Press, 2003).

13. See Wolfe's essay "Uncle Remus and the Malevolent Rabbit."

14. John Bird in *Mark Twain and Metaphor* points out that "the controversy over the ending was a dominant critical concern beginning in the 1950s, and in many ways continues today. A bibliography of critical comment would be voluminous in itself; a good introduction and overview is provided in Gerald Graff and James Phelan's edition of *Adventures of Huckleberry Finn*" (Boston: Bedford/St. Martin's, 2004), 277–355.

15. See also Stephanie McCurry, *Masters of Small Worlds: Yeoman Households, Gender Relations, and the Political Culture of the Antebellum South Carolina Low Country* (New York: Oxford University Press, 1995).

16. For more information regarding Missouri slave laws and social and cultural mores, see Terrell Dempsey, *Searching for Jim: Slavery in Sam Clemens's World* (Columbia: University of Missouri Press, 2003).

17. For more information regarding the publication history of the collection of tales Charles Chesnutt sent to the editor of the *Atlantic Monthly*, Walter Hines Page, see Brodhead, "Introduction."

18. See Catherine Clinton and Michele Gillespie, eds., *The Devil's Lane: Sex and Race in the Early South* (New York: Oxford University Press, 1997).

19. Susan K. Harris observes that Roxy "can be seen as a trickster" and that Roxy "evolves from slave trickster to female rogue" (163).

20. For information regarding the duel, see former South Carolina governor John Lyde Wilson's *The Code of Honor; or, Rules for the Government of Principals and Seconds in Duelling* (Charleston, SC: James Phinney, 1835).

21. Two particularly insightful literary treatments of this issue are William Faulkner's short story "Dry September" and Richard Wright's "Big Boy Leaves Home."

Conclusion

1. The subtitle signifies on Langston Hughes's 1930 novel *Not without Laughter*.

Bibliography

Abrahams, Roger D. *Deep Down in the Jungle: Negro Narrative Folklore from the Streets of Philadelphia*. New York: Aldine, 1963.

———. "Playing the Dozens." *Mother Wit from the Laughing Barrel: Readings of Afro-American Folklore*. Ed. Alan Dundes. Jackson: University Press of Mississippi, 1990. 295–309.

———. "Rapping and Capping: Black Talk as Art." *Black America*. Ed. John F. Szwed. New York: Basic Books, 1970. 132–42.

———. *Talking Black*. Rowley, MA: Newbury House, Series in Sociolinguistics, 1976.

Alexander, Robert. *I Ain't Yo' Uncle: The New Jack Revisionist Uncle Tom's Cabin*. Woodstock, IL: Dramatic, 1991.

Anderson, Lisa M. "From Blackface to 'Genuine Negroes': Nineteenth-Century Minstrelsy and the Icon Of the 'Negro.'" *Theatre Research International* 21.1 (Spring 1996): 17–23.

Andrews, William L. "Inter(racial)textuality in Nineteenth-Century Southern Narrative." *Influence and Intertextuality in Literary History*. Ed. Jay Clayton and Eric Rothstein. Madison: University of Wisconsin Press, 1991. 298–317.

Anonymous. "The Duty of Southern Authors." *Southern Literary Messenger* 16 (October 1856): 241–47.

Anonymous. "Notice of New Works: *Uncle Tom's Cabin; or Life among the Lowly*." *Southern Literary Messenger* 18.10 (October 1852): 630–39.

Bahktin, M. M. *The Dialogic Imagination: Four Essays*. Ed. Michael Holquist. Trans. Caryl Emerson and Michael Holquist. Austin: University of Texas Press, 1981.

Bailey, Frankie Y. *Out of the Woodpile: Black Characters in Crime and Detective Fiction*. Westport, CT: Greenwood Press, 1991.

Baker, Houston A., Jr. *Blues, Ideology, and Afro-American Literature: A Vernacular Theory*. Chicago: University of Chicago Press, 1987.

———. *Long Black Song: Essays in Black American Literature and Culture*. Charlottesville: University of Virginia Press, 1972.

Baldwin, James. "Everybody's Protest Novel." *Notes of a Native Son*. Boston: Beacon Press, 1955. 13–23.

Barthes, Roland. "From Work to Text." *The Norton Anthology of Theory and Criticism*. 2nd ed. Ed. Vincent B. Leitch. New York: W. W. Norton, 2010. 1326–31.

Baudrillard, Jean. *Simulations*. Trans. Paul Foss, Paul Patton, and Philip Beitchman. Cambridge: Semiotex[e] and MIT Press, 1983.

Bell, Bernard W. "Twain's 'Nigger' Jim: The Tragic Face behind the Minstrel Mask." *Satire or Evasion? Black Perspectives on Huckleberry Finn*. Ed. James S. Leonard, Thomas A. Tenney, and Thadious M. Davis. Durham, NC: Duke University Press, 1992. 124–40.

Bickley, Bruce R., Jr. *Joel Chandler Harris: A Biography and Critical Study*. Athens: University of Georgia Press, 1978.

———. "John, Brer Rabbit, and Babo: The Trickster and Cultural Power in Melville and Joel Chandler Harris." *Trickster Lives: Culture and Myth in American Fiction*. Ed. Jeanne Campbell Reesman. Athens: University of Georgia Press, 2001. 97–109.

———. *The Method of Melville's Short Fiction*. Durham, NC: Duke University Press, 1975.

Bird, John. *Mark Twain and Metaphor*. Columbia: University of Missouri Press, 2007.

Blassingame, John W. *The Slave Community: Plantation Life in the Antebellum South*. New York: Oxford University Press, 1972.

Brasch, Walter M. *Brer Rabbit, Uncle Remus, and the "Cornfield Journalist": The Tale of Joel Chandler Harris*. Macon, GA: Mercer University Press, 2000.

Brickhouse, Anna. "The Writing of Haiti: Pierre Faubert, Harriet Beecher Stowe, and Beyond." *American Literary History* 13.3 (2001): 407–44.

Brodhead, Richard H. "Introduction." *The Conjure Woman and Other Conjure Tales*. Durham, NC: Duke University Press, 1995. 1–21.

Brown, Henry "Box." "Narrative of Henry 'Box' Brown." 1849. *The Great Escapes: Four Slave Narratives*. Ed. Daphne A. Brooks. New York: Barnes and Noble, 2007. 93–139.

Bruce, Dickson. "Politics and Political Philosophy in the Slave Narrative." *The Cambridge Companion to the African American Slave Narrative*. Ed. Audrey Fisch. Cambridge: Cambridge University Press, 2007. 28–43.

Campbell, Kermit E. "The Signifying Monkey Revisited: Vernacular Discourse in African American Personal Narratives." *Journal of Advanced Composition* 14.2 (1994): 463–73.

Caponi, Gena Dagel. "Introduction: The Case for an African American Aesthetic." *Signifyin(g), Sanctifyin', and Slam Dunking: A Reader in African American Expressive Culture*. Ed. Gena Dagel Caponi. Amherst: University of Massachusetts Press, 1999. 1–41.

Carpio, Glenda R. *Laughing Fit to Kill: Black Humor in the Fictions of Slavery*. New York: Oxford University Press, 2008.

Chadwick-Joshua, Jocelyn. *The Jim Dilemma: Reading Race in "Huckleberry Finn."* Jackson: University Press of Mississippi, 1998.

Chesnut, Mary Boykin. *A Diary from Dixie*. Ed. Isabella D. Martin and Myrta Lockett Avary. New York: D. Appleton, 1905.

Clegg, Jennifer. "Exploding the Semantic Horizon." *Philosophy, Psychiatry, and Psychology* 14.3 (2007): 233–35.

Cochran, Robert. "Black Father: The Subversive Achievement of Joel Chandler Harris." *African American Review* 38.1 (2004): 21–34.

Cowan, William Tynes. *The Slave in the Swamp: Disrupting the Plantation Narrative*. New York: Routledge, 2005.

Craft, William. "Running a Thousand Miles for Freedom." 1860. *The Great Escapes: Four Slave Narratives*. Ed. Daphne A. Brooks. New York: Barnes and Noble, 2007. 221–86.

Davis, David Brion. *Inhuman Bondage: The Rise and Fall of Slavery in the New World*. New York: Oxford University Press, 2006.

Delbanco, Andrew. *Melville: His World and His Work*. New York: Vintage, 2006.

Douglass, Frederick. "Narrative of the Life of Frederick Douglass." *The Classic Slave Narrative*. Ed. Henry Louis Gates Jr. New York: Mentor, 1987. 299–403.

———. *My Bondage and My Freedom*. New York: Miller, Ortan and Mulligan, 1855.

Downes, Paul. "Melville's *Benito Cereno* and the Politics of Humanitarian Intervention." *South Atlantic Quarterly* 103.2/3 (2004): 465–88.

DuBois, W. E. B. *Black Reconstruction in America*. Ed. Henry Louis Gates Jr. New York: Oxford University Press, 2014.

———. *The Souls of Black Folk*. 1903. New York: Signet, 1982.

Dundes, Alan, ed. *Mother Wit from the Laughing Barrel: Readings of Afro-American Folklore*. Jackson: University Press of Mississippi, 1990.

Earl, Riggins R., Jr. *Dark Symbols, Obscure Signs: God, Self, and Community in the Slave Mind*. New York: Orbis Books, 1994.

Egan, Ken, Jr. *The Riven Home: Narrative Rivalry in the American Renaissance*. Selingsgrove, PA: Susquehanna University Press, 1997.

Ellison, Ralph. "Change the Joke and Slip the Yoke." *Shadow and Act*. New York: Random House, 1953. 45–59.

———. *Going to the Territory*. New York: Random House, 1986. 104–12.

———. *Invisible Man*. New York: Vintage Books, 1947.

———. "What Would America Be Like without Blacks." *Going to the Territory*. New York: Random House, 1986. 104–12.

Evans, Robert C. "The Trickster Tricked: Huck Comes Out of the Fog in Mark Twain's *The Adventures of Huckleberry Finn*." *The Trickster*. Ed. Harold Bloom. New York: Infobase, 2010. 1–8.

Felman, Shoshana. "Psychoanalysis and Education: Teaching Terminable and Interminable." *Contemporary Literary Criticism: Literary and Cultural Studies*. 4th ed. Ed. Robert Con Davis and Ronald Schleifer. New York: Longman, 1998. 410–29.

Fischer, David Hackett. *Liberty and Freedom*. New York: Oxford University Press, 2005.

———. *Albion's Seed: Four British Folkways in America*. New York: Oxford University Press, 1989.

Fishkin, Shelley Fisher. "Interrogating 'Whiteness,' Complicating 'Blackness': Remapping American Culture." *American Quarterly* 47.3 (1995): 428–66.

———. *Lighting Out for the Territory*. New York: Oxford University Press, 1996.

———. *Was Huck Black? Mark Twain and African-American Voices*. New York: Oxford University Press, 1993.

Floyd, Samuel A., Jr. "Ring Shout! Literary Studies, Historical Studies, and Black Music Inquiry." *Signifyin(g), Sanctifyin', and Slam Dunking: A Reader in African American Expressive Culture*. Ed. Gena Dagel Caponi. Amherst: University of Massachusetts Press, 1999. 135–56.

Ford, Lacy K. *Deliver Us from Evil: The Slavery Question in the Old South*. New York: Oxford University Press, 2009.

Fox-Genovese, Elizabeth. *Within the Plantation Household: Black and White Women of the Old South*. Chapel Hill: University of North Carolina Press, 1988.

Fredrickson, George M. *The Black Image in the White Mind: The Debate on Afro-American Character and Destiny, 1817–1914*. New York: Harper and Row, 1971.

Gates, Henry Louis, Jr. *The Annotated Uncle Tom's Cabin*. Ed. Henry Louis Gates Jr. and Hollis Robbins. New York: W. W. Norton, 2007.

———. *Figures in Black: Words, Signs, and the "Racial" Self*. New York: Oxford University Press, 1989.

———. "Editor's Introduction: 'Race,' Writing, and the Difference It Makes." *"Race," Writing, and Difference*. Ed. Henry Louis Gates Jr. Chicago: University of Chicago Press, 1986. 1–20.

——. *The Signifying Monkey: A Theory of African-American Literary Criticism*. New York: Oxford University Press, 1989.

——. "Talkin' That Talk." *"Race," Writing, and Difference*. Ed. Henry Louis Gates Jr. Chicago: University of Chicago Press, 1986. 402–9.

——. "*Uncle Tom's Cabin* Reconsidered: A Conversation with Henry Louis Gates Jr., Hollis Robbins, and Margo Jefferson." Moderated by Thelma Golden. Nov. 29, 2006. South Court Auditorium. New York Public Library. www.nypl.org/live.

Genovese, Eugene D. *Roll, Jordan, Roll: The World the Slaves Made*. New York: Vintage, 1972.

Gillman, Susan. *Dark Twins: Imposture and Identity in Mark Twain's America*. Chicago: University of Chicago Press, 1989.

——. "'Sure Identifiers': Race, Science, and the Law in *Pudd'nhead Wilson*." *Mark Twain's "Pudd'nhead Wilson": Race, Conflict, and Culture*. Ed. Susan Gillman and Forrest G. Robinson. Durham, NC: Duke University Press, 1990. 86–104.

Goldberg, Shari. "*Benito Cereno*'s Mute Testimony: On the Politics of Reading Melville's Silences." *Arizona Quarterly* 65.2 (2009): 1–26.

Gray White, Deborah. *Ar'n't I a Woman? Female Slaves in the Plantation South*. New York: W. W. Norton, 1999.

Greenberg, Kenneth S. *Honor and Slavery*. Princeton, NJ: Princeton University Press, 1996.

Grimwood, Michael. *Heart in Conflict: Faulkner's Struggles with Vocation*. Athens: University of Georgia Press, 1986.

Gubar, Susan. *White Skin, Black Face in American Culture*. New York: Oxford University Press, 1997.

Guild, June Purcell. *Black Laws of Virginia*. Lovettsville, VA: Willow Bend Books, 1996.

Gunning, Sandra. *Race, Rape, and Lynching: The Red Record of American Literature 1890–1912*. New York. Oxford University Press, 1996.

Hahn, Steven. "The Yeomanry of the Nonplantation South: Upper Piedmont Georgia, 1850–1860." *Class, Conflict, and Consensus: Antebellum Southern Community Studies*. Ed. Orville Vernon Burton and Robert C. McMath Jr. Westport, CT: Greenwood Press, 1982. 29–56.

Hale, Dorothy J. "Bakhtin in African American Literary Theory." *ELH* 61.2 (1994): 445–71.

Hamilton, Virginia. *The People Could Fly: American Black Folktales*. New York: Alfred A. Knopf, 1985.

Harris, Ashleigh. "Speaking the 'Truth by Dissembling': Necessary Ambiguities in the Tar-Baby Tale." *Journal of Literary Studies* 16.3-4 (2000): 58–75.

Harris, George Washington. *Sut Lovingood Yarns Spun by a "Nat'ral Born Durn'd Fool."* New York: Dick and Fitzgerald, 1867.

Harris, Joel Chandler. *Balaam and His Master and Other Sketches and Stories*. New York: Freeport Press, 1891.

——. *The Complete Tales of Uncle Remus*. Ed. Richard Chase. Boston: Houghton Mifflin, 1983.

——. *Free Joe, and Other Georgian Sketches*. New York: International Association of Newspapers and Authors, 1901.

——. "Introduction." *The Complete Tales of Uncle Remus*. Ed. Richard Chase. Boston: Houghton Mifflin, 1983. xxi–xxvii.

——. *Mingo, and Other Sketches in Black and White*. Boston: J. R. Osgood, 1884.

——. *On the Plantation: A Story of a Georgia Boy's Adventures during the War*. New York: Appleton, 1929.

———. *Stories of Georgia*. New York: American Book Company, 1896.

Harris, Susan K. "Mark Twain's Bad Women." *Studies in American Fiction* 13 (1985): 157–68.

Harvey, Paul. *Moses, Jesus, and the Trickster in the Evangelical South*. Athens: University of Georgia Press, 2012.

Hemenway, Robert. "Introduction: Author, Teller, and Hero." *Uncle Remus: His Songs and His Sayings*. New York: Penguin, 1982. 7–31.

Hildebrand, Jennifer. "'I Awluz Liked Dead People, en Done All I Could for 'Em': Reconsidering Huckleberry Finn's African and American Identity." *Southern Quarterly: A Journal of the Arts in the South* 47.4 (2010): 151–90.

Horth, Lynn, ed. *Correspondence: The Writings of Herman Melville*. Vol. 14, scholarly ed. Evanston, IL: Northwestern University Press, 1993.

Howe, Lawrence. "Property and Dialect Narrative in *Huckleberry Finn*: The 'Jim Dilemma' Revisited." *Mark Twain Annual* (2009): 5-21.

Hughes, Langston, and Arna Bontemps. *The Book of Negro Folklore*. New York: Dodd, Meade, 1959.

Hyde, Lewis. "Where Are the Women Tricksters?" *Trickster Lives: Culture and Myth in American Fiction*. Ed. Jeanne Campbell Reesman. Athens: University of Georgia Press, 2001. 185–93.

Inge, M. Thomas, and Edward Piacentino. "Introduction: The Humor of the Old South; or, Transgression *He* Wrote." *Southern Frontier Humor: An Anthology*. Eds. M. Thomas Inge and Edward Piacentino. Columbia: University of Missouri Press, 2010. 1–23.

Irving, Washington. *The Legend of Sleepy Hollow*. 1819. Elegant Ebooks, 2015.

Isacc, Rhys. *The Transformation of Virginia 1740–1790*. Chapel Hill: University of North Carolina Press, 1982.

Jackson, John P., Jr., and Nadine M. Weidman. *Race, Racism, and Science: Social Impact and Interaction*. New Brunswick, NJ: Rutgers University Press, 2006.

Jacobs, Harriet. *Incidents in the Life of a Slave Girl*. San Diego: Harvest, 1973.

Jehlen, Myra. "The Ties That Bind: Race and Sex in *Pudd'nhead Wilson*." *Mark Twain's "Pudd'nhead Wilson": Race, Conflict, and Culture*. Ed. Susan Gillman and Forrest G. Robinson. Durham, NC: Duke University Press, 1990. 105–20.

Johnson, Charles S. *Patterns of Negro Segregation*. Notre Dame, IN: University of Notre Dame Press, 2001.

Johnson, Walter. *Soul by Soul: Life inside the Antebellum Slave Market*. Cambridge, MA: Harvard University Press, 1999.

Jones, Paul Christian. *Unwelcomed Voices: Subversive Fiction in the Antebellum South*. Knoxville: University of Tennessee Press, 2005.

Joyner, Charles. *Down by the Riverside: A South Carolina Slave Community*. Urbana: University of Illinois Press, 1985.

———. *Shared Traditions: Southern History and Folk Culture*. Urbana: University of Illinois Press, 1999.

Karcher, Carolyn L. "Herman Melville." *The Heath Anthology of American Literature: Early Nineteenth Century 1800–1865*. Vol. B. 5th ed. Ed. Paul Lauter. Boston: Houghton Mifflin, 2006. 2621–25.

———. "The Riddle of the Sphinx: Melville's 'Benito Cereno' and the *Amistad* Case." *Critical Essays on Herman Melville's "Benito Cereno."* Ed. Robert E. Burkholder. New York: Macmillan, 1992. 196–229.

———. *Shadow over the Promised Land: Slavery, Race, and Violence in Melville's America*. Baton Rouge: Louisiana State University Press, 1980.

Kelley, Wyn. "An Introduction to *Benito Cereno*." *Benito Cereno*. Ed. Wyn Kelley. Boston: Bedford/St. Martin's, 2008. 5–32.

Kennedy, John Pendleton. *Swallow Barn; or, A Sojourn in the Old Dominion*. 1832, rev. 1852. Baton Rouge: Louisiana State University Press, 1986.

Kinney, James. *Amalgamation! Race, Sex, and Rhetoric in the Nineteenth-Century American Novel*. Westport, CT: Greenwood Press, 1985.

———. "Race in the New South: Joel Chandler Harris' 'Free Joe and the Rest of the World.'" *American Literary Realism* 33.3 (2001): 235–51.

Kolchin, Peter. *American Slavery: 1619–1877*. New York: Hill and Wang, 1993.

Kristeva, Julia. *Revolution in Poetic Language*. Trans. Margaret Waller. New York: Columbia University Press, 1984.

Lauzon, Autumn Rhea. "Just Another 'Poke in the Ribs': Calvinist Humor in *Uncle Tom's Cabin*." *Studies in American Humor* 3.24 (2011): 15–29.

Lee, Julia Sun-Joo. "Knucklebones and Knocking-Bones: The Accidental Trickster in Ellison's *Invisible Man*." *African American Review* 40.3 (2006): 461–73.

Levine, Lawrence W. *Black Culture and Black Consciousness: Afro-American Folk Thought from Slavery to Freedom*. New York: Oxford University Press, 1978.

Levine, Robert S. "Introduction." *Dred: A Tale of the Great Dismal Swamp*. Ed. Robert S. Levine. New York: Penguin Books, 2000. ix–xxx.

———. "Race, Slavery, Prejudice." *Clotel; or, The President's Daughter*. Ed. Robert S. Levine. Boston: Bedford/St. Martin's, 2000. 328–34.

———. "*Uncle Tom's Cabin* in *Frederick Douglass' Paper*: An Analysis of Reception." *American Literature* 64.1 (1992): 71–93.

Litwack, Leon F. *Trouble in Mind: Black Southerners in the Age of Jim Crow*. New York: Alfred A. Knopf, 1998.

Lock, Helen. "The Paradox of Slave Mutiny in Herman Melville, Charles Johnson, and Frederick Douglass." *College Literature* 30.4 (2003): 54–70.

Longstreet, Augustus B. *Georgia Scenes: Characters, Incidents, &c. in the First Half-Century of the Republic*. 1835. Savannah, GA: Beehive, 1975.

Lott, Eric. *Love and Theft: Blackface Minstrelsy and the American Working Class*. New York: Oxford University Press, 1993.

———. "Mr. Clemens and Jim Crow: Twain, Race, and Blackface." *The Cambridge Companion to Mark Twain*. Ed. Forrest G. Robinson. Cambridge: Cambridge University Press, 1995. 129–52.

Lynn, Kenneth S. *Mark Twain and Southwestern Humor*. Boston: Little, Brown, 1959.

MacKethan, Lucinda. "Introduction." *Swallow Barn; or, A Sojourn in the Old Dominion*. Baton Rouge: Louisiana State University Press, 1986. xi–xxxii.

———. "Plantation Fiction." *The Companion to Southern Literature: Themes, Genres, Places, People, Movements, and Motifs*. Ed. Joseph M. Flora and Lucinda MacKethan. Baton Rouge: Louisiana State University Press, 2002. 650–52.

———. "Trickster." *The Companion to Southern Literature: Themes, Genres, Places, People, Movements, and Motifs*. Eds. Joseph M. Flora and Lucinda MacKethan. Baton Rouge: Louisiana State University Press, 2002. 913–15.

Mason, Theodore O., Jr. "Signifying." *The Oxford Companion to African American Literature*. Ed. William L. Andrews, Frances Smith Foster, and Trudier Harris. New York: Oxford University Press, 1997. 665–66.

Mayfield, John. *Counterfeit Gentlemen: Manhood and Humor in the Old South*. Gainesville: University Press of Florida, 2009.

McCurry, Stephanie. *Masters of Small Worlds: Yeoman Households, Gender Relations, and the Political Culture of the Antebellum South Carolina Low Country*. New York: Oxford University Press, 1995.

McLaurin, Melton A. *Celia, a Slave: A True Story of Violence and Retribution in Antebellum Missouri*. Athens: University of Georgia Press, 1991.

McWilliams, Dean. *Charles W. Chesnutt and the Fictions of Race*. Athens: University of Georgia Press, 2002.

Meer, Sarah. *Uncle Tom Mania: Slavery, Minstrelsy, and Transatlantic Culture in the 1850s*. Athens: University of Georgia Press, 2005.

Melville, Herman. *Bartleby and Benito Cereno*. New York: Dover, 1990.

———. *Redburn: His First Voyage*. New York: Harper and Brothers, 1849.

Mensh, Elaine, and Harry Mensh. *Black, White, and Huckleberry Finn: Re-Imagining the American Dream*. Tuscaloosa: University of Alabama Press, 2000.

Mixon, Wayne. "The Ultimate Irrelevance of Race: Joel Chandler Harris and Uncle Remus in Their Time." *Journal of Southern History* 56.3 (1990): 457–80.

Mitchell-Kernan, Claudia. "Signifying, Loud-Talking and Marking." *Signifyin(g), Sanctifyin', and Slam Dunking: A Reader in African American Expressive Culture*. Ed. Gena Dagel Caponi. Amherst: University of Massachusetts Press, 1999. 309–30.

Moody-Turner, Shirley. *Black Folklore and the Politics of Racial Representation*. Jackson: University Press of Mississippi, 2013.

Morgan, Winifred. "Signifying: The African-American Trickster and the Humor of the Old Southwest." *The Enduring Legacy of Old Southwest Humor*. Ed. Edward Piacentino. Baton Rouge: Louisiana State University Press, 2006. 210–26.

———. *The Trickster Figure in American Literature*. New York: Palgrave Macmillan, 2013.

Morris, Linda A. *Gender Play in Mark Twain: Cross-Dressing and Transgression*. Columbia: University of Missouri Press, 2007.

Morrison, Toni. *Beloved*. New York: Signet, 1987.

———. *Song of Solomon*. 1977. New York: Penguin, 1987.

———. *Playing in the Dark: Whiteness and the Literary Imagination*. New York: Vintage, 1992.

———. "Unspeakable Things Unspoken: The Afro-American Presence in American Literature." *Michigan Quarterly Review* 28.1 (1989): 1–34.

Nowatzki, Robert. *Representing African Americans in Transatlantic Abolition and Blackface Minstrelsy*. Baton Rouge: Louisiana State University Press, 2010.

Obenzinger, Hilton. "'Pluck Enough to Lynch a Man': Mark Twain and Manhood." *Critical Insights: Mark Twain*. Ed. R. Kent Rasmussen. Pasadena, CA: Salem Press, 2011. 89–109.

Oriard, Michael. "Shifty in a New Country: Games in Southwestern Humor." *Southern Literary Journal* 12.2 (1980): 1–28.

Osofsky, Gilbert. *Puttin' on Ole Massa*. New York: Harper and Row, 1969.

Page, Thomas Nelson. *In Ole Virginia; or, Marse Chan and Other Stories*. Nashville: J. S. Sanders and Company, 1991.

Patton, Phil. "The Most Positive yet Most Racist Stereotype: Mammy." *Star-News* (Wilmington, NC). Sept. 26, 1993, 5E.

Pettit, Arthur G. "The Black and White Curse: *Pudd'nhead Wilson* and Miscegenation." *Pudd'nhead Wilson and Those Extraordinary Twins*. Ed. Sidney E. Berger. New York: W. W. Norton, 2005. 346–60.

Piacentino, Edward. "Stowe's *Uncle Tom's Cabin*." *Explicator* 58.3 (2010): 135–38.

Prince, Gerald. *A Dictionary of Narratology*. Lincoln: University of Nebraska Press, 1987.

———. "Introduction to the Study of the Narratee." *Essentials of the Theory of Fiction*. Ed. Michael J. Hoffman and Patrick D. Murphy. Durham, NC: Duke University Press, 1988. 213–33.

Rampersad, Arnold. "*Adventures of Huckleberry Finn* and Afro-American Literature." *Satire or Evasion? Black Perspectives on "Huckleberry Finn."* Ed. James S. Leonard, Thomas A. Tenney, and Thadious M. Davis. Durham, NC: Duke University Press, 1992. 216–27.

Reed, Ishmael. *Flight to Canada*. New York: Scribner, 1976.

Reilly, John M. "Giving Bigger a Voice: The Politics of Narrative in *Native Son*." *New Essays on "Native Son."* Ed. Kenneth Kinnamon. Cambridge: Cambridge University Press, 1990. 35–62.

Reinhardt, Mark. *Who Speaks for Margaret Garner?* Minneapolis: University of Minnesota Press, 2010.

Reynolds, David S. *Mightier Than the Sword: "Uncle Tom's Cabin" and the Battle for America*. New York: W. W. Norton, 2011.

Robbins, Sarah. "Gendering the History of the Antislavery Narrative: Juxtaposing *Uncle Tom's Cabin* and *Benito Cereno*, *Beloved*, and *Middle Passage*." *American Quarterly* 49.3 (1997): 531–73.

Roberts, John W. *From Trickster to Badman: The Black Folk Hero in Slavery and Freedom*. Philadelphia: University of Pennsylvania Press, 1989.

Robinson, Forrest G. *The Author-Cat: Clemens's Life in Fiction*. New York: Fordham University Press, 2007.

Rock, Chris. *Rock This!* New York: Hyperion, 2000.

Romine, Scott. *The Narrative Forms of Southern Community*. Baton Rouge: Louisiana State University Press, 1999.

Rose, Alan Henry. "The Image of the Negro in the Pre-Civil-War Novels of John Pendleton Kennedy and William Gilmore Simms." *Journal of American Studies* 4.2 (1971): 217–26.

Rosenthal, Debra J. "'I've only to say the word!': *Uncle Tom's Cabin* and Performative Speech Theory." *Legacy* 27.2 (2010): 237–56.

Ryan, Susan M. *The Grammar of Good Intentions: Race and the Antebellum Culture of Benevolence*. Ithaca, NY: Cornell University Press, 2003.

Scheick, William J. "The Spunk of a Rabbit: An Allusion in Huckleberry Finn." *Mark Twain Journal* 15 (1971): 14–16.

Schwartz, Marie Jenkins. *Born in Bondage: Growing Up Enslaved in the Antebellum South*. Cambridge, MA: Harvard University Press, 2000.

Scott, Kevin Michael. "'There's More Honor': Reinterpreting Tom and the Evasion in *Huckleberry Finn*." *Studies in the Novel* 37.2 (2005): 187–207.

Simpson, Lewis P. *The Dispossessed Garden: Pastoral and History in Southern Literature*. Athens: University of Georgia Press, 1975.

Sloane, David E. *"Adventures of Huckleberry Finn": American Comic Vision*. Boston: Twayne, 1988.

Smedley, Audrey. *Race in North America: Origin and Evolution of a Worldview*. 3rd ed. Boulder, CO: Westview Press, 2007.

Smith, Ayana. "Blues, Criticism, and the Signifying Trickster." *Popular Music* 24.2 (2005): 179–91.

Smith, David L. "Huck, Jim, and American Racial Discourse." *Satire or Evasion? Black Perspectives on "Huckleberry Finn."* Ed. James S. Leonard, Thomas A. Tenney, and Thadious M. Davis. Durham, NC: Duke University Press, 1992. 103–23.

Smith, Jeanne Rosier. *Writing Tricksters: Mythic Gambols in American Ethnic Literature*. Berkeley: University of California Press, 1997.

Soitos, Stephen F. *The Blues Detective: A Study of African American Detective Fiction*. Amherst: University of Massachusetts Press, 1996.

Stauffer, John. *The Black Hearts of Men: Radical Abolitionists and the Transformation of Race*. Cambridge, MA: Harvard University Press, 2002.

Stephenson, Mimosa. "Humor in *Uncle Tom's Cabin*." *Studies in American Humor* 3.20 (2009): 4–20.

Stowe, Harriet Beecher. *A Key to Uncle Tom's Cabin*. 1853. Bedford: Applewood Books, 1998.

———. *Uncle Tom's Cabin; or, Life among the Lowly*. 1852. Edited by David S. Reynolds. New York: Oxford University Press, 2011.

Stuckey, Sterling. *African Culture and Melville's Art: The Creative Process in "Benito Cereno" and "Moby-Dick."* New York: Oxford University Press, 2009.

———. *Going through the Storm: The Influence of African American Art in History*. New York: Oxford University Press, 1994.

Sundquist, Eric J. "Slavery, Revolution, and the American Renaissance." *The American Renaissance Reconsidered*. Ed. Walter Benn Michaels and Donald E. Pease. Baltimore: Johns Hopkins University Press, 1985. 1–33.

———. *To Wake the Nations: Race in the Making of American Literature*. Cambridge, MA: Harvard University Press, 1993.

Taliaferro, Hardin E. *Fisher's River (North Carolina) Scenes and Characters*: New York: Harper and Brothers, 1859.

Tawil, Ezra. *The Making of Racial Sentiment*. Cambridge: Cambridge University Press, 2006.

Thomas, H. Nigel. *From Folklore to Fiction: A Study of Folk Heroes and Rituals in the Black American Novel*. New York: Greenwood Press, 1988.

Thompson, William Tappan. *Major Jones's Sketches of Travel, Comprising the Scenes, Incidents and Adventures in His Tour from Georgia to Canada*. Philadelphia: T. B. Peterson, 1847.

Tolson, Nancy D. "The Butler Didn't Do It so Now They're Blaming the Maid: Defining a Black Feminist Trickster through the Novels of Barbara Neely." *South Central Review* 18.3–4 (2001): 72–85.

Tracy, Susan. *In the Master's Eye: Representations of Women, Blacks, and Poor Whites in Antebellum Southern Literature*. Amherst: University of Massachusetts Press, 1995.

Turner, Darwin T. "Daddy Joel Harris and His Old-Time Darkies." *Southern Literary Journal* 1. 1 (1968): 20–41.

Twain, Mark. "A True Story, Repeated Word for Word as I Heard It." *Atlantic Monthly* 34 (1874): 591–94.

———. *Adventures of Huckleberry Finn*. 3rd ed. Ed. Thomas Cooley. 1884. New York: W. W. Norton, 1999.

———. *Autobiography of Mark Twain*. Vol. 1. Ed. Harriet Elinor Smith. Berkeley: University of California Press, 2010.

———. "How to Tell a Story." 1895. *The Complete Essays of Mark Twain*. Ed. Charles Neider. Garden City, NY: Doubleday, 1963. 155–59.

———. *Pudd'nhead Wilson*. Ed. Sidney E. Berger. 1894. New York: W. W. Norton, 1980.

———. "Sociable Jimmy." *New York Times* 29 (1974), 7.

———. "The United States of Lyncherdom." *The Complete Essays of Mark Twain*. Ed. Charles Neider. Garden City: Doubleday, 1963. 673–78.

Valkeakari, Tuire. "Huck, Twain, and the Freedman's Shackles: Struggling with *Huckleberry Finn* Today." *Atlantis, revista de la Asociación Española de Estudios Anglo-Norteamericanos* 28.2 (2006): 29–43.

Wald, Elijah. *The Dozens: A History of Rap's Mama*. New York: Oxford University Press, 2012.

Walker, Alice. "Uncle Remus, No Friend of Mine." *Georgia Review* (special issue, Fall 2012): 635–37.

Wallace-Sanders, Kimberly. *Mammy: A Century of Race, Gender, and Southern Memory*. Ann Arbor: University of Michigan Press, 2008.

Walters, Wendy W. "'One of Dese Mornings, Bright and Fair,/Take My Wings and Cleave De Air': The Legend of the Flying Africans and Diaspora Consciousness." *MELUS* 22.3 (Fall 1997): 3–29.

Washington, Booker T. "Up from Slavery." *Three Negro Classics*. New York: Avon Books, 1965.

Watkins, Mel. *African American Humor: The Best Black Comedy from Slavery to Today*. Chicago: Lawrence Hill Books, 2002.

———. *On the Real Side: Laughing, Lying, and Signifying—The Underground Tradition of African-American Humor That Transformed American Culture, from Slavery to Richard Pryor*. New York: Simon and Schuster, 1994.

Webb, James. *Born Fighting: How the Scots-Irish Shaped America*. New York: Broadway Books, 2004.

Wells, Jeremy. *Romances of the White Man's Burden: Race, Empire, and the Plantation in American Literature, 1880–1936*. Nashville, TN: Vanderbilt University Press, 2011.

Williamson, Joel. *The Crucible of Race: Black-White Relations in the American South since Emancipation*. New York: Oxford University Press, 1984.

Wolfe, Bernard. "Uncle Remus and the Malevolent Rabbit." *Mother Wit from the Laughing Barrel: Readings in the Interpretation of Afro-American Folklore*. Ed. Alan Dundes. Jackson: University of Mississippi Press, 1990. 524–40.

Woodard, Fredrick, and Donnarae MacCann. "Minstrel Shackles and Nineteenth-Century 'Liberality' in *Huckleberry Finn*." *Satire or Evasion? Black Perspectives on "Huckleberry Finn."* Ed. James S. Leonard, Thomas A. Tenney, and Thadious M. Davis. Durham, NC: Duke University Press, 1992. 141–53.

Wright, Richard. *Uncle Tom's Children*. New York: Harper and Row, 1938.

Yarborough, Richard. "Strategies of Black Characterization in *Uncle Tom's Cabin* and the Early Afro-American Novel." *New Essays on "Uncle Tom's Cabin."* Ed. Eric J. Sundquist. Cambridge: Cambridge University Press, 1986. 45–84.

Yellin, Jean Fagan. *The Intricate Knot: Black Figures in American Literature, 1776–1870*. New York: New York University Press, 1972.

Index

CPSIA information can be obtained at www.ICGtesting.com
Printed in the USA
LVOW11*2057090216

474395LV00005B/33/P